THE LIBRARY
ST. MARY'S COLLEGE OF MARYLAND
ST. MARY'S CITY, MARYLAND 20686

081551

S0-BJI-177

Salem, Massachusetts, 1626-1683

A Covenant Community

Salem, Massachusetts

1626-1683
A Covenant Community

Richard P. Gildrie

University Press of Virginia
Charlottesville

THE UNIVERSITY PRESS OF VIRGINIA
Copyright © 1975 by the Rector and Visitors
of the University of Virginia

First published 1975

Library of Congress Cataloging in Publication Data
Gildrie, Richard P.   1945-
   Salem, Massachusetts,   1626-1683 : a covenant community
   Bibliography: p.
   Includes index.
   1. Salem, Mass. — History.   2. Salem, Mass. —
Religious life and customs.   I. Title.   F74.SlG5   917.44'5
74-20841   ISBN 0-8139-0532-X

Printed in the United States of America

For

Burr C. Brundage, William A. Koelsch, and William C. Wilbur

Contents

Tables

Maps

Preface

If, as a wise friend recently remarked, Colonial American studies are in danger of becoming "balkanized," then this work may seem part of that trend. By studying individual towns, persons, and events, historians have rediscovered diversity within seventeenth-century New England. They have given new historiographic meaning to the old political dictum that Boston is not Massachusetts, nor Massachusetts, New England. Yet the goal of such studies is both analysis and comparison; a synthesis is at least implied. I have tried to make mine explicit.

I conceive of the experiences of Massachusetts towns as a spectrum ranging from the stable, usually inland, agricultural communities where Puritan organicism remained essentially unchanged for decades to the rapidly changing port of Boston where institutions adapted swiftly to the pressures engendered by the town's commercial and political role. Between these poles are intermediary points; for instance, agricultural communities wracked by dissension over land use and distribution and farming towns that gradually became commercial centers.

Salem, a coastal village that developed into a commercial town, belongs in the latter category. Its transition took over three decades and was painful as its citizens tried to reconcile the organicism of Puritan ideals with the atomization encouraged by economic growth. Salem, like other Puritan communities, attempted to create an orderly, mutually dependent society. But its hopes were frustrated by conflicts between older settlers and newcomers and by both mercantile and agricultural expansion. This study will explore Salem's original character and its transformation in order to illuminate both this part of the spectrum and the town's significant role in many of the Bay Colony's political and religious controversies.

The various Salem covenants are central to the story. Facing a social void in the New England wilderness and living in a world in which religious concepts were crucial intellectual tools, the Puritan leadership regarded covenants as more than creeds. The covenants were social compacts as well. Through them the community defined its values, its aspirations, its problems and the means of resolving them. The changing content of the Salem covenants reflected and affected the town's social and political development. This interpretation of the significance of the covenants is a moot point among modern historians. A basic purpose of this book is to show the importance of covenants in New England and their usefulness to historians.

Scholarly effort, like sin, is an individual responsibility. But, also like the sinner, the writer is usually inspired and abetted by others. Acknowledging debts, however inadequately, to those who helped should not impute to them any guilt for the errors that remain.

The web of inspiration and aid that grew during the six years of this book's development cannot be completely untangled nor can all those who participated even be mentioned. I am indebted to the staff of the University of Virginia Library and especially to David Little, Director of the Essex Institute of Salem, Massachusetts, and his fine staff of courteous and patient librarians. Copies of this study in its dissertation form are available at the Essex Institute and the University of Virginia Library. My colleagues at Austin Peay State University, Clarksville, Tennessee, gave me critical financial assistance through a Tower Fund Grant in 1972. D. Alan Williams has patiently seen this work through from its inception in his seminar at the University of Virginia. William W. Abbot and David H. Flaherty read and criticized the manuscript skillfully. Without these three it would not exist. Ken Wibking of the Austin Peay State University geography department has kindly prepared the maps for this volume.

The three men to whom this book is dedicated were the members of the history department at Florida Presbyterian College, now Eckerd College, in St. Petersburg while I was a student there. They are inspirational, profound teachers who convinced me that the study of history is a way of life. Finally I would like to acknowledge the support of my wife, Meredith, and our Elizabeth, who only knows that sometimes "Daddy can't play now, 'cause he's doing his ABC's." They make a home, the heart of all sustained effort.

Clarksville, Tennessee
August 1974

Salem, Massachusetts, 1626-1683

A Covenant Community

Chapter I

Origins of the Implicit Covena
1626-1630

The founding of Salem was a complex event, crucial to the history of New England Puritanism. Salem is the oldest town in the Bay Colony; its creation even antedated the formation of the Massachusetts Bay Company in 1629. The earliest settlers of the town made decisions concerning church and civil polity that influenced not only its subsequent character but that of the whole colony. Because the founders of Salem were not homogeneous, understanding its earliest institutions necessitates examination of the various groups that participated in their creation and the differing conceptions of an ideal society that they held. What emerged at Salem during these first few years was a rough consensus, an implicit covenant which provided definition, an institutional framework for the infant community.

In the spring of 1626 a group of twenty Englishmen—together with their wives, children, and cattle—abandoned their small settlement on Cape Ann and walked to the base of the cape where a number of rivers emptying into the sea formed a harbor safe from the blasts of northeast storms. The Indians called this site Naumkeag. In 1629 the settlers gave it an English and biblical name, Salem.

These pioneers from Cape Ann were the remnants of a defunct West Country trading and fishing venture, the Dorchester Company. After its collapse the company offered to transport its employees home to England, and most did return in 1626. However, Roger Conant, governor of the Cape Ann settlement just before its failure, determined not to abandon the idea of colonization. Some of the original stockholders concurred, most notably two West Country ministers of the Established Church, Conant's older brother John of Lymington, Somerset, and John White of Dorchester, Devon, who had been the moving spirit behind the original Dorchester venture. These two men immediately sought new settlers and new capital among West Country merchants and gentry, the London financial community, and the East Anglian aristocracy.[1] In two years reinforcements began arriving at Naumkeag.

---

[1] Bernard Bailyn, *The New England Merchants in the Seventeenth Century* (paperback ed., New York, 1964), pp, 17-18; Frances Rose-Troup, *John White, the Patriarch of Dorchester and the Founder of Massachusetts, 1575-1648* (New York, 1930), p. 105.

Meanwhile Roger Conant held the settlement together. Called the Old Planters, these original settlers, with Conant at their head, remained a coherent and significant group in the life of Salem into the 1660s. Conant was an archetypal seventeenth-century political leader. In the social hierarchy of the time he ranked significantly higher than any of his original companions; his brother's prominence complemented his own reputation as a moderately successful London merchant. After his arrival in Plymouth Colony in 1623, he took up independent trading in fish and furs and became founder of Nantasket as well as governor of the Cape Ann venture.[2] He was a leader by virtue of his personality, wealth, birth, and connections in England and America. His followers too were of a common type. All of the Old Planters whose English origins are known came from a sixty-mile-square area whose center was the Reverend John Conant's parish.[3] Many of the immigrants sent by the New England Company to join them at Salem came from the same region; John Conant was probably recruiting local men of useful trades and sending them to join his brother.

During their experience together before 1628 the Old Planters developed a sense of common identity. As new settlers arrived, the Old Planters became a coherent interest group within the larger community. In addition to fishing and fur trading, they were especially interested in commercial agriculture to service the itinerant fishermen and traders who worked along the coast between Newfoundland and Plymouth. They had chosen Naumkeag not only for its fine harbor but also for the "considerable quantity of planting land near adjoining thereto."[4]

As an old man Conant claimed another motive as well for remaining at Naumkeag; he had settled there "secretly conceiving in his mind, that in following times, (as since is fallen out) it might prove a receptacle for such as upon the account of religion would be willing to begin a foreign plantation in this part of the world of which he gave some intimation to his friends in England."[5] The word "secretly" perplexes. It is possible that subsequent events colored the memory of the old patriarch or even that he claimed a religious motive to impress the ardent young minister William Hubbard with his prescience. In any case Conant's assertion opens the question of the religious commitments of the first Salem

[2] Clifford K. Shipton, *Roger Conant: A Founder of Massachusetts* (Cambridge, Mass., 1945), pp. 3-59.

[3] Charles E. Banks, "The 'West Country' Origin of Salem's Settlement," *Essex Institute Historical Collections* 66 (1930): 317-24.

[4] William Hubbard, *A General History of New England from the Discovery to 1680* (1680; Cambridge, Mass., 1815), p, 101.

[5] Ibid., p. 107.

settlers. The word "secretly" even suggests that Conant's vision of the future of the settlement differed somewhat from that of his companions.

This problem of Old Planter beliefs is important in understanding subsequent events, and yet it is hard to resolve. Were they Anglicans or Puritans? The answer seems to be that they were something in between. The English church in the period between the Elizabethan Settlement and the Civil War "was a spectrum, in which the ultimate extremes of colour are clear enough, but the intermediate tones merge imperceptibly."[6] The Old Planters fell to the left of the Anglicans but somewhat to the right of the Puritan leadership that later came to New England.[7]

Before 1628 a number of experiences in America revealed the religious attitudes of Conant and his followers and shaped their response to later immigrants. A major one was the mutual suspicion that arose between them and the Pilgrims. As usual with seventeenth-century disputes, religious, political, and economic motivations are impossible to disentangle. Although they also actively pursued the fisheries and the fur trade, the Pilgrims were intent on forming a new community, separate from the "corruptions" of England. Being Separatists, they rejected the entire institutional framework of the English church. At Plymouth they sought to implement their separatist organic ideal by creating one church, one town, and one economic unit with minimum dependence on outsiders.

In 1623 that communal order of the Pilgrim Colony was seriously undermined by the arrival of new settlers, among them Roger Conant. These people were called "Particulars" because they had financed their own transportation and consequently were not subject to the joint-stock obligations of the original settlers. In fact they tended to compete with the Pilgrims. The diversity they introduced was not merely economic, for many of them were out of sympathy with the religious and social ideals of the Pilgrims.

Conant, as a Particular, was profoundly dissatisfied with life at Plymouth. He and his wife stayed only a year and left at the first decent opportunity to join another community. Not being part of the joint-stock company, the Particulars in Plymouth were denied participation in public affairs while "being subject to the general government." Willaim Bradford, governor of the colony, wrote in *Of Plymouth Plantation*, "Those that came on their particular looked for greater matters than they found or could attain unto, about building great houses, and such pleasant situations for them,

---

[6] Patrick Collinson, *The Elizabethan Puritan Movement* (Los Angeles, 1967), p. 17.
[7] Shipton, p. 69.

as themselves had fancied; as if they would be great men and rich all of a sudden"[8]

The hostility between the groups soon found religious expression. During the dispute Bradford made a list of the Particulars' objections to Pilgrim religious practices:

1st objection was diversity about religion.
2nd objection: Neglect of family duties on the Lord's day.
3rd objection: Want of both sacraments.
4th objection: Children not catechized nor taught to read.[9]

The Particulars did not object to Separatism or any of the doctrines being propounded. Instead they were criticizing the lack of a communal belief that would supersede doctrinal precision and unify the settlers. In response Bradford spoke of a tacit union: "Here was never any controversy or opposition, either public or private (to our knowledge) since we came." The other three objections of the Particulars hit at the same point. The second and fourth are concerned with perpetuation of pious tradition and social discipline, and the third, with the proper symbolic reaffirmation of a sense of community with each other and God.

Both the Pilgrims and the Particulars desired an organic, communal order. The difference arose over the nature of the community to be sought. The Pilgrims, being Separatists, tended to define the good society in exclusive terms; social and political arrangements were designed to protect the pure, i.e., the Leyden Congregation, and their control over the colony's life. Other people were tolerated but not considered to be really part of the community. The Particulars, on the other hand, regarded the ideal community as inclusive, not merely because they were outsiders but also because they were in the non-Separatist tradition. That tradition, embracing both Puritan and Anglican beliefs, held that society and church ideally should serve the interests of both regenerate and unregenerate; a major goal was the salvation of the "poor in spirit" rather than their exclusion.

The Pilgrims used doctrinal tests as a method of excluding strangers and individuals who held different social and religious ideas. The paradoxical result of such a policy was to exacerbate the very diversity they sought to avoid. Non-Separatists tried either to find a common denominator that would preserve the community or, conversely, to convince the offender that the community's ideas were more correct than his own. Exclusion for

[8]Bradford, *Of Plymouth Plantation, 1620-1647* (1647; ed. Samuel Eliot Morison, New York, 1952), p. 133.
[9]Ibid., pp. 142-43.

them was a painful last resort rather than an instinctive first reaction.

After leaving Plymouth, Conant and the Old Planters who were accumulating around him continued to differ with the Pilgrims. At both Nantasket in 1624 and Cape Ann in 1625 they used the Book of Common Prayer in services conducted by John Lyford, a minister the Pilgrims had expelled. At Cape Ann, Conant was barely able to prevent violence between Plymouth men and Dorchester Company employees, including various Old Planters, over fishing rights.

By the time the Old Planters had settled at Naumkeag their hostility toward the Pilgrims was deep. They had shown themselves to be thorough non-Separatists, willing to conform to practically any doctrinal or ceremonial position within the spectrum of the English church but unwilling to accept exclusion. In this context Conant may have kept the notion of recruiting Puritans to himself. Knowing well his companions' distaste for the Pilgrims, Conant may have felt that the Old Planters would suspect that the newcomers would too closely resemble the Pilgrims.

Conant was having a hard time holding the settlers at Naumkeag. Accustomed to movement, they grew restless after two years and were strongly tempted to follow their minister Lyford, who accepted an invitation to Virginia. In order to keep his friends at Naumkeag Conant threatened to remain there alone, if need be, "to wait the providence of God." He assured them that they "should soon have more company," but presumably he did not say where White was going for help.[10]

At home White and John Conant had succeeded in garnering financial support through the creation of the New England Company, which tapped greater sources of wealth than had been available for earlier West Country ventures. The new organization also meant an infusion of new men. Of seventy subscribers to the joint stock, only six were former members of the Dorchester Company, including White. The membership of the company was overwhelmingly aristocratic. There were only seven merchants and two merchant knights, a highly unusual situation since merchants generally dominated overseas ventures. However, the gentry tended to be more interested in actual colonization than in purely trading ventures, and the projected New England Company was designed for commercial agriculture, which would intail settlement. For governor of the company in England, this largely gentry

[10]Hubbard, p. 108.

organization chose Matthew Cradock, a merchant who had invested heavily in the East India Company and the New Merchant Adventurers.[11]

Like the stockholders of many seventeenth-century ventures, the members of the New England Company desired both a pious and a profitable community. They wanted discipline, piety, and order on their ships and in their settlements just as Puritans favored these virtues at home. In addition to the problem of temptation in distant lands, the companies also had to consider danger to the settlements from either the native population or European competitors. The threat of both internal disorder and external attack predisposed company planners toward the creation of semifeudal military garrisons and trading posts.[12] A suitable governor of such a settlement in America would be a pious soldier of some social standing. The New England Company found such a man in John Endecott.

Little is known about Endecott before he arrived in Massachusetts.[13] He was born in Devonshire in 1588 and went to London sometime before 1617. There is some indication that he was connected with Sir Edward Coke. He was a strong admirer of both Roger Williams and Hugh Peter and asked that either of them be sent to minister to the settlement, but since both these Puritan divines were connected with the New England Company, his knowledge of them may not have antedated his joining the organization. It is a tempting conjecture that Endecott got his title of captain, his militant piety, and his strong attachment to Hugh Peter, onetime minister to the English church at Rotterdam, while serving in the Dutch Wars. But there is no hard evidence. In any case he was married to a cousin of Matthew Cradock, which gave him entree into London's mercantile, colonizing circles and a relatively high social standing.

Endecott arrived at Naumkeag on September 6, 1628, with about fifty or sixty new settlers, of whom only a quarter were adult males. The migration of families was a sign of the company's intention to create a permanent agricultural settlement. The contingent more than doubled the hamlet's population. Such an

[11]Theodore K. Rabb, *Enterprise and Empire: Merchant and Gentry Investment in the Expansion of England, 1575-1630* (Cambridge, Mass., 1967), pp. 35-48, 104, 108, 257, 273, 401.

[12]Louis B. Wright, *Religion and Empire: The Alliance between Piety and Commerce in English Expansion, 1558-1625* (Chapel Hill, N.C., 1943), p. 136; Howard Mumford Jones, *O Strange New World: American Culture, the Formative Years* (New York, 1952), p. 188.

[13]Lawrence Shaw Mayo, *John Endecott: A Biography* (Cambridge, Mass., 1936), is the most thorough and scholarly account of his life.

influx in early fall meant that both the newcomers and the Old Planters had to devote their full energies to preparing for winter. There were shelters to build and the harvest to gather. That winter a number of colonists died of the seasoning process. Facing these difficulties and having as yet no minister, Endecott put off making decisions about church and civil government until the following spring and summer.

Despite the pressures of necessity, or perhaps because of them, some tension arose between Endecott and Conant's followers. Endecott was an abrasive and imperious man, and the Old Planters, who had doubts about staying at Naumkeag anyway, probably resented his replacement of Conant as leader of the settlement. The Old Planters suspected that they might be kept from becoming an integral part of the community, just as they had been excluded in Plymouth. They feared that the powers that the patent gave the incorporators of the New England Company would "make them slaves."[14] Meanwhile Conant once more had to talk his companions into staying. He argued that the problem "should not disturb the peace of good Christians, that came so far to provide a place where to live in christian amity and concord."[15]

Conant was visualizing an inclusive godly community that would be free of the strife of England and of the problems he had experienced so far in America. And it was on this basis that the Old Planters, the new settlers, and the company came to a lasting agreement. The instructions that arrived from London in late June stressed that the Old Planters "shall be incorporated into this society." Furthermore the only criteria for prospective participants in the "privileges and profits" of the settlement were that they "be peaceable men, and of honest life and conversation, and desirous to live amongst us, and conform themselves to good order and government." The company buttressed these good intentions toward the Old Planters with several more specific guarantees. Economically "They should have some benefit by the common stock." They were to be secure in "those lands which formerly they have manured" plus "such a further proportion as, by the advice and judgment of yourself and the rest of the Council, shall be thought fit for them or any of them." Since the governor and Council enjoyed wide local powers, the company sought to assure the Old Planters some voice in this governing body. They were to "choose two of the discreetest and judicial men" to join the eleven men appointed by the company in London. Also they were to

[14] Edmund S. Morgan, *The Founding of Massachusetts: Historians and the Sources* (New York, 1964), p. 454.

[15] Hubbard, pp. 109-10; Shipton, pp. 71-72.

have strong influence in the future development of institutions
and laws; "we would have their consent (if it may be) in making
wholesome constitutions for government."[16]

The directors of the company had made a wise and thorough
attempt to assuage the Old Planters' suspicions, and they were
successful. To both Endecott's and Conant's followers "the late
controversy" seemed so unfortunate and the reconciliation so
complete that they decided to change the name of the settlement
to Salem "in remembrance of a peace."[17] Henceforward as new
waves of immigrants entered the town the Old Planters and
Endecott's followers grew closer together. Overwhelmingly West
Countrymen and holding the same religious and social views, they
acted in rough concert. Hereafter they are referred to jointly as
the Old Planter or West Country faction.

The fleet of five ships that carried the instructions guaranteeing
Conant and his companions an influential role in the life of the
settlement also brought well over three hundred new immigrants.
Although "above forty" of the newcomers were "from Dorchester
and other places thereabouts," the immigrants had been recruited
from all over England. Their motives and their social and religious
ideas varied. Robert Moulton, a skilled shipwright commanding
five other artisans, came from Great Ormsby, Norfolk. He and
Thomas Scruggs, also of Norfolk, both became Antinomians in
1637. Richard Waterman, of Essex and London, became a
supporter of Roger Williams in 1633 and later a Gortonist in
Rhode Island. Lawrence Leach, a farmer of Somersetshire, was
quickly assimilated into the Old Planter faction. The company had
applied only their usual criteria of virtue and usefulness. Wrote
Cradock to Endecott: "We desire you to take notice of one
Lawrence Leach, whom we have found a careful and painful man,
and we doubt not but he will continue his diligence; let him have
deserving respect. The like we say of Richard Waterman, whose
chief employment will be to get you good venison."[18]

However, when Cradock contemplated the four ministers who
had emigrated in the fleet, he had intimations of "some
distractions among you." Francis Bright, who sailed with the
Dorchester contingent, was a "Conformist" and a protégé of John
White. Samuel Skelton and Francis Higginson, of East Anglia and
the Midlands respectively, were both silenced Puritan preachers.
Although Skelton tended more toward Separatism than Higginson,

[16]Morgan, pp. 453-54.

[17]John White, *The Planters Plea* (London, 1630), rept. in *Proceedings of the
Massachusetts Historical Society*, 3d. ser., 62 (1929): 378-79; Hubbard, p. 109.

[18]Morgan, p. 462.

their differences were not obvious, and the company detected nothing irreconcilable between them, or even between them and Bright. Ralph Smith was another matter. He, unlike the others, had not been hired by the company, but had merely "desired passage." Suspecting that Smith was strongly committed to Separatism, the company considered not sending him. But Cradock believed that, despite "his difference of judgment in some things from our ministers," Smith could be included in the community because "we have a very good opinion of his honesty."[19] Actually Smith was not long at Salem. He quickly gravitated toward Plymouth, whose church he served for several years.[20]

Cradock's belief in the infant settlement's ability to absorb four ministers ranging from Conformist to Separatist was part of the intense optimism that pervaded both the company and the settlers as they began to create civil and ecclesiastical institutions. Such optimism seems foreign to men of generally Calvinist bent; men who believed that the natural course of society is degenerative, that strong faith and dedicated action are necessary just to keep human society from regressing, much less progressing. The primary basis of their high expectations was that while God was about to afflict England, He had ordained settlement in America. Therefore, "We doubt not but God will in Mercy give a blessing upon our labors."[21]

Besides the good will of the Lord, they felt that the success of their efforts was assured by two things. The first was the high quality of the men sent to fill responsible positions. The company felt it had taken the advice that John White was later to put into print and had sent "not the weak, unfit and prodigal," but "good Governors, able Ministers, Physicians, Soldiers, Schoolmasters, Mariners, and Mechanics of all sorts." The hope was that once "the frame of the body is thus formed and furnished with vital parts, and knit together with firm bands and sinews, the bulk may be filled up with flesh, that is with persons of less use and activity, so they be pliable and kept in life."[22]

The other basis for optimism was the American environment. This sense of the New England wilderness as a promising opportunity to form new pure societies can be found both in the promotional tracts of White, who never saw the coasts and forests,

[19] Ibid., p. 457.

[20] George D. Langdon, Jr., *Pilgrim Colony: A History of New Plymouth, 1620-1691* (New Haven, 1966), pp. 117-18.

[21] Morgan, p. 450.

[22] White, pp. 391-92.

and in the writings of Francis Higginson, who came to Salem and was one of the important figures in the formation of its Church. At least one of Higginson's works, *New Englands Plantation* (London, 1630), must have been influential and appealing to his contemporaries, for it went through three editions in one year.[23] Arriving in New England during summer after a harrowing voyage, Higginson saw a warm, balmy, green land, heavy with the fragrance of flowers and trees. "Now what with fine woods and green trees by land, and these yellow flowers painting the sea, made us all desirous to see our new paradise of New England, whence we saw such forerunning signals of fertility afar off." "Paradise," a new Garden of Eden, was a concept not used lightly by Calvinist ministers in the seventeenth century.[24] Once ashore he did not change his mind. "The fertility of the Soil is to be admired at ... and I am told that about three miles from us a Man may stand on a little hilly place and see diverse thousands of acres of ground as good as need to be, and not a Tree in the same." This enthusiasm was more than an appeal to English land hunger. To Higginson the bountiful land almost guaranteed that England's social problems of overpopulation and poverty would never appear in Massachusetts. Even "little children here by setting of Corn may earn more than their own maintenance." Among the drawbacks of New England, like the severity of winter and the mosquitos, he included the lack of a "good company of honest christians" to use the land and remarked, "Great pity it is to see so much good ground for Corn and Grass as any is under the Heavens, to lie altogether unoccupied when so many honest Men and their Families in old England through the populousness thereof, do make a very hard shift to live one by the other."[25]

Is it not possible that there lurked just below the surface of minds like Higginson's the belief that for the first time in history there was a chance of approximating the prelapsarian bliss for which Christians have always hungered? In New England, Calvinists seemed to have their first opportunity to give their social theories full application without the qualifications forced upon them in Europe.

[23]*New Englands Plantation* and a letter from Higginson are in Morgan, pp. 138-57. Moses Coit Tyler, *A History of American Literature during the Colonial Period, 1607-1765* (abridged ed., Ithaca, N.Y., 1949), pp. 29-30.

[24]Francis Higginson, *A True Relation of the Last Voyage to New England* (London, 1630), rept. in *Proceedings of the Massachusetts Historical Society*, 3d. ser., 62 (1930): 295-96; Richard P. Gildrie, "Francis Higginson's New World Vision," *Essex Institute Historical Collections* 106 (1970): 182-89.

[25]Higginson, *New Englands Plantation*, pp. 140-41, 146-47.

The Calvinist doctrines of social ethics which Salem's early settlers sought to apply had their roots deep in covenant theology. For Calvinists the covenant was a central concept, so important that some modern theologians regard the idea as "almost exclusively the preserve of the Puritans."[26] Calvinists made a radical distinction between the actual social order and the new order sought by God.[27] Consequently, social and political traditions had no automatic sanction. The traditional order, although not totally repudiated, was suspect since it was corrupted by disobedience to God's will, that is, by sin. The Calvinist's chief loyalty, therefore, rested with the coming new order of the Lord, the cornerstone of which was the covenant. A covenant was a voluntary assumption of mutual obligations. Christian action had to express a voluntary, consensual commitment first to God and then to fellow Calvinists. Covenants provided the means of breaking one's bonds with an old order and of creating new institutions. A new world free of the encumbrances of long history and entrenched custom presented Calvinists an excellent foundation on which to build a new society.

In the euphoric atmosphere of the summer of 1629, the leaders of Salem set out to form lasting institutions. The new institutions partook of this mood; they were informal and covenanted. The company had provided for a resident governor and Council made up of leading settlers, merchants, and ministers as a government. Apparently Endecott felt that this government, imposed from London, was unlikely to hold the loyalty of the settlers; so he hit upon a voluntary association, or covenant.

The only surviving account of the civil covenant is a hostile and caustic one by Thomas Morton. He was incensed against Endecott, who had that previous May taken a leading part in the suppression of Morton's little settlement at Merrymount. Morton had been engaged in more than debauchery around his Maypole; he had been selling firearms and alcohol to the Indians in exchange for furs, contrary to a proclamation made by the Crown in 1622. Nonetheless, the main outlines of Endecott's proposal emerge from his account.

Endecott "summoned a general appearance at the worshipful town of Salem" of all living within the New England Company's grant and "there in open assembly was tendered certain Articles, devised between him and their new Pastor Master Eager

---

[26] *The Heart Prepared: Grace and Coversion in Puritan Spiritual Life* (New Haven 1966), p. 13n.

[27] David Little, *Religion, Order and Law: A Study in Pre-Revolutionary England* (New York, 1969), p. 127.

[Skelton] . . . . To these Articles every Planter, old and new, must sign." The alternative to signing was expulsion from the area of the grant. The binding contract that Endecott sought was simple and direct, saying nothing more, according to Morton, then "that in all causes, as well Ecclesiastical, as Political, we should follow the rule of God's Word." Morton stressed that he was aware of this "very mousetrap to catch somebody by his own consent" and demanded the addition, "so as nothing be done contrary, or repugnant to the Laws of the Kingdom of England."[28] Since Morton did not say that this amendment was rejected, we can assume that it was amiably included. In fact, since Morton was not above altering facts in the interests of making a hero of himself, the qualifying phrase may have been there from the beginning, although the possibility of conflict between the Word of God and the laws of England, if both were properly interpreted, was inconceivable to non-Separatists.

There are a number of interesting things about this civil covenant. First was its inclusiveness. All adult males were required to sign and hence were to be an integral part of the community. This was in sharp contrast to the Pilgrims' Mayflower Compact, which was signed only by the Leyden Congregation. Endecott's articles were similar to that compact in their lack of specificity; both were open-ended toward the future. Further, the articles were designed, like the compact, to preserve not only order but also the social hierarchy. The goal was to assure obedience to the governor and Council. After all, both the Word of God and the laws of England enjoined proper deference, mutual obligations, and peace within a community.

The community was to be inclusive economically as well as politically. According to Morton, Endecott offered everyone in the area of the patent participation in the general stock; "every man to put in a part: and every man, for his person, to have shares alike: and for their stock according to the ratable proportions was put in: and this to continue for twelve months and then to call an account." Morton, suspecting that the motive was to rob the Particulars, suggested more restrictions to the effect that the accounts be taken after six months and that the salaried managers be paid from "clear profit" rather than stock.[29] These suggestions too were taken, but he still refused to sign. Although it was not long before the joint stock began losing money and had to be

---

[28] Thomas Morton, *New English Canaan* (Amsterdam, 1637; facsimile ed. Amsterdam, 1969), pp. 158-59.

[29] Ibid., pp. 159-60.

abandoned, the attempt was a significant effort to weld disparate elements into an integrated economic community.

The most important institution created that summer was the church, an event which probably preceded the civil covenant and the stock offering. The only certain date of that summer's activities is the week of the church's creation, July 29 to August 6. The formation of the Salem church was a pivotal act in Salem's history and in the history of New England Puritanism, for the Salem church was the first in the Bay Colony and set a precedent that was generally followed by its successors.

The New England Company was primarily interested in religion as the substructure of a moral environment rather than as a set of doctrines, and it recruited its ministers accordingly. For example, Francis Higginson, a stranger to Endecott, was introduced in the company's instructions simply as "a grave man, and of worthy commendations." Cradock's suspicion of Separatists like Ralph Smith was based on fear of "needless questions to stir up strife . . . (most commonly in things indifferent)." Endecott was exhorted "that if any such disputes shall happen among you, that you suppress them, and be careful to maintain peace and unity." The particular adjustments necessary to gain that end were left to Endecott and the ministers. "For the manner of exercising their ministry, and teaching both our own people and the Indians, we leave that to themselves, hoping they will make God's Word the rule of their actions, and mutually agree in the discharge of their duties."[30]

Thus the company, following the general procedure in such cases, granted great latitude to its agents. As John White later explained when the charges of Separatism in New England had reached a high pitch in London, "Nay I see not how we can expect from them a correspondence in all things to our State civil or Ecclesiastical: Wants and necessities cannot but cause many changes . . . and the consideration of their own necessities will certainly enforce them to take away many things that we admit, and introduce many things that we reject." He reiterated the only criteria by which the company would judge the settlement: "Piety, sobriety and austerity." Apparently even the ministers, while preparing to emigrate, were unwilling to decide "upon their form of church government" before they reached Salem. Like the company's officials, they felt strongly that the new environment would impose new conditions and fresh opportunities. They wished to remain flexible.[31]

[30] Morgan, pp. 453, 462.
[31] White, p. 412; Hubbard, p. 118.

Before the fleet arrived in Massachusetts, Endecott gave some thought to the problem of church government. During the winter of 1628/29 Deacon Samuel Fuller of Plymouth had come to Salem to help care for the sick, and he and Endecott discussed the issue. On May 11, 1629, Endecott wrote Governor Bradford, "I am by him satisfied touching your judgments of the outward form of God's worship." He went on to say that he had held the same general opinions since his conversion and that he was glad that the Pilgrims were not as Separatist as "common report" held.[32] Endecott was careful to note that he had accepted "the outward form," that is, the congregational organization of the Plymouth church. He said nothing about its exclusionist rationale. In the secular areas of the community's life the company's instructions and his efforts had stressed inclusiveness instead. The company was urging "peace and unity." The consent mechanism of congregational church formation undoubtedly appealed to Endecott for much the same reasons as did the civil covenant. It was a means of cementing the community.

By the time the fleet bearing the new immigrants and the ministers arrived in late June 1629, Endecott had apparently decided on some form of covenanted church order but probably little else. Hubbard later described the majority of the leaders as "honest minded men, studious of reformation, that only had disliked some things in the discipline and ceremonies of the church of England, but were not precisely fixed upon any particular order or form of government, but . . . fit to receive any impression, that could be delineated out of the word of God." Into this malleable environment came Samuel Skelton, whom the company had especially sought "for that we are informed yourself have formerly received much good by his ministry." Skelton, an East Anglian of Separatist bent, became the first of Endecott's spiritual advisers.[33]

It did not take Francis Bright, the conformist, long to see what was afoot, and he returned to England the next year. Francis Higginson, who was "a stranger" to Endecott and must have exercised less influence on him, decided to stay. His strong hope that a new world might mean new institutions made him acquiesce in the planned course "although in some points of church discipline Mr. Higginson's principles were a little discrepant from theirs of Plymouth," according to Hubbard.[34]

Late in July Endecott declared "a solemn day of humiliation for the choosing of a pastor and teacher." Skelton was chosen

[32] Bradford, pp. 223-24.
[33] Hubbard, p. 117; Morgan, p. 453.
[34] P. 119.

pastor and Higginson teacher "by election," and there followed "the imposition of hands" by "three or four of the gravest members of the church." It is now generally agreed that this procedure was not necessarily Separatist and involved no repudiation of the Church of England. Later when the founders of the Boston church used the same method they explicitly denied any Separatist intent.[35]

The founders of both the Salem and the Boston churches were not concerned with doctrine but with the sense of community. The only questions asked of Skelton and Higginson concerned their "calling." The ministers acknowledged two kinds; inward, from God, and outward, "from the people." The ministers were operating within the intellectual framework of the covenant idea. The point was made clear on August 6, when the Salem church members framed their covenant. It said simply, "We covenant with the Lord, and one with another and do bind ourselves in the presence of God to walk together in all his ways, according as he is pleased to reveal himself unto us in his Blessed Word of Truth." [36]

The founders felt no need for anything more than this statement. After a month or more of consultation they felt they knew each other, enjoyed the blessing of the Lord, and agreed sufficiently about their mission to forgo more explicit religious tests. Events had allowed the saints to recognize each other without tests, and true saints would build a true church. As non-Separatists they decided to allow some latitude on all issues peripheral to the core of Reformed belief, just as the company had advised. Until 1633, when Roger Williams introduced tighter standards, this looseness characterized the church. According to Hubbard, "Those that were afterward admitted unto the church fellowship, were with the confession of their faith required to enter into a like covenant engagement with the church, to walk according to the rules of the gospel, . . . but for the manner and circumstances, it was left to the wisdom and faithfulness of the elders, to be so ordered as was judged most conducive to the end, respect by themselves had to the liberty and ability of persons."[37]

This character of implicitness helped to make the church's form more acceptable to the mass of settlers. Even the new pattern was not totally unfamiliar. The animating desire for one church, one

---

[35] Charles Gott's letter in Bradford, pp. 224-25, is the only firsthand account. Edmund S. Morgan, *Visible Saints: The History of a Puritan Idea* (New York, 1963), pp. 80-87; John Winthrop, *Winthrop's Journal, 1630-1649* (1649; 2 vols., ed. James K. Hosmer, New York, 1908), I, 31-32.

[36] Williston Walker, *The Creeds and Platforms of Congregationalism* (1893; rept. Boston, 1960), pp. 106, 116.

[37] Pp. 119-20.

community, was in spirit a re-creation of the ideal English parish around which every individual's life revolved. The whole community attended services, as in England, and the parish was a basic element in the governing of all aspects of local life. That the church was not democratic would scarcely have concerned anyone. There were only thirty initial members of the church, probably the same men who comprised the social, political, and economic leadership of the town. These thirty chose the church officers, and the officers exercised great power, as Hubbard hinted above. Although their titles might have been somewhat unfamiliar to most of the townspeople, their powers were not, for they were similar to those of the vestry of local parishes in England.

Despite the flexibility and familiarity of the form and the great influence of the men who created it, there was a strong challenge. As the new deacon Charles Gott put it, the church had been founded "notwithstanding all opposition that hath been here and elsewhere." To be effective, dissent had to come from the ranks of the leadership, and, in fact, it was led by two members of the Council, the Browne brothers, "both of them amongst the number of the first patentees, men of estates, and men of parts and port in the place."[38]

According to Nathaniel Morton in his *New Englands Memorial* (1669), "They began to raise some trouble . . . observing that the ministers did not at all use the Book of Common Prayer, and that they did administer baptism and the Lord's supper without the ceremonies, and that they professed also to use discipline in the congregation against scandalous persons, by a personal application of the word of God, as the case might require, and that some that were scandalous were denied admission into the church." Although these critics urged an inclusive and traditional form, they were willing to use a Separatist method to pursue their own beliefs. Shattering the unity of the community, "these two brothers gathered a company together, in a place distinct from the public assembly, and there, sundry times, the Book of Common prayer was read unto such as resorted thither."[39]

Apparently it was because of this action rather than for their opinions that Endecott decided to act against the Brownes. Revealing both his uncertainty in the face of religious questions and his determination to keep the community together, Endecott called a public meeting in which the Brownes voiced their complaint that the ministers were "departing from the orders of

[38] Bradford, p. 224; Mayo, pp. 42-48.
[39] Nathaniel Morton, *New Englands Memorial* (1699; facsimile ed., Boston, 1903), p. 147.

the Church of England, that they were Separatists, and would be anabaptists, etc. but for themselves, they would hold to the orders of the Church of England." In reply, the ministers took a conciliatory line, one that was to characterize Massachusetts Puritanism for the rest of the century. They claimed that they were not separating from the English church "but only from the corruptions and disorders there," an appeal to the general Puritan criticism of English society and to the common belief in a reformed church order as the solution. The outcome of the debate was inevitable. "The governor and council, and the generality of the people, did well approve of the ministers' answer; and therefore finding those two brothers to be of high spirits, and their speeches and practices tending to mutiny and faction, the governor told them that New England was no place for such as they." Endecott sent them back to the company in England, explaining that they were "factious."[40]

By swift and drastic action and by liberal interpretation of his instructions Endecott had managed to save Salem from a possibly fatal schism. But his course bewildered and shocked the company's managers in London, who were understandably nervous about anything "which may have ill construction with the State here, and make us obnoxious to any adversary." In October 1629, after nearly a month of deliberation, the company delivered a mild rebuke to both Endecott and the ministers. All this occurred several months after John Winthrop and his East Anglian connection had become prominent within the company. Although both Winthrop and White had taken Endecott's side in the company's formal debate, it is clear from the company's letters that they were contending not that Endecott had established the correct order, only that the company should suspend judgment. The company grudgingly accepted Endecott's decision, but it is probable that discomfort over his course helped lead the company to replace him with John Winthrop at the next election.[41]

Endecott's summary rejection of the Browne's complaints strongly indicates that the Pilgrims had some influence at Salem. It would have been strange had it been otherwise. By the very act of separating from the Church of England, the Pilgrims had been forced into working out the implications of Puritan doctrine for many years before the problem was faced by non-Separatists. They had been in America adapting their notions to the new American environment for nine years. Furthermore, they constituted the only organized church within easy communication of

[40] Ibid., p. 148.
[41] Morgan, *Founding of Mass.*, pp. 370-71, 373, 380, 477-79.

Salem and were eager to assist their neighbors. Leyden Separatists had been passing through Salem on their way to Plymouth, taking advantage of the company's more frequent ships from Europe. Also, Deacon Fuller, who seems to have had the greatest influence on Endecott before Skelton's arrival, was one of the more articulate Separatist theorists in the Pilgrim colony.

Nevertheless, Endecott, with the company's encouragement, was bent on creating a more inclusive and flexible society than that devised by the Pilgrims. He had in mind a theologically centered commonwealth, a common concept not only among Puritans but throughout all the colonizing powers of Europe. Central to all these experiments was some method of coercion, a centripetal force to counter the natural fragmenting influence of the unstructured environment.[42] The Pilgrims used the device of a covenant as a means of discipline. Endecott pushed the concept even further. Instead of using it as a pact among the regenerate in order to control the unregenerate, Endecott attempted to make everyone a party to the agreement, especially in the civil and economic spheres. In a sense he had no other option; it was necessary to include, for example, Conant's Old Planters on an equal basis since they were men of some stature and wealth. Also the company was sensitive to the need of keeping the Old Planters and other Particulars in order to strengthen the colony. The status lines, unlike Plymouth's, were not clear, and some way had to be found to cement the society and insure Endecott's leadership.

Endecott's decision to cope with Salem's initial pluralism by involving as many settlers as possible in implicit covenants had a pronounced effect on the town's institutions for decades. In the church, the governing process among the thirty or so original communicants appears to have been remarkably egalitarian. As late as 1642 Thomas Lechford could contrast the Salem and Boston churches sharply. "In Boston, they rule, by unanimous consent, if they can, both in admissions, and censures, and other things. In Salem, they rule by the major part of the church: you that are so minded hold up your hands; you that are otherwise minded, hold up yours." In Boston, when agreement could not be reached, the final decision was made by select committee. For the system to work there had to be within the church a clearly defined leadership that made policy to be ratified by the membership; the Boston church contained "a speaking aristocracy" and "a silent democracy."[43] In Salem the whole church seems to have been the

---

[42] Jones, pp. 74-75.

[43] Lechford, *Plain Dealing; or, News from New England* (1642; ed. J. Hammond Trumbull, Boston, 1867), p. 38.

speaking aristocracy with the rest of the society comprising a silent democracy. At times the result was cacophony with an internally divided church that split the town into factions.

The unusual organization of the Salem church hints at another peculiarity of Salem society that was to last for some time. The necessity of combining the Old Planters on a basis of equality with the leaders of Endecott's migration created an unusually large upper class. Part of the company's compromise with the Old Planters was a guarantee of two hundred acres for each family, the same amount of land given to each member of the company who contributed the rather lordly sum of £50. Those individuals who came over on their own expense but did not contribute £50 were to receive only fifty acres and another fifty if they brought servants. The effect of this land policy remained visible when the land records began in 1636. Holders of over one hundred acres comprised about one quarter of the adult male population, an unusually large proportion.[44] It seems probable that the ratio of these large landholders to the generality was about the same in 1629-30, although at that early date a claim to two hundred acres was a promise of future landed wealth than an economic reality since everyone lived on the peninsula and farmed very few acres indeed.

Endecott, with Conant's help, succeeded in welding a community together that showed strength but contained elements of instability, the most crucial of which was this large leadership group. Many of these leaders, then and later, had their own followings within the town. Endecott did not preside over a clearly defined hierarchy. Instead he enjoyed an uneasy hegemony over a group of equals whom he kept in tenuous alliance. Another indication of future troubles lay in the fact that although the society was overwhelmingly West Country, not one of the six men who held church offices in the year 1629-30 was a West Countryman. All but Francis Higginson, who came from the Midland town of Leicester, were from East Anglia.[45] This tendency of East Anglians to take a leading role in church affairs was to prove a source of disruption under the ministry of Roger Williams in 1633-36.

[44]Morgan, *Founding of Mass.*, pp. 340, 357-62, 388; Philip J. Greven, Jr., *Four Generations: Population, Land, and Family in Colonial Andover, Massachusetts* (Ithaca, N.Y., 1970), p. 44.

[45]Sidney Perley, *The History of Salem, Massachusetts*, 3 vols. (Salem, 1924-27); James Duncan Philips, *Salem in the Seventeenth Century* (Boston, 1933), esp. p. 357.

Chapter II

The Crisis of the Implicit Covenant
1630-1636

By the summer of 1630 Endecott had managed to weld together
the community of Salem through implicit and inclusive covenants.
Because a covenant is a pledge of mutual obligations, the various
practical compromises designed to keep the Old Planters within
the community were an integral part of the early covenant system.
Of greater long-range significance was the notion of the covenant as a rudimentary social contract whose purpose, unlike
eighteenth-century formulations of the theory, was to incorporate
political necessities into a religious vision.[1] Thus Endecott,
Conant, and the ministers not only found that two keys of
Calvinist theory—voluntarism and universalism—were practically
useful but also believed that they were divinely required. For
thirty more years this vision would be an important element in the
thought of many of Salem's leaders.

Salem's earliest covenant system lacked specific guidelines for
either doctrine or behavior. The assumption was that there would
be a consensus defining "the rule of God's word" among those
who agreed "to walk together in all his ways." The leadership, like
John White, felt that this lack of specificity allowed necessary
flexibility. However, the increasing diversity of Salem undermined
the possibility of implicit consensus. The immigration of the
1630s into Salem and the Bay brought economic, political, and
social problems that were insoluble within so simple a system.
New people with different experiences and ideas could not easily
adapt to, or even completely understand, religious and political
institutions in which standards of belief and behavior were not
clearly expressed. The "rule of God's word" meant different
things to different people. The problems were further complicated
by confusion between Separatist and non-Separatist attitudes at
Salem during the early 1630s. Consequently the town, and to
some extent the entire Bay Colony, was torn by disagreements
and confusion.

Initially Endecott's efforts seemed successful. He had established his leadership within the community. But the relative

---

[1] David Little, *Religion, Order and Law: A Study in Pre-Revolutionary England* (New
York, 1969), p. 129.

position and authority of lesser leaders was confused. Clashes among these men were frequent, and the situation worsened during the 1630s. At first the problem seemed slight since Endecott's prestige was as yet unassailable and the village was small, not above two hundred people. He probably had high hopes that with continuing personal interaction among the settlers, cooperation from men like Conant, and effective preaching from the ministers, the Christian society envisioned in the covenants would emerge.

The core of a successful Christian community was, of course, the church. Although founding the Salem church with thirty "pillars" instead of the more common seven or eight in congregational organizations may have been a concession to the large number of Salem townsmen of high status, it was also a step toward the non-Separatist ideal of universality. The means of attaining this end was not to allow "things indifferent," i.e., peripheral doctrinal matters, to prevent people from "owning the covenant." "In the beginning of things they only accepted of one another, according to some general profession of the gospel, and the honest and good intentions they had one towards another."[2]

The attainment of that goal was soon hindered when the Salem church began to manifest a Separatist psychology in the summer of 1630. Francis Higginson, who might have successfully resisted the trend, became mortally ill during the winter and died in August. Samuel Skelton became the sole minister and, strongly supported by his fellow East Anglians who held lay offices in the church, embarked on a Separatist course. Skelton "did in some things not only imitate and equal, but strongly endeavor to go beyond that pattern of separation set up before them in Plymouth, in pressing of some indifferent things, that savored as much or more than they of Plymouth did, of the same spirit." As specific examples Hubbard mentioned "enjoining all women to wear veils, under penalty of noncommunion, urging the same as a matter of duty and absolute necessity, as is by some reported, as well as in refusing communion with the church of England."[3]

As an outward sign of Eve's temptation, the requirement of veils was revelatory of the Separatist mind. Refusing communion with the Church of England was, of course, the major debating point between Separatist and non-Separatist Puritans, the main doctrinal issue on which they diverged.[4] When the initial

[2] William Hubbard, *A General History of New England from the Discovery to 1680* (1680; Cambridge, Mass., 1815), pp. 181-82.
[3] Ibid., p. 117.
[4] Raymond P. Stearns and D. H. Brawner, "New England Church 'Relations' and Continuity in Early Congregational History," *Proceedings of the American Antiquarian Society* 75 (1965): 18-19.

contingents of the Massachusetts Bay Company arrived during June and July 1630, Skelton denied their leaders communion with the Salem church because Winthrop and his associates were not members of a church organized by a particular covenant. The rejection of such prestigious persons contradicted the non-Separatist policy of accepting people to membership on the basis of their apparent individual piety and behavior. Skelton was substituting a doctrinal test for "honest intentions," a tendency that often led to dissension and schism in Separatist congregations.[5] If he could deny membership to men in whose East Anglian connection he had once belonged, one wonders how he regarded the West Countrymen of Salem, especially Conant's followers.

Possibly Skelton was distinguishing between a unified Salem community and newcomers, but John Cotton, the influential Puritan vicar in Boston, England, feared otherwise. He wrote a letter rebuking Skelton: "Say not . . . that Saints are gathered out of the world. What though many scandalous gospelers be tolerated amongst us? that argueth the neglect of Discipline, not the nullity of a church." He also suspected, with typical non-Separatist logic, that such a policy of exclusion disrupted the social fabric by undermining the communal sense of charity: "Have pity also upon these poor creatures that die among you and (as it is said) some for lack of necessaries: call upon the richer sort for a compassionate heart and hand."[6] Exhortation to Christian love was to Cotton a far more preferable course for a minister than the quest for dogmatic purity.

Skelton's course ran counter to Endecott's earlier intent. Endecott probably could have prevented the trend, but he did not; in fact, he encouraged Separatist actions until 1636. There are several possible explanations. The least complimentary motive was possible pique at being replaced by Winthrop as governor. Endecott was acutely sensitive about his authority and prestige; in May 1631 he was fined £40 for attacking a man who provokingly challenged a decision he had made as justice of the peace.[7] To see Winthrop insulted by Skelton may not have bothered him since he may have felt similarly treated. Separatism, at least that applied to the new arrivals, may also have been a way for Endecott to

[5] Edmund S. Morgan, *Visible Saints: The History of a Puritan Idea* (New York, 1963), chap. 2.

[6] David D. Hall, "John Cotton's Letter to Samuel Skelton," *William and Mary Quarterly,* 3d ser., 22 (1965): 482-85.

[7] Lawrence Shaw Mayo, *John Endecott: A Biography* (Cambridge, Mass., 1936), pp. 61-63.

preserve his authority in Salem. The decision of Winthrop and his followers to settle around Massachusetts Bay was probably motivated as much by tact as by the attractiveness of the Bay.[8] If Winthrop and the other gentry who were with him had stayed in Salem, Endecott would have been replaced as leader there as well. The refusal of church membership may have been a broad hint which Winthrop quickly understood. Endecott's tendency to rely heavily on advice from ministers whom he respected also must be taken into account. Although often politically astute, he could make serious political errors in the name of religion. Besides, being impressed with the use of covenants, he would not have found uncomfortable the idea that only covenanted churches were true churches.

Serious conflict between Salem and the Massachusetts Bay settlers did not occur immediately, largely because the latter group was no more certain about the proper form of church government than Endecott had been the previous summer. Just as the new immigrants were forming their first congregation, Providence seemingly intervened to give the Plymouth-Salem pattern added legitimacy. Interpreting their severe seasoning process as divine chastisement, Winthrop and his followers wrote to Salem asking them to consider "what was to be done to pacify the Lord's Wrath." The Salem church consulted with Plymouth and then, in a predictable response, urged a day of humiliation during which "such godly persons that are amongst them, and known to each other, may . . . solemnly . . . enter into covenant with the Lord to walk in his ways."[9]

The congregational pattern of Massachusetts churches had been set. The younger churches continued to seek advice from Salem and Plymouth until 1633 when Thomas Hooker and John Cotton became the arch-theorists of the New England Way. For example, the Boston church in 1632 was concerned over whether or not the same person could be a ruling elder and a civil magistrate simultaneously and whether "there might be diverse pastors in the same church." Salem and Plymouth gave a strong negative to the first and were "doubtful" about the second.[10] At least until 1633 the relationship among the churches was as loose as that among

[8] Edmund S. Morgan, *The Puritan Dilemma: The Story of John Winthrop* (Boston, 1958), p. 58.

[9] William Bradford, *Of Plymouth Plantation, 1620-1647* (1647; ed. Samuel Eliot Morison, New York, 1952), p. 235.

[10] John Winthrop, *Winthrop's Journal, 1630-1649* (1649; 2 vols., ed. James K. Hosmer, New York, 1908), I, 81; Larzer Ziff, *The Career of John Cotton: Puritanism and the American Experience* (Princeton, N.J., 1962), pp. 78-82.

individuals within each church. Each town and church developed its own variant of the same basic congregational pattern.

The issue of Separatism, however, had not been resolved. Roger Williams brought the problem out in the open. He arrived in Boston in 1631 with an excellent reputation and was immediately offered the post of teacher in the Boston church. That he was known as a Separatist probably did not disturb the non-Separatists of Boston, for they felt that they had worked out a reasonable modus vivendi with Salem and Plymouth. But Williams could not be absorbed into a system that sought consensus by tolerating diversity over "things indifferent." To his mind there were no minor points when perfection was the goal. He refused both the post and membership in the Boston church. He objected to fellowship with the Bostonians because they would not publicly repent of their former ties with the Church of England or openly repudiate the connection. That such a declaration might bring down the wrath of a sensitive English government upon infant Massachusetts seemed to him irrelevant.[11] After refusing Boston, Williams went to Salem, transforming the problem from a local concern in Boston to a colonywide issue. Before he could be formally installed as Skelton's assistant, the Bay Colony's leadership wrote a letter to Endecott protesting the choice as an insult to the non-Separatists and an incitement to division.[12] Salem heeded the warning, and Williams, finding Salem not as Separatist as he had hoped, departed for Plymouth.

Salem's decision was not due solely to the letter from Boston. The deciding factor was the power relationships within Salem. In 1631, despite the East Anglian monopoly on church offices, the town was still overwhelmingly West Country. Williams had been invited by the church officers, but Conant and the Old Planters resisted his settlement. Conant had accepted the exclusion of Winthrop and the 1630 immigrants, probably for political reasons. Yet he could not accept a pastor who would demand that he repent his membership in the Church of England. Conant's father and grandfather had been churchwardens. His brother and his friend John White were both respected ministers of the Church of England.[13] Furthermore, Williams's strict attitude on this and other points would call into question the right of Conant and the Old Planters to belong to the church and hence threaten their power and status within the community.

[11] Edmund S. Morgan, *Roger Williams: The Church and the State* (New York, 1967), pp. 24-26.

[12] Winthrop, I, 52-53.

[13] Clifford K. Shipton, *Roger Conant: A Founder of Massachusetts* (Cambridge, Mass., 1945), pp. 100-101.

The Old Planters were successful in opposing Williams in 1631 because they were in a highly strategic position both within the town and the colony. They were the bulk of the town's political community. Of the twenty-two Salem men who took the freeman's oath on May 18, 1631, at least twelve were West Countrymen. Eight of them were Conant's followers. The only known East Anglians on the list—Charles Gott, John Horne, Samuel Skelton, and Roger Williams—were officers of the church.[14]

After 1633 Old Planter influence in Salem politics was challenged by newcomers. In 1634, the year the freemen of the towns began sending deputies to the General Court, Salem elected three representatives. Joining Roger Conant and Francis Weston was a recent immigrant from East Anglia, John Holgrave.[15] The appearance of East Anglians in the high position of deputy was attended by political confusion, judging from the rapid turnover in that office from 1634 to 1637 (table 1). Salem was changing its

Table 1. Elections of Salem deputies, 1634-39

Year	West Countrymen	East Anglians	Others	Total
1634	2	1	–	3
1635	3	3	1	7
1636	2	2	1	5
1637	2	2	3	7
1638	1	–	3	4
1639	1	–	2	3

Sources: James Duncan Phillips, *Salem in the Seventeenth Century* (Boston, 1933), p. 358; Sidney J. Perley, *The History of Salem, Massachusetts*, 3 vols. (Salem, 1924-27), I.

delegation to almost every meeting of the General Court. During that period Salem's representation varied from two to three seats; yet in 1635 alone seven different men held the posts. Over the whole four-year span eighteen men were elected, none more than three times. To some extent the turnover was normal in communities where potential political leaders had to be tested. Boston, for example, sent ten different men from 1634 to 1636.[16] But in the same period the smaller and older town of Salem sent fifteen. Clashes between East Anglians and West Countrymen apparently accounted for Salem's difficulties in sorting out its

[14] Sidney Perley, *The History of Salem, Massachusetts*, 3 vols. (Salem, 1924-27), I, 197.

[15] James Duncan Phillips, *Salem in the Seventeenth Century* (Boston, 1933), pp. 358-59, provides a convenient list of Salem's representatives in the colonial government.

[16] Darrett B. Rutman, *Winthrop's Boston: Portrait of a Puritan Town, 1630-1649* (Chapel Hill, N.C., 1965), pp. 74-75, 81-82.

leadership. Note that in the last three years men who were neither East Anglians nor West Countrymen became prominent, and in the final two years no East Anglians were elected, while the number of deputies chosen stabilized. Also in the last three years the turnover was drastically reduced. Only one of the seven men elected in that period had not served previously.

These shifts in Salem's representation in the General Court reflected demographic, social, political, and religious changes that forced modifications in the covenant system. The social and political order that characterized Salem through the 1650s had its roots in this period of tension from 1634 to 1637. The years 1638 and 1639 marked the beginning of a new order based on more explicit and formal institutional frameworks. Understanding the collapse of the earlier implicit system is essential to grasping the character of Salem from the late 1630s until the late 1650s.

The cause of the crisis was the influx of East Anglians into Salem, beginning in 1633. Salem garnered few if any new settlers from the first great East Anglian migration of 1630; these people followed their leaders into the area around Boston. During 1631 and 1632 there was a hiatus in emigration. The few who came were a later element of the first great movement, and most also went to the Bay. By 1633 seven churches had been founded in the colony, all but Salem a result of the Winthrop migration. Salem from 1630 to 1633 grew slowly, if at all, and its West Country cast was not significantly altered. Then in 1633 large-scale East Anglian migration was renewed, reaching a peak in 1635 and tapering off through 1638. Having less intense ties to the leaders of the Winthrop migration, some of these East Anglians chose to settle in Salem.[17] Although it is not possible to discover both the origins and the dates of first arrival in Salem for all the new immigrants, some approximate measure is feasible. Before and during 1633 there were forty recorded families living in Salem.[18] From 1633 to 1635 fifty-three new families settled in the town. Of these fifty-three, twenty-five can be identified as East Anglian. Only eleven other families are known to have come from other parts of England, and of these eleven only four were West Country. Not only did the town's population more than double between 1633 and 1635, but about two-thirds of the newcomers were not West Countrymen. The influx continued through 1636 and 1637, with fifty-seven new families settling in the town, most of whom were East Anglian.

[17] N. C. P. Tyack, "Migration from East Anglia to New England before 1660" (PhD. diss., University of London, 1951), pp. 33, 37; Phillips, pp. 74-75.

[18] Phillips, pp. 343-56, provides lists of known settlers before 1650.

The problem that the East Anglians posed was one of redefining the community. The community had been formed on implicit covenants, an intangible web of intimate personal relationships. From 1629 to 1633 the people of Salem had been judging each other's "honest intentions" and settling into as frictionless a hierarchy in church and civil government as they could. But the influx of strangers from 1633 to 1638, outnumbering the original inhabitants, greatly complicated the process. The newcomers had to be judged and absorbed into the system. If all the immigrants had been strangers to each other the problem would have been simpler. But, typical of seventeenth-century New England immigrants, the newcomers were tied to each other in various ways, by marriage and blood, by birth in the same towns and villages, or by membership in the same English churches. For example, seventeen of the immigrant families came from Great Yarmouth, Norfolk, and a number of these were related by marriage. Since many of these people were familiar with each other, they had undoubtedly formed opinions about the relative worthiness of members of their own groups. The question was whether the settled population would concur. Somehow the leading men of the immigrant groups had to be judged and then accommodated within the town's structure.

In addition to bringing new leaders into the town, the East Anglian influx reinforced the power of East Anglians who were resident before 1633. It is reasonable to suppose that Thomas Scruggs and Robert Moulton owed a great deal of the influence that made them selectmen in 1636-37 to the settlement in Salem by so many of their former neighbors from Great Yarmouth.

The East Anglians would not necessarily have forced a reconsideration of the town's basic character. But during the mid-1630s they clashed with the West Countrymen over issues too basic to be easily compromised. The two groups had somewhat differing ideals of the kind of community they wished to create, which affected a number of practical issues, like land use and distribution, division of political authority, and doctrinal details. The implicit covenants of the early period did not provide guidance except in the vaguest possible terms. As a result, disturbances broke out in Salem and in a number of other towns.[19]

The East Anglians' motives in emigrating were roughly the same as the West Countrymen's and similarly mixed. They both sought

---

[19]John J. Waters, "Hingham, Massachusetts, 1631-1661: An East Anglian Oligarchy in the New World," *Journal of Social History* 1 (1968): 351-70; Winthrop, I, 157, 176-77, 182-84.

to escape the social and economic problems of England and saw in America the opportunity to create godly model communities for reform-minded Englishmen to follow. Yet the West Country and East Anglian conceptions of the ideal community differed in material ways. Salem's West Countrymen had originated in an area of dispersed farms, with no tradition of open-field husbandry. Scattered through the West Country were hamlets and, along the coasts, fishing villages, whose inhabitants combined farming in enclosed lots with various artisan trades. On the other hand, East Anglia, despite some enclosure, especially in Essex, had strong open-field traditions, and East Anglians tended to see the ideal community as a compact village surrounded by fields worked in common.[20]

The most obvious area of conflict was religion, for seventeenth-century men and particularly Puritans used religious symbols as the core of their thought and conceived of most of their differences within its terminology. East Anglia was the heart of that region of England stretching from London and Kent north and east through Lincolnshire where dissenting zeal was traditionally strongest and most articulate. The deepening sense of crisis in England, especially during and after 1633, made the East Anglian immigrants of this period even more intense and certain of their religious convictions than were the people of Winthrop's migration. Laudian pressure, while not effective enough to suppress Puritan preaching or prevent emigration, heightened the tension in East Anglia and, in fact, encouraged emigration of the disaffected. There is a close correlation between areas of greatest Laudian effort and greatest migration to New England. A related result of the tension, according to a recent student of East Anglian migration, was "the creation of a general atmosphere of spiritual intolerance," an attitude many of these people brought to America.[21]

The Laudian campaign against Puritanism was directed primarily against the nonconformist preachers, and they came to New England in some numbers during these years, some thirty-two in all from East Anglia. Only one of these men, John Fiske of South Elmham, Suffolk, is known to have settled in Salem, but the impact on the colony and on Salem of the immigration of so many experienced and talented Puritan ministers can hardly be

---

[20]Tyack, pp. 56, 93, 95-97, 100; Carl Bridenbaugh, *Vexed and Troubled Englishmen, 1590-1642* (New York, 1968), pp. 38-39, 65, 69-70, 203-6; Waters, pp. 355-56.

[21]Tyack, pp. 287, 345; William Haller, *The Rise of Puritanism* (paperback ed., New York, 1957), pp. 227-69.

exaggerated, for among their number were those two preeminent theorists of Congregationalism, Thomas Hooker and John Cotton. According to William Hubbard it was these two divines "who did clear up the order and method of church government, according as they apprehended was most consonant to the Word of God."[22] Cotton and Hooker were only the two most prominent of the East Anglian immigrants whose presence and zeal forced a fundamental readjustment of the covenant order. For the new immigrants, and most especially the ministers, the much-sought-after unity could only be based on "God's pure truth" found in the Bible and natural law. All issues could become "fundamental and principal points."[23]

Salem's East Anglians managed to form a degree of unity based on their zeal, their common problems as newcomers, and their differences from the West Countrymen. Their most basic problem was establishing their status in the community in order to form a society consistent with their ideals and traditions. The West Countrymen, having their own ideals, interests, and traditions, did not accord the newcomers the respect and power the East Anglians felt they deserved. As longtime residents with more developed farms and large land claims, the West Countrymen held an economic position that they were intent upon preserving; neither would they voluntarily surrender much political power. The result was a clash between social, rather than purely economic, classes, for social class structure is "a prestige order, determined by how people rate others in their community."[24]

The relative economic worth of the groups was not the major source of conflict since the immigrants varied tremendously in wealth, as did the West Countrymen. Yet the peculiar economic conditions of early Massachusetts complicated the problem of sorting out the "prestige order." One of the traditional means of determining status, by occupation, was collapsing in the New England wilderness. The vast amount of uncleared land and the influx of people needing homes and farms put a premium on skilled artisans and even on unskilled labor.[25] The consequences of the breakdown of traditional occupational signs of status were rather striking in Salem. Of Salem's first ten selectmen, all of whom held office in 1636, one (Conant) had been a merchant in

---

[22] Hubbard, p. 182; Tyack, pp. 286-344, 414; Rutman, p. 108.

[23] Rutman, p. 111; Morgan, *Puritan Dilemma*, pp. 131-33.

[24] Jackson Turner Main, *The Social Structure of Revolutionary America* (Princeton, N.J., 1965), p. 5.

[25] Bernard Bailyn, *The New England Merchants in the Seventeenth Century* (paperback ed., New York, 1964), p. 53.

England, one a soldier (Endecott), three fishermen, one a carpenter, one a maltster, one a ropewalker, and two farmers of indeterminate status. Half of these men did not emigrate until after 1633, and three of them arrived during 1635.

In 1634, when the town record began, Salem had just begun the process of formally laying out the town's land.[26] In the midst of this status confusion, determining the size of grants and defining policy was not easy. Phrases such as "after a large discourse" and "diverse speeches" often appear in the records. The situation was complicated. Not only were many of the settlers strangers to each other, but new people were pouring into the settlement during the whole period. In addition, many of the early settlers, mostly West Countrymen, had large land claims left over from their various agreements with the New England Company. It was not until 1637, three years later, that the whole system could be laid out and the necessary adjustments and compromises reduced to writing.

Individual settlers, and especially the newcomers, who had come from communities in which the behavioral standards and status lines were much clearer than Salem's tended to feel frustration and discontent. In a society as fluid as Salem's and yet one in which such importance was placed on openly judging each individual's worth to the community, many people wanted to have their own sense of worth and their own values unambiguously interpreted and reinforced by their social surroundings. As a result, people often joined mutually exclusive groups that reinforced the members' claims to status while disparaging the claims of outsiders.[27]

Such groups search out an institutional framework to enforce their beliefs. They also seek a leader who shares their attitudes and who is capable of interpreting the situation in a way that helps the group establish its self-esteem.[28] Salem's East Anglians gravitated toward the church, and in Roger Williams who was invited back to Salem in 1633, they found a skilled and passionate leader. The West Countrymen, more secure in their position and more intimately connected to each other, had less need of a charismatic spokesman to weld them together and articulate their claims. The

----

[26] The town records of Salem from 1634 to 1691 are in three volumes; the first volume is in *Essex Institute Historical Collections* 9 (1868), and the two subsequent volumes were published separately by the Essex Institute in 1913 and 1934 (hereafter cited as *Town Recs*). *Town Recs.*, I, 8-19, 38.

[27] Norman F. Washburn, *Interpreting Social Change in America* (New York, 1954), pp. 30-31.

[28] Ibid., pp. 24, 26; James G. March and Herbert A. Simons, *Organizations* (New York, 1958), pp. 60-61.

most important man in the struggle was John Endecott, and it was his influence in conjunction with the great numbers of the East Anglians that overcame temporarily the initial advantages held by the West Countrymen.

For Salem's East Anglians the church provided an ideal means of coping with the West Countrymen and establishing their own claims. The church was seen, even by the West Countrymen, as the center of the community, and proper church discipline seemed a necessary means of social control if a godly society was to appear. The inchoate state of the town's civil institutions before 1636 further enhanced the importance of the church. It was not until 1636 that the board of selectmen and the town meeting appeared as formal institutions. Endecott, as magistrate, apparently ran the town, taking advice from whomever he chose. Business was conducted in freemen's meetings and by committee. The constable, West Countryman John Woodbury, had been chosen by the town in 1630 and confirmed by the General Court. The deputies, once their position as formal representatives of all the town's freemen had been established, were chosen by the assembled freemen. Although some Salem settlers had gained freemanship before the General Court restricted that privilege to church members in 1631, for all practical purposes "the freemen assembled" and the male church members were identical.

The East Anglians were able to use this situation to challenge the political power of the West Countrymen. At the height of the controversy in 1635 Salem sent two East Anglian deputies to the General Court, one of whom was a deacon, Charles Gott. Although a deacon was not a ruling elder and a deputy was not a magistrate, Gott's election was a violation, at least in spirit, of the Salem church's 1632 statement that due separation must be maintained between church and state by not electing ruling elders to civil positions.

Another important element in the role of the church was the gradually developing Separatism of that body, which reached a peak under Roger William's pastorate from 1633 to 1635. Within the context of Salem's life Williams's opinions made sense, especially to recent immigrants. A good example and one that greatly incensed the Massachusetts authorities was Williams's belief that the king of England had no right to grant land in New England, for it belonged to the Indians. East Anglians must have found this notion appealing when they considered the vast land claims held by the Old Planters and guaranteed in 1628.

Of greater importance were the explicitly Separatist ideas that gave doctrinal and moral support to the East Anglians' sense of alienation toward the older residents and their need to assert their own worth. In an admonition to Salem about Williams's brand of Separatism, the Boston church singled out these beliefs as "tending to the disturbance of religion and peace, in family, church and commonwealth."[29] The Boston church put their understanding of Williams's position into five propositions, which may be reduced to two basic points.

The first point was that regenerate persons had no obligations to help or even to associate spiritually with the unregenerate. They were not to admonish or "to call upon an unregenerate man to pray for himself." Nor did Williams believe it "lawful for a regenerate man to pray with his carnal family." The second point was that magistrates could play no part in asserting or maintaining a sense of community. Traditionally the oath of allegiance to the state was a civic symbol of mutual interdependence and trust. Williams held not merely that it was wrong "to take an oath of fidelity from unregenerate men" but even that "it is not lawful for magistrates to take an oath of fidelity from the body of subjects, though regenerate and members of the churches. " A natural corollary of denying magistrates this role in the community was to assert that the civil power had no right to enforce the First Table of the Decalogue, that is, those commandments having to do with spiritual life.

The obvious implication of these beliefs was to shatter any communal unity based on secular relationships. Within this system the only significant psychological community was the regenerate in the church. The explicit renunciation of magisterial power either to symbolize communal unity or to interfere with church affairs was more than a mere doctrinal consequence of Separatism. It also provided a means of denying the civil authorities, West Countrymen locally and Winthrop's cohorts colonially, significance or status as essential functioning parts of a Christian society.

Williams and his followers were drastically altering Salem's definition of itself. The degree of change emerges clearly from a comparison of Williams's use of the Garden image with Francis Higginson's a few years earlier. Higginson had visualized the wilderness of New England as the Garden whose great natural abundance could provide an environment which might prove redemptive for large numbers of individuals. But Williams persistently used the Garden symbol to describe the church, not the land itself or the society. The church was a walled Garden in which

[29]Nathaniel Morton, *New Englands Memorial* (1669; facsimile ed., Boston, 1903), pp. 155-56.

Christ kept the Saints from the world. To pull out worldly weeds was a necessity, for weeds do not make a garden.[30]

There is no way of knowing how many—or if any—West Country "weeds" were cast out while Williams's power over the Salem church was secure. However, as his control waned during the town's struggles, he began to enforce his belief stringently. When "the more prudent and sober part of the church," according to Nathaniel Morton, refused to declare themselves separate from the Bay churches, Williams "never came to the church assembly more, professing separation from them as antichristian, and not only so, but withdrew all private religious communion from any that would hold communion with the church there, insomuch as he would not pray nor give thanks at meals with his own wife nor any of his family, because they went to church assemblies."[31]

One might suspect that such extreme Separatism would have a limited appeal even among the East Anglians. In fact, the atomistic implications of Williams's doctrines did erode his strength, when they emerged late in his Salem career. But earlier Williams encouraged a number of church practices that helped create a sense of unity among sympathetic members. Some of these practices became so popular and so deeply ingrained that they remained features of the Salem church long after Williams left. One was "prophesying," an integral part of Separatist thought. At Salem prophesying, or lay preaching, became a regular part of the church service. It must have enhanced the status of the participants, giving the East Anglian majority a chance to be vocal in the community. Even women, though shamed by the mandatory veils, were allowed to "speak for themselves, for the most part, in the church." Apparently this right was not restricted to their initial confessions of faith but extended to all church business. This freedom must have had a tremendous psychological impact. Nathaniel Morton observed that "diverse women that were zealous in their way" were among Williams's most determined adherents.[32]

By their peculiar path, Williams and the Salem church were serving the East Anglian needs both in doctrine and practice while alienating West Countrymen whose sense of disorientation in America was not nearly as profound. Nevertheless, one aspect of Williams's Separatism had some appeal for Salem townsmen no

[30] Higginson, *New Englands Plantation* (1630), rept. in Edmund S. Morgan, *The Founding of Massachusetts: Historians and the Sources* (New York, 1964), p. 149; Morgan, *Roger Williams*, p. 28.

[31] P. 153.

[32] Thomas Lechford, *Plain-Dealing; or, News from New England* (1642; ed. J. Hammond Trumbull, Boston, 1867), p. 23; Morgan, *Roger Williams*, p. 21.

matter what their origins or length of time in America. This was his emphasis on Salem's independence from outside interference. When Williams arrived in town during the autumn of 1633, the church under the leadership of the mortally ill Skelton was protesting the fortnightly meetings of the Bay ministers, "fearing it might grow in time to a presbytery or superintendencey, to the prejudice of the churches' liberty."[33] This suspicion of the Bay towns, especially Boston, had political and economic as well as religious roots.

A strong sense of localism permeated early Massachusetts, but Salem had a particularly intense feeling of uniqueness. Some of the West Countrymen, most notably Conant and Endecott, envisioned Salem as the center of a great colony. Under the New England Company, Endecott had every reason to assume that that hope would be realized and that he would continue to be the leading figure. Far into the 1640s Salem political leaders assumed that their town should, by precedence, be the capital of the colony. But as early as 1633 Boston's power was secure and Salem's hopes expressed jealousy rather than potentiality. At the same time rapid growth of the Bay settlements threatened to turn Salem into an economic backwater, a distant outpost, rather than a leading town in the colony. Endecott, like the other magistrates, prized his local power and knew that to some extent his influence in colonial affairs depended upon the position of his town. He encouraged Separatism not merely as a means of expressing resentment at Boston's leadership but also as a means of asserting Salem's. His public arguments with John Cotton about veils for women and his cutting of the cross, "a superstitious thing and a relic of antichrist," out of the English ensign were manifestations not only of his religious zeal but also of his desire to extend Salem's influence and to assert its particularity as a Christian community.[34]

Because their reasons for favoring Separatism differed, Endecott's support of Williams was not absolute. Endecott did not agree that the colony's land claims were fraudulent, and under urging from Winthrop, Endecott convinced Williams to recant. Williams soon reneged, and Endecott once again attempted to protect the minister. But his doubts were growing. The turning point seems to have been the ensign episode. As Endecott wrote to John Winthrop, Jr., in London, "The Cross is much stood for, and I am like to suffer in it."[35] Suffer he did. The General Court in May

[33]Winthrop, I, 116-17.
[34]Shipton, p. 118; Winthrop, I, 125, 137, 146-47, 150, 156.
[35]Winthrop, I, 122-23; *Winthrop Papers*, 7 vols. (Boston, 1947), III, 146-49, 176.

1635 strongly censured Endecott, deeming the act "rash and without discretion." In its rebuke the court shrewdly examined the temptations to which Endecott succumbed: "taking upon him more authority than he had, and not seeking advice of the court, etc. uncharitable, in that he, judging the cross, etc., to be a sin, did content himself to have reformed it at Salem, not taking care that others might be brought out of it also; laying a blemish, also upon the rest of the magistrates, as if they would suffer idolatry." Realizing that Endecott's motives were a mixture of piety and desire to exercise power, the court assessed the perfect punishment; "they adjudged him worthy of admonition, and to be disabled for one year from bearing any public office; declining any heavier sentence, because they were persuaded he did it out of tenderness of conscience, and not of any evil intent."[36]

As time went on Endecott became increasingly easier to convince of the wrongness of some of Williams's positions. The Massachusetts authorities resorted to a traditional method of dealing with dissent, as well as the best means of convincing the theologically unsophisticated Endecott, and staged public debates between the Bay ministers and Williams which the latter and Endecott were required to attend. The debates caused Endecott to change his mind and Williams to remain adamant.

In Salem the West Country faction grew stronger as Endecott's doubts and the pressures from the government increased. In the spring of 1635 the two East Anglians deputies, Deacon Gott and Henry Bartholomew, were denied their seats by the General Court because of the intransigence of these men in their defense of Williams. As further punishment the court also refused the town additional territory. This resulted in a Salem letter, now lost, to the other churches protesting the court's actions. When the churches refused support and Williams demanded that the Salem church declare its separation from them because they were "papist," the local church split. Williams and his supporters seceded.[37]

At this juncture in September 1635, the West Countrymen were able to elect three of their own as deputies. The court now felt ready to proceed against Williams and his adherents in earnest. It began by ordering the Salem deputies to return to Salem to get either an apology from the freemen for the letter "or else the arguments of those that will defend the same with the subscription of their names." When Endecott objected he was threatened "by

[36]Winthrop, *Journal,* I, 158; Mayo, chap. 8.
[37]Phillips, pp. 106-7; Winthrop, *Journal,* I, 164.

general erection of hands" with jail. He backed down. Then the court pronounced banishment upon Williams and ordered the ruling elder of the Salem church, Samuel Sharp, to appear before the next meeting either "to acknowledge his offense" or justify the church's course. Apparently Sharp also repudiated Williams.[38]

The influence of Williams over the official institutions of Salem was broken. But the divisions and tensions within the town remained. Williams and his supporters, separate from the church, met in private homes, a practice that they continued after he left for Rhode Island. The situation was serious enough to prompt the governor, Henry Vane, to send a letter to the Salem constable ordering the suppression of these meetings.[39]

Their meetings duly suppressed and their leader banished, a few of the more determined Separatists gradually drifted into Rhode Island.[40] Since a number of their names are known, some analysis of Williams's hard-core support is possible. The bulk of them came from East Anglia or the areas immediately around London. Of the ten adult males known to have followed Williams, only three came from other parts of England, and all three of them arrived in Salem after 1633 and therefore shared the East Anglian problems. Their economic and social status, measured by landholdings, varied from the semiliterate Stukely Westcott's one acre to the merchant Robert Cole's three hundred acres.

The only thing the men who left Salem seem to have had in common besides similar geographic origins was their relative lack of influence within the town. Only one of them, Joshua Verin, was close to a position of power, being the son of Philip Verin who was elected selectmen in 1636. He later regretted his decision, which was apparently more his wife's than his own, and returned to Salem.[41] Williams's other supporters who had some influence in Salem decided to remain there, despite the discomfort of their position. Bartholomew, for example, was unable to rejoin the church until 1637 and did not regain political office until the early 1640s.

As a consequence of the struggle, the East Anglians, despite their high percentage of the town's population, were once again underrepresented in political office. The West Countrymen, whose proportion of the population was dropping steadily, were in command, but their power was waning. Because of their pre-

---

[38] Nathaniel B. Shurtleff, *Records of the Governor and Company of the Massachusetts Bay in New England,* 5 vols. in 6 (Boston, 1853-54), I, 156-58, 160-61. (hereafter cited as *Mass. Recs.*).

[39] Perley, I, 288.

[40] Ibid., I, 269, lists these men.

[41] Ibid., I, 272.

carious political position, the West Countrymen had sought allies in their fight against the Williams faction and later in governing the town. They found the necessary help in men who had come from parts of England other than the West Country and East Anglia, most notably Wiltshire, Berkshire, and Hampshire.

Of the nine most influential men of Salem (that is, those most likely to be assigned economic or political tasks before the formal creation of the board of selectmen), there were five West Countrymen, counting Endecott and Conant, and two East Anglians. Two men, Philip Verin and Edmund Batter, who were from Salisbury, Wiltshire, made up the remainder.[42] Gradually this third element was strengthened, most notably by the arrival of William Hathorne, and new concerns and new lines of political debate emerged after 1637. But the more immediate result of the banishment of Williams was a fundamental reexamination of the town's institutions. This introspective mood was not restricted to Salem. The mid-1630s witnessed a whole series of crises in Massachusetts, of which the Williams episode was but the first.[43]

Since October 1630 the Court of Assistants, composed of the colony's ten to twelve local magistrates, had elected the governor and deputy governor, had passed laws and had chosen the men to enforce them. Until 1634 the General Court, which included the magistrates and all the colony's freemen, existed mainly to advise the Court of Assistants. Many of the freemen concluded that this highly personal and restricted system denied them their right to participate fully in the colony's government and was also incapable of coping adequately with the rapid influx of strangers and the scattering of towns. In the May 1634 session of the General Court deputies elected by the freemen of the towns passed resolutions which won more power for the freemen by making the General Court a more influential body.[44]

At that session the deputies formally established the right of the freemen to elect two or three representatives from each town to act for them at the General Court, which until 1644 generally contained about twenty deputies together with the assistants and the governor and deputy governor. They then declared that the court had exclusive right "to choose and admit freemen," to make law, to appoint and remove officers, to raise taxes, and to "dispose of lands." The right to trial by jury was guaranteed and the longer,

[42] *Town Recs.*, I, 8-19; Perley, I, 317.

[43] Emery Battis, *Saints and Sectaries* (Chapel Hill, N.C., 1962), pp. 94-95.

[44] George Lee Haskins, *Law and Authority in Early Massachusetts: A Study in Tradition and Design* (New York, 1960), pp. 26-31.

more explicit freeman's oath to which Roger Williams so strenu-
ously objected was instituted. Citizens were ordered "upon
warnings" from the constables "to attend upon public service."[45]
Although directed against the great influence of the magistrates, or
assistants, the court's actions also seem designed to discipline the
magistrates' town power bases in order to assure the towns'
loyalty and subordination to the whole central government and
not exclusively to their leading men.

The quest for order began almost immediately to solve the
problem in the churches. In March 1635 the General Court, largely
under the stimulus of Roger Williams's challenges of the role of
magistrates in spiritual affairs, declared: "This Court doth entreat
of the elders and brethren of every church within this jurisdiction
that they will consult and advise of one uniform order of
discipline in the churches, agreeable to the scriptures, and then to
consider how far the magistrates are bound to interpose for the
preservation of that uniformity and peace of the churches." A
year later, after having watched the Salem Separatists secede from
their church and form new ones meeting in private homes,
Winthrop proposed an order to the General Court "to prevent
future inconveniences of unnecessary multiplication of Church
society and disturbance both to State and Churches." He
suggested that it be made unlawful for new churches to be formed
"without consent of the General Court and approbation of
neighbor churches" and, further, that no "ministry or Church
administration" be allowed to exist in any town "in opposition to
that which is openly and publicly observed and dispensed by the
settled and approved Minister of the place."[46]

As the year 1636 opened, the most prominent men in the
colony had come to agree that the colony's institutions on all
levels had to be strengthened in order to gain that uniformity of
purpose and opinion which they had formerly assumed was
implicit in the fact of immigration to America. Under the impact
of immigration, social and economic mobility, and various
religious outlooks, Salem and the rest of the Bay Colony were
forced to create more rigorous institutional frameworks. New
frameworks meant explicit covenants, which necessarily involved
an altered definition of the "Errand into the Wilderness." Salem,
with its new pastor Hugh Peter, set out to forge for itself a new
definition and to find the "uniformity and peace" that had eluded
the town for so long.

[45]*Mass. Recs.*, I, 116-18; Winthrop, *Journal*, I, 178.
[46]*Mass. Recs.*, I, 168; *Winthrop Papers*, III, 231.

Chapter III

Institutions of the Explicit Covenant
1636-1638

The problems and crises of the mid-1630s forced the leadership of Salem and the Bay to reform and to solidify the institutions of both church and state. The general direction of the reforms was to make explicit covenants, to create more formal and diversified institutions, so that communication and enforcement of the values of the society would be easier and more predictable. As usual the leadership saw the problems in largely religious terms, which made the ministers important in the reforms.

During most of 1636 Salem, however, struggled along without a settled ministry. Without a pastor to crystallize the issues and with the Williams episode fresh in their minds, the townsmen apparently allowed their doctrinal differences to remain dormant. The town, for all practical purposes, had divided into sects, each enjoying its own prophesying.

Although Salem seemed relatively quiet, its problems were not resolved. Despite the emergence of other pressing matters, the town was a dominant concern of the Massachusetts leadership. Religious unity had to be achieved and the authority of the central government over the colony's oldest town exerted. In February 1636 the Bay churches invoked the customary renewal of their covenants to rededicate their membership to a unified assault on the colony's problems. Heading Winthrop's list of troubles were the "distractions" in the Salem church.[1]

Hugh Peter, a highly experienced and respected Puritan pastor, arrived at Boston in October 1635 and was soon deeply involved in the colony's attempt to find a viable order.[2] Although he arrived in New England relatively late, Peter had been intimately connected with the Massachusetts Bay Company from its inception. He was familiar with all its leading men, including Endecott, who had suggested him in 1629 as a possible minister for Salem. Although Peter was under contract to the newly created New Haven Colony when he immigrated, he turned his abundant talent

---

[1] *Winthrop's Journal, 1630-1649* (1649; 2 vols., ed. James K. Hosmer, New York, 1908), I, 181.

[2] Raymond P. Stearns, *The Strenuous Puritan: Hugh Peter, 1598-1660* (Urbana, Ill., 1954), is the standard biography.

and energy to the difficulties of the older colony. In January 1636 he helped instigate a meeting of ministers and magistrates in Boston designed to head off incipient factionalism "among the magistrates and some other persons of quality" over whether the government should carry on its business "with more lenity" or "more severity."[3] The issue was whether or not the colony needed more discipline and more uniformity. An affirmative answer meant more formal institutions, more explicit covenants.

John Winthrop and Thomas Dudley, both leading magistrates who were often elected governor and deputy governor, held conflicting views of government, with the result that "factions began to grow among the people" as well as within the leadership. Essentially tolerant, Winthrop believed in leniency and, more important, in discretion on the part of the magistrates. He felt "that in the infancy of plantations, justice should be administered with more lenity than in a settled state, because people were then more apt to transgress, partly of ignorance of new laws and orders, partly through oppression of business and other straits." The best course was judicial discretion rather than legal precision. His argument for lenient but arbitrary government expressed the spirit of the implicit covenant. Dudley believed the opposite. Reputedly "skilled at law," Dudley believed in definite rules, strictly enforced.[4]

After receiving assurances from both Winthrop and Dudley that their personal "breach was healed" and that each would abide by the decision of the meeting, the participants turned the main question of government policy over to the ministers "to set down a rule in the case." After a day of consultation, the ministers determined "that strict discipline . . . was more needful in plantations than in a settled state, as tending to the honor and safety of the gospel." The way was cleared for more explicit covenants. The ministers also recommended that in a society in which people did not have an intimate knowledge of each other and in which diversity was becoming common, the magistrates should maintain unity among themselves and make an impressive show of their authority in order to discourage factionalism. The ministers were shrewd enough to realize that the rapidly increasing population and the scattering of settlements necessitated more decentralization of institutions. They suggested "that trivial things, etc. should be ordered in towns, etc."[5] They were recommending a

[3] Winthrop, I, 177-79, gives an account of the meeting.

[4] George Lee Haskins, *Law and Authority in Early Massachusetts: A Study in Tradition and Design* (New York, 1960), pp. 54, 106; Edmund S. Morgan, *The Puritan Dilemma: The Story of John Winthrop* (Boston, 1958), p. 105.

[5] Winthrop, I, 177-79.

strengthening of the authority and power of the magistrates in both colonial and local affairs. To some extent, they were urging a reversal of the General Court's policy of trying to centralize power in the court.

Henry Vane, a highborn young man of twenty-three who had been in Massachusetts only a year, was elected governor in May 1636 and Winthrop, deputy governor. Although more personable than Dudley, Vane shared the same uncompromising zeal for absolute truth, a passion that would one day force him to an English scaffold. Vane's election meant another rebuke to Winthrop, who had lost the governorship to Dudley in 1634 when he resisted the political reforms of that year and again to John Haynes in 1635. It was another sign of the colony's new approach to order.

The earlier meeting of the General Court, held in early March 1636, was one of the most momentous in the history of early Massachusetts. The court accepted the suggestions of the ministers and laid out in detail a decentralized, federal, secular constitution for the colony. At the same time the court, in its provisions for local government, attempted the forestall the possibility of another episode like that involving Roger Williams.

The General Court began by appointing Winthrop and Dudley as members of a standing council of vague powers for life. The new governor was chosen president for his year term. The legislators also created the Quarterly Court system, to "be kept in several places for the ease of the people." The courts, presided over by locally resident magistrates and commissioners especially chosen for the task, were to meet at Ipswich, Salem, Newtown, and Boston. The dispersal of judicial bodies for civil and noncapital matters not only would enhance the influence of the magistrates and provide convenient trials for the populace but also, it was hoped, would serve to curb "disorder" in the towns and churches.[6]

The court next turned its attention to the storm centers of the colony, the churches and the towns. The legislators passed in modified form Winthrop's proposal for regulating the formation of churches. The order was prefaced with a renunciation of what was going on in Salem, lamenting the formation of separate churches or meetings within towns. New churches had to be recognized by "the greater part" of the colony's elders and magistrates, who had to approve of "their intentions."[7]

The towns were granted the exclusive right of "ordering their own affairs," which included the "power to dispose of their own

---

[6] *Mass. Recs.*, I, 167, 169; Winthrop, I, 184-85.
[7] *Mass. Recs.*, I, 168; Winthrop, I, 185.

lands, and woods, with all the privileges . . . of the said town, to grant lots, and make such orders as may concern the well ordering of their own towns, not repugnant to the laws and orders here established by the General Court." The court, concerned about good civil order, required each town to have two constables so that "they may attend more carefully upon the discharge of their office." The constables were also "liable to give their accounts to this Court when they shall be called thereunto." All local officers were to be chosen by the "freemen of the town, or the major part of them."[8] The court was trying to guarantee that the towns would live up to the corporate, non-Separatist ideal by delegating local civil initiative to them. Although the "freemen of the town" and the male church membership were almost identical, it seems apparent that the General Court was creating local institutions that embodied the civil life of the communities as formally as the churches embodied the religious.

Under the impetus of the March orders Salem began the formal explication of the town's civil institutions. The central one was the town meeting, whose function, like that of the congregation in the ecclesiastical sphere, was to express the corporate will of the community. Its purpose was to provide a means by which local policy could be set. In order to assure that all concerned understood the decisions reached, attendance by all the townsmen was encouraged. Often long discussions occurred, votes were taken, and the orders were written out for future perusal in case of disagreement. The town meeting also chose local officers empowered to carry out and enforce the decisions made in the meeting. The ideal was to attain and maintain "peace and unity."[9]

Significant and potentially dominant power rested in the town meeting or in any of the most popular branches of various Puritan institutions largely because of their belief that all men, even respected leaders, were subject to temptation and needed restraints imposed by others. As John Cotton was saying in Boston, "Let all the world learn to give mortal men no greater power than they are content they shall use, for use it they will."[10] Popular power was conceived as reining rather than initiating action. The social and political ideal was essentially a static society in which

[8]*Mass. Recs.*, I, 168, *Town Recs.*, I, 7-8.

[9]Michael Zuckerman, "The Social Context of Democracy in Massachusetts," *William and Mary Quarterly*, 3d ser., 25 (1968): 523-44; Darrett B. Rutman, *Winthrop's Boston: Portrait of a Puritan Town, 1630-1649* (Chapel Hill, N.C., 1965), pp. 59-60.

[10]Cotton, "Limitation of Government," in *The Puritans: A Sourcebook of Their Writings*, eds. Perry Miller and Thomas H. Johnson (paperback ed., 2 vols., New York, 1963), I, 212.

"order and precedency" were maintained. In that hierarchically minded age the concept of democracy had pejorative connotations of disorder, even for American Puritans. The initiative rightly should lie with the leading men, and within the Salem town meeting their voices were the dominant ones. Besides the rather informal operation of deference within the town meeting, there were more formal structures that embodied the hierarchical conception. One of these was the distinction between freemen and inhabitants, a status that was legally defined in 1637. In the wording of the General Court, local control passed to "the freemen of each town, or the greater part of them." For Salem this was a confirmation of the town's custom since its records began in 1634, wherein it was noted that land grants and ordinances were voted "by the freemen of Salem."[11]

Yet the inhabitants were not excluded from town government. They enjoyed an unlimited right of attendance and speech in the town meeting. Despite the fact that the General Court did not formally recognize the right until 1647, the Salem freemen, apparently feeling need to maintain the notion of general consent, allowed inhabitants some limited right to vote. In the records distinctions soon appeared between gatherings "at a general Town Meeting of freemen," where votes were taken for colonial officers and for commissioners to the Salem Quarterly Court, and others "by the town in general," in which land was granted and selectmen were chosen.[12]

Despite the differences between the two types of town meeting, there is reason to believe that a relatively small group of prominent men controlled both. Since the goal of these meetings was to gain a consensus, not to be a representative democracy, the situation is hardly surprising. If the town's leading men could agree on policy, dissent from the generality was unlikely. Once the local customs and policies of the town had become stable, there was even less cause for general interest, and attendance at the town meetings was sporadic despite attempts to encourage greater participation. In August 1639 the town bylaws declared that "the whole town [is] to be lawfully warned and the special occasions [topics on the agenda] manifested together with the warning: a day before the meeting." But sparse attendance was evidently still expected, for a quorum was set at "above the number of six persons," who could carry on business "provided that the said persons have been together or have stayed an hour after the time

[11]*Mass. Recs.*, I, 96; *Town Recs.*, I, 14-15.
[12]*Town Recs.*, I, 48, 142, 168, 183.

first appointed." At that time there were no less than 90 freemen and some 230 adult males in Salem.[13]

In some towns, for example Dedham and Boston, the business of gaining a consensus was so simple that the town meeting was called only a couple of times a year and effective local government passed to the selectmen except for electoral purposes and occasional ratification of particularly important transactions. In Salem the process of maintaining a consensus was more difficult, despite the great influence of its leading men. In fact, most of the signs of dissension that survive involve these leaders, not the people. The town clerk, Ralph Fogg, inserted this shorthand note into the records: "Ed. Giles [a leading freeman] said I was the strangest troublesome man, a falling out and quarreling." Fragmentary and confused as the Salem records for this period are, the town meetings seem more frequent and often of longer duration than those of Boston and Dedham.[14] Table 2 shows the large number of recorded meetings held in Salem at the end of the 1630s, when the town's customs were being solidified. Salem's leadership apparently felt the need to give their fellow townsmen the opportunity to listen to and to pass judgment on their agenda. The poor attendance was not the result of any overt action on the part of the leadership but rather of the sense of deference that the generality held toward their superiors.

Table 2. Civic meetings in Salem, 1637-40

Year	Town meetings	Selectmen sessions
1637	5	10
1638	5	7
1639	6	20
1640	4	3

Source: *Town Recs.*, I.

The other organ of town government, the board of selectmen, authorized by the General Court in 1636, embodied even more clearly the controlling influence of "the better sort." Formally the selectmen were a governing board of the general town meeting, elected by and responsible to that body. The selectmen's authority was almost coterminous with that of the town meeting and almost as vague. They too granted land, adjudicated minor disputes,

[13] Ibid., I, 88, 101-4; Sidney Perley, *History of Salem, Massachusetts*, 3 vols. (Salem, 1924-27), I, 196-97.
[14] Rutman, pp. 81-82; Kenneth A. Lockridge, *A New England Town: The First Hundred Years, Dedham, Massachusetts, 1636-1736* (New York, 1970), pp. 41-42; *Town Recs.*, I, 49.

passed local ordinances, and appointed lesser town functionaries. On the other hand, elections of major officers and establishment of the town rates took place exclusively within the full town meeting. Within these amorphous boundaries the board of selectmen became in Salem, as in other New England towns, a very powerful body. One of the reasons the board of selectmen quickly became a powerful institution was its convenience. Governing through the town meeting was cumbersome, even when attendance was low. It required planning to prepare agenda and to "warn" the town. Moreover, much of the town's business was routine, and it did not make sense to interrupt everyone's workday to process these questions. The selectmen could meet swiftly and handle problems more efficiently.

More important to the board's power than these institutional factors was the type of man who became a selectman. During the first few years the size of the board fluctuated from a high of thirteen down to seven. Twenty different men served as selectmen from 1636 to 1638. The list contains all the powerful men of Salem who were not holding a church office. It is headed by Endecott and Conant. In 1637 William Hathorne, whose power and prestige came to rival Endecott's, served the first of his many terms. Such men came to the office with influence which the position only reinforced. Kenneth Lockridge has remarked of Dedham's selectmen, "As in the politics of any age, power led to experience and experience enhanced power."[15]

An analysis of all twenty of the early selectmen gives a clear picture of where power lay in those years. Although West Countrymen probably comprised only about one third of the population by this time, ten of the twenty were West Countrymen. All but two of the West Countrymen, Endecott and Thomas Gardner, were closely allied with Conant. On the other hand, all the prominent East Anglians who had not been too closely linked to Williams also served. Moulton, Scruggs, Townshend Bishop, and Ralph Fogg all held the office and other posts as well. The mediating group who originated from Wiltshire and Bedfordshire were represented by Batter, Hathorne, and Philip Verin.

Economically the twenty selectmen represented Salem's wealth. Their landholdings ranged from Endecott's 500 acres to Fogg's 89. They averaged over 380 acres; the town average was 25. In occupation they ranged from artisan to merchant to farmer. Eighteen of the twenty are known to have been church members.

Despite their influence within the community, in the first years the selectmen did not take their power for granted. The selectmen

[15] P. 41.

scattered phrases such as "if the town shall agree thereunto" through their deliberations as if uncertain of their position. On occasion their decisions were challenged, especially on land grants. In March 1637 the selectmen entered this apology: "After much discourse about the equity of the proportions of Land to be Laid out to these inhabitants. It is agreed that wherein we have not walked by order & Rule in the proportioning of Land, that it should be rectified." Significantly Endecott and Conant were not present at this meeting. This challenge apparently originated from within the board itself rather than from the generality. A month later the dissension among the selectmen appeared even more clearly in the record. "Mr. Scruggs & our brother Ray fined 6d a piece to be distrained for disorderly standing & neglecting to speak to Town business." Again Conant and Endecott were absent. Although the nature of the quarrel is vague, it involved the West Country-East Anglian split over land. Both Scruggs and Daniel Ray were East Anglians, while the majority of the selectmen were West Countrymen.[16]

Salem's civil government was in the hands of men of relative wealth as measured in land. Their influence pervaded all aspects of the town's life in the 1630s. But control by "the better sort" did not guarantee peace for Salem any more than it did for the larger societies of Massachusetts Bay or England itself. Leading men, each with their own connections, could and did fall out. The problem of governing Salem was to suppress this tendency, to gain a consensus, not among all the classes, but within the ruling class. The town meeting and board of selectmen were means to that end. These institutions provided forums in which reconciliation was sought and policy determined. They were important elements in forging a more definite, explicit system.

Complementing this town civil system were the Quarterly Courts. Their jurisdiction was both criminal and civil, subordinate to the Court of Assistants meeting in Boston. The grand jury of each court was "to inform of the breaches of any order, or other misdemeanors, that shall know or hear to be committed by any person." There were petit juries with the power to summon and to pay witnesses in order to establish fact. The courts had the use of the commonwealth marshal and his deputies to carry out their orders and also the right to choose arbiters to resolve conflicts before passions and expenses had risen too high for "Christian carriage." The new court system, in replacing many of the local responsibilities of the Court of Assistants, also formally installed town officers.[17]

[16] *Town Recs.*, I, 38, 45.

[17] Mass. Recs., I, 143; Rutman, p. 235.

Endecott was the magistrate in the Salem area and presided over the court until he moved to Boston in 1655. Each year until the colony was divided into counties in 1643 the freemen of Salem and Lynn elected commissioners to join him on the bench. In 1636 to 1638 these included Bishop, Conant, Scruggs, Hathorne, Moulton, Holgrave for Salem. The juries also were generally composed of leading freemen.

In sum, the freemen of Massachusetts had created under the auspices of the March 1636 laws a federal system of civil institutions stretching from the towns, through the Quarterly Courts, to the Court of Assistants and the General Court. The system was admirably suited to cope with the massive population growth and the dispersal of towns. More basically, these institutions provided the means for defining a Christian community, for making the covenant among men more explicit.

Meanwhile Hugh Peter was analyzing the colony's ills and began to formulate remedies that complemented the efforts of the General Court. His approach was two-pronged, economic and ecclesiastical. In November 1635, just a month after his arrival, Peter preached sermons in the port towns of Boston and Salem on the necessity of raising a capital stock for the fishing trade. His goal was to create an independent commerce for the colony that would employ "many idle hands." With this encouragement the keel of a 120-ton ship, the *Desire*, was laid in Salem during the spring, and a 150-ton ship was started at Boston. The capital was also used in less ambitious ways of equal benefit to the colony's economy. "The intent was to set up a magazine of all provisions and other necessaries for fishing, that men might have things at hand, and for reasonable prices; whereas now the merchants and seaman [of England] to advantage to sell at most excessive rates." It was hoped that such measures would allow more stable economic growth than an economy based so strongly on provisioning new immigrants and the English fisheries.[18]

In May 1636 Peter was still considering the relationship between the economy and the stability of the social order. In a sermon delivered that month in Boston he urged that the colonists "take order for employment of people, (especially women and children, in the wintertime) for he feared that idleness would be the ruin both of church and commonwealth." The main burden of the sermon, however, was more concerned with making the church covenant explicit in order to eliminate future dissension. Specifically he urged the devising of a uniform pattern of church organization, "that a form of church government might be drawn

[18]Winthrop, I, 173, 176; Stearns, pp. 95-96.

according to the scriptures." Cotton and Hooker had been considering this problem since 1633. Peter suggested to the Boston church "that they would spare their teacher, Mr. Cotton, for a time, that he might go through the Bible, and raise marginal notes upon all the knotty places of the scriptures."[19] The goal here was to create an authoritative New England theology written by so prestigious a cleric that serious disagreement would be difficult even among the learned.

In the same sermon he focused attention on one of the greatest problems of Puritanism, religious psychology. The difficulty, which lay at the heart of the distinction between Separatism and non-Separatism, was distinguishing the Elect from the unregenerate. At issue was not only the psychology of conversion, or justification, but also subsequent behavior, or sanctification. In New England the problem was aggravated by rapid immigration and by the fact that church membership often led to political power and social status. Hypocrisy was too great a danger. The problem was so basic that it remained a major source of heresy and church disturbance far into the eighteenth century. Peter's suggested solution was a Puritan version of empirical psychology, "that a new book of martyrs might be made, to begin where the other had left." Puritan martyrology, biography, and autobiography were written and read in a Baconian spirit, to establish models of the ways through which the Holy Spirit worked on the human soul and the soul's response. Such a guide, brought up to date, would give the "soul physicians" some diagnostic certainty in dealing with their people and would provide exemplars by which individuals could judge their own spiritual estate.[20]

In this sermon and his other activities Hugh Peter showed a strong interest in and a keen understanding of the problems facing the colony and most especially towns like Salem. His energetic pursuit of capital and his programs for its use impressed the Massachusetts leadership. In the January 1636 meeting about leniency versus discipline he had revealed talent as a mediator among the proud and powerful. So, when his contract with New Haven expired and he became available for a pastorate in Massachusetts, he was sought by the colony's troubled churches. In late fall of 1636 Peter went to both Lynn and Salem to look over the possibilities and to deliver trial sermons. He chose Salem,

[19]Winthrop, I, 186.

[20]Raymond P. Stearns and D. H. Brawner, "New England Church 'Relations' and Continuity in Early Congregational History," *Proceedings of the American Antiquarian Society* 75 (1965): 39-40, 43; Daniel B. Shea, *Spiritual Autobiography in Early America* (Princeton, N.J., 1968), pp. 87-91.

and Salem's leaders were delighted to accept him. Peter had preached there often, and the town officers had been trying to convince him to settle with them. As early as November 1635 they had given him a two-acre house lot.[21]

Just as Hugh Peter was being installed as Salem's pastor in December 1636, the Antinomian Crisis broke. Although Antinomian strength was concentrated in Boston and the nearby towns of Charlestown and Roxbury, there was some support for the movement in Salem. Doctrinally and psychologically the new heresy had much in common with Roger Williams's brand of Separatism.[22] Mrs. Anne Hutchinson and her followers maintained that any regenerate person could discern the spiritual state, and hence the worth, of others regardless of the outward signs of status and behavior. Also, the regenerate could not be subject to social control. Antinomianism, like Salem's Separatism, was an assertion of personal worth and autonomy without reference to the values or needs of the whole community.

In Boston, Antinomianism strongly appealed to merchants and craftsmen who were church members but who were also under suspicion because their business practices clashed with Puritan communal ethics.[23] Salem's Separatists, however, were not an occupational grouping, although merchants like Bartholomew were involved. Instead they were latecomers with social and religious ideals differing from those of the resident population. Given the psychological similarity between the two movements, it is not surprising that nine Salem men were connected with the Antinomians, five of whom were committed enough to sign Wheelwright's petition to the General Court to repeal his conviction for sedition and consequently had their weapons seized by the authorities in 1637.

What Salem's Antinomians lacked in numbers they more than made up for in quality. Among those disarmed were two selectmen, Scruggs and Moulton, who were the two most important East Anglian political leaders in the period just after Williams's banishment. At least five of the nine were East Anglians, and seven of the nine had arrived in Salem after 1635. Both of the West Countrymen who were involved, William King and William Alford, were late arrivals and merchants. The outbreak of Antinomianism in Salem complicated the problem of molding a strong communal identity. The authorities responded

[21]Stearns, pp. 106, 109.
[22]Morgan, p. 140.
[23]Emery Battis, *Saints and Sectaries* (Chapel Hill, N.C., 1962), pp. 56, 67-68, 99-100, 103, 296.

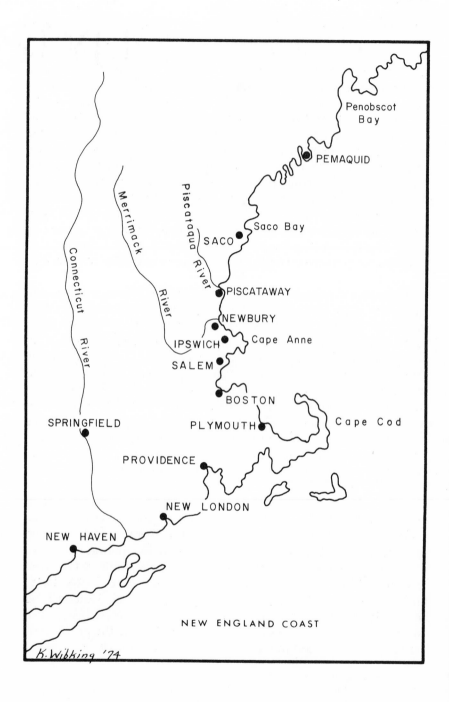

K. Wibking '74

NEW ENGLAND COAST

with severity. Besides the disarming ordered by the General Court, the town of Salem never again elected any of these men to a responsible position.

Hugh Peter took a major role in the suppression of Antinomianism throughout the Bay, probably because he was alarmed by the complexity of the problems at Salem, where both Separatist and Antinomian currents ran deep.[24] He attended and took an active part in the meetings and trials that led to Anne Hutchinson's exile in 1638. Typical of his method, particularly in dealing with the powerful, was an exchange in December 1636 with young Governor Vane, who exhibited Antinomian sympathies. The governor had taken umbrage at the fact that some of the ministers, at Peter's instigation, had met without his knowledge to draw up questions for John Cotton in order to determine Cotton's responsibility for the crisis. According to Winthrop, "Mr. Peter told him plainly of it, (with all due reverence), and how it sadded the ministers' spirits, that he should be jealous of their meetings, or seem to restrain their liberty, etc." The governor excused his speech as "sudden and upon a mistake." Having gotten Vane to admit one error, Peter pressed the attack. He "also besought [Vane] humbly to consider his youth, and short experience in the things of God, and to beware of peremptory conclusions, which he perceived him to be very apt unto." Seeds of doubt were thus planted in the mind of the introspective governor, and his support for the Antinomians diminished significantly.[25]

During that crowded month of December 1636 Peter turned the same method of defining positions and then working on dissenters to the particular problems of Salem. He wrote a new church covenant, containing a lengthy preamble and nine articles, that specifically condemned Separatist behavior and reaffirmed the Puritan communal ideal.[26] The members of the church were to sign it; those who would not were excommunicated. Salem's enlarged covenant shows how anxious Hugh Peter and the original signers were to avoid further dissension. It seemed to them that the way to prevent difficulty was to define Christian community more carefully. The mood was not restricted to Salem. The Dedham church, founded in 1636 and without Salem's difficulties, wrote a covenant of five articles taking up two pages of the town's records.[27]

---

[24] Stearns, pp. 112-25.

[25] Winthrop, I, 208-9.

[26] Williston Walker, *The Creeds and Platforms of Congregationalism* (1893; rept. Boston, 1960), pp. 116-18.

[27] Lockridge, pp. 4-7.

The preamble to Salem's new covenant began with an analysis of the church's problems framed as a confession.

We whose names are here under written, members of the present Church of Christ in Salem, having found by sad experience how dangerous it is to sit loose to the Covenant we make with our God: and how apt we are to wander into bypaths, even to the losing of our first aims in entering into Church fellowship: Do therefore solemnly in the presence of the Eternal God, both for our own comforts, and those which shall or may be joined unto us, renew that Church Covenant we find this Church bound unto at their first beginning.

Having renewed the original covenant, the signers pledged that they "do more explicitly in the name and fear of God, profess and protest to walk as followeth through the power and grace of our Lord Jesus," in ways itemized in the nine clauses following.

The clauses did not define doctrine but rather behavior. The first two clauses contained the closest thing to doctrine and were hardly more explicit than the original covenant. The first clause reasserted the primacy of the Lord. It also reaffirmed that the signers were "his people in the truth and simplicity of our spirits." This was followed by a statement on the authority of the "Lord Jesus Christ and the word of his grace, for the teaching, ruling and sanctifying of us in matters of worship, and Conversation." The doctrinal details were being left to the minister and the church officers. In the last phrase of the second clause the signers pledged to "oppose all contrary ways, canons, and constitutions of men in his worship." With this statement Peter bound the signers to support actively orthodoxy as he defined it.

The next three articles bore down on what were considered the worst effects of Separatism. In dealing with their "brethren and sisters," church members were to avoid "all jealousies, suspicions, backbitings, censurings, provokings, secret risings of spirit against them." From the officers and fellow members the signers promised to "be willing to take advice for ourselves and ours as occasion shall be presented." This statement provided an explicit justification for "working in a church way" when behavioral or doctrinal problems arose. Another clause constituted an attempt to discipline prophesying: "We will not in the Congregation be forward either to show our own gifts or parts in speaking or scrupling, or there discover the failings of our brethren and sisters but attend an orderly call thereunto."

Articles six and seven contradicted the ecclesiastical and political implications of Separatism. The members were to "study the advancement of the Gospel in all truth and peace, both in regard of those that are within, or without," which was an acceptance of the responsibility of the Elect for the spiritual health of the whole community. They explicitly repudiated Williams's battle with the Bay churches when they pledged to carry on their work in "no way slighting our sister churches, but using their Counsel as need shall be." Then they promised "all lawful obedience to those that are over us, in Church or Commonwealth, knowing how well pleasing it will be to the Lord, that they should have encouragement in their places, by our not grieving their spirits through our Irregularities."

The last two clauses concerned the economy and the social order. In the eighth they promised to pursue their occupations or "particular callings" diligently, "shunning idleness as the bane of any State." They combined that declaration with the pledge "nor will we deal hardly, or oppressively with any, wherein we are the Lord's stewards." Together the phrases constituted a good summary of communal Puritan economic ethics. The last article, the ninth, stressed the obligation "to teach our children and servants, the knowledge of God and his will, that they may serve him also." Here the centrality of the well-regulated family to the non-Separatist ideal of a godly community was reaffirmed.

Hugh Peter's new covenant reversed the dominant Separatist tendencies of the Salem church, tendencies that reached back to the time of Francis Higginson's death in 1630. Many of the East Anglians must have found it painful to repudiate what little New England past they had. Indeed, a number of them never were fully reconciled to the new order.

Realizing the difficulty and wishing to be as inclusive as possible, Peter compromised a little by allowing the retention of a number of church practices probably unique to Salem. The "rule by the major part of the Church" rather than controlled unanimity was still characteristic. The new covenant permitted lay prophesying, "notwithstanding, it is generally held in the Bay, by some of the most grave and learned men amongst them, that none should undertake to prophesy in public, unless he intend the work of the Ministry." Women still held the right to speak, but only "upon the week days." Peter may well have been willing to preserve these customs both to prevent arguments over nonessentials and to learn the spiritual state of the membership. Also he probably recognized that these practices could not be totally eradicated.[28]

Initially forty-seven men and thirty-three women, only about

[28]Thomas Lechford, *Plain-Dealing; or, News from New England* (1642; ed. J. Hammond Trumbull, Boston, 1867), pp. 23, 38, 42.

one-fifth of the adult population, signed the covenant.[29] Some very significant men did not sign, among them Moulton, Bartholomew, and Deacon Gott, and were excommunicated.[30] Yet a number of important East Anglian names did appear: the ruling elder, Samuel Sharp, and his wife, Holgrave, Bishop, Scruggs, who was not yet deeply involved with the Antinomians, and Elias Stileman. Endecott, Conant, and all the influential West Countrymen signed. The signatures on the covenant were another indication of the power, respectability, and non-Separatism of the West Countrymen, especially of Conant's Old Planters. Although West Country people comprised only about one-third of the town's population by late 1636, they provided forty-two, or a little over half, of the initial signers of the new covenant. The name of every one of Conant's old associates was on the list.

The intention, of course, was to include eventually in membership all the town's inhabitants, without sacrificing the quality of the church. Some towns, like Dedham and Sudbury, almost succeeded.[31] Salem never did, but under Hugh Peter's ministry, church membership, gaining about 200 over the original 80 signers, did increase more rapidly than the adult population. In the period 1637 to 1643 the total population, including children, rose approximately from 900 to 1,200. Peter's efforts apparently had the same salutary effect on the Salem church that Cotton had had in Boston during the first year of his tenure.[32] Salem's development was finally beginning to fit the general non-Separatist pattern.

The new covenant and subsequent efforts succeeded in integrating the East Anglians and the West Countrymen into the same religious community. After 1638 religious dissent was sporadic and diverse and did not threaten the unity of the community until the outbreak of Quakerism in 1656-57. Although West Countrymen and East Anglians continued to differ occasionally over issues like land use, the conflict between the two groups had peaked. The townsmen tended to divide along economic and political lines. Means, not goals, became the issues of the 1640s.

The most significant effort made by an outsider to reintegrate Salem into the Bay Colony and to interpret the town's Separatist

---

[29] James Duncan Phillips, *Salem in the Seventeenth Century* (Boston, 1933), app. C.

[30] In reclaiming the excommunicated the church had some success, but it is impossible to gauge how much because membership before 1636 is largely a matter of conjecture. Bartholomew, for example, rejoined, but others, like Moulton, never regained membership.

[31] Lockridge, pp. 30-31; Sumner Chilton Powell, *Puritan Village: The Formation of a New England Town* (Middleton, Conn., 1963), p. 144.

[32] Battis, pp. 88-89.

traditions for the larger community was a sermon preached at Salem by the renowned John Cotton in July 1636, six months before Peter took office.[33] In the sermon Cotton explicitly reversed the position he had taken some seven years earlier in his letter to Skelton and affirmed the necessity of a particular covenant as a criterion of a true church. Yet, masterful interpreter of ambiguity that he was, Cotton absorbed this Separatist notion into a non-Separatist framework. The idea of the covenant, which Separatists saw as a means of protecting the Elect from the corruptions of the world, became in his hands the basis of an inclusive community, perpetual in time, with its strongest emphasis on the non-Separatist ideal of good behavior. "Now this covenant of God consisteth of moral laws, and statutes and judgments, unto all which He doth require obedience." Since this was the Covenant of Works it included the non-Elect, "the poor in spirit."

Cotton went on to insist that once such a covenant is made it cannot be broken. In short, separation from a covenanted church, such as Williams's departure from the Salem church, is not possible without renouncing Christ. In fact, one of the criterion of an "everlasting covenant" is the concern the Elect show to bring the unregenerate "nearer and nearer to Jesus Christ." To make his point even clearer Cotton concluded: "Therefore if you belong to Christ, He will show it is not the water of separation that will serve your turn, but getting Christ Jesus, and sitting closer to Him, and to your brethren, by admonishing and reproving them, if you see them defiled. This will keep you clean, and your hearts clean, and your soul comfortable: That the Lord hath made an everlasting covenant with you that never shall be forgotten."[34]

By 1637 the ideals of non-Separatism dominated Salem's life. These ideals had not only been strongly stated to the townsmen by prestigious leaders but also explicitly embodied in a renewed church covenant and in new secular institutions. The meaning of Christian community at Salem had been defined, and means of pursuing that end had been created. In future years the problem would be to adapt those ideals and institutions to changing social and economic conditions.

[33] *A Sermon . . . Deliver'd at Salem, 1636* (Boston, 1713), rept. in Larzer Ziff, *John Cotton on the Churches of New England* (Cambridge, Mass., 1968), pp. 41-68.
[34] Ibid., pp. 65-68.

Chapter IV

The Social Structure of Salem
1636-1650

In both his actions and the 1636 covenant, Hugh Peter operated on the common belief that "peace and unity" involved not only religious and political practices but the economy and the social structure as well. In Puritan thought and Massachusetts reality all these aspects of life were closely intertwined. As the townsmen elaborated their religious and political institutions, they also solidified the social structure.

The foundation to that order was the land. During the 1630s and 1640s the vast majority of Salem's population were farmers. Even most of the merchants and artisans were at least part-time agriculturalists. Fishermen seem to have been the only significant exception; in order to encourage that trade, they were restricted to small lots of between a half acre and five acres on Winter Island and Marblehead.[1]

The land provided more than a common economic interest. It was also a generally agreed upon, easily measured standard of status. Since the delicate Puritan merging of both hierarchical and collective ideals depended so heavily upon clarity of status, land was a convenient and emotionally significant symbol, and since the power to grant land and regulate its sale and use rested with the town, the town was in a good position to reward and punish in the general interest. In their land divisions the Puritans operated on the principle that clearly defined status lines, a man for every place and a place for every man, would lead to "peace and unity."

As might be expected, land policy during the years of rapid immigration and conflict over Roger Williams was confused. In January 1635 the town determined "after discourse" that "the least family shall have 10 acres, but greater families may have more, according to their numbers." In the contemporary home county of Kent it was generally believed that five to ten acres was sufficient to support the occupier and his family, less if the farmer held grazing rights in a nearby common. Salem, then, was attempting to assure everyone a decent standard of living, a hedge against the ills of England. But by January 1637 the new immigrants were so numerous that the selectmen rescinded the guarantee and de-

[1] *Town Recs.*, I, 15-17, 27-28.

termined that "such lots are to be set out according to the discretion of the town."[2]

Although it is difficult to gauge the full effect of this change in policy because the records are fragmentary, it is important to keep the change in mind. Most of the statistical knowledge of Salem during 1636-50 is based on two surviving lists of landholders. The first list, dated 1636 and in town clerk Ralph Fogg's shorthand, is of landholders and their acreage.[3] Fogg's surviving record was not the final copy but a working copy in the "waste book" and therefore replete with erasures and repetitions. The large number of blanks after the names implies that at the time this copy was made no final ·decision on the acreage had been reached. Of 163 names, 32 fall into this category, or some 20 percent. The deficiency can be partially remedied by a careful reading of the town record. For example, neither Samuel Sharp's nor James Standish's land grants appear on Fogg's list, but the record indicates that they were given 300 and 20 acres respectively during 1637. With such corrections Fogg's list yields a reasonably clear picture of Salem's social structure at about the time Hugh Peter became the town's pastor (table 3).

Table 3. Landholding in Salem, 1636-37

Acreage	No. of families
300+	6
100-299	23
60-99	15
30-59	39
10-29	52
½-9	0
Blank	28
Total	163

Sources: *Town Recs.*, I, 18-61; Sidney J. Perley, *The History of Salem, Massachusetts*, 3 vols. (Salem, 1924-27), I, 454-65.

Grants of 100 acres or more were a significant sign of status and power.[4] Salem gave large grants as rewards for service and as inducements for the recipients to remain in the town in order to maintain a stable ruling class. Almost all the men who played a leading role in the town's affairs received such grants, including Endecott, Conant, Peter, Sharp, Scruggs, Hathorne, and Batter.

[2] Ibid., I, 8, 10, 28; C. W. Chalklin, *Seventeenth-Century Kent: A Social and Economic History* (London, 1965), p. 68.

[3] *Town Recs.*, I, 18-27.

[4] Compare with Edward S. Perzel, "Landholding in Ipswich," *Essex Institute Historical Collections* 104 (1968): 303, 312.

These large landholders of 1636-37 and those who later joined their ranks held a near monopoly on important town offices until 1650. For several years before and after 1650, men who held less land but had gained status through other means were granted larger acreage in an attempt to absorb them into the existing status system and prevent its disruption. The acreage possessed by the men who held the offices of deputy and selectmen before 1650 reveals something of the stability of the structure (table 4). Of the twenty-nine heads of families holding over 100 acres, only five never held any town office. The lack of participation of three of the five can be readily explained; one was a widow, the second was a nonresident London merchant, and the third was in exile with Williams.

Table 4. Officeholding in Salem before 1650

	Deputy	Selectman
Men who held 100+ in 1636-37	13	16
Men who gained 100+ later	3	9
Men who held less than 100	3	4
Total	19	29

Sources: *Town Recs.*, I; James Duncan Phillips, *Salem in the Seventeenth Century* (Boston, 1933), pp. 358-62.

Such a concentration of power in the hands of a landed elite was the usual pattern in seventeenth-century Massachusetts. The vast majority of the Massachusetts deputies and all the assistants between 1634 and 1637 were large landholders. In towns like Dedham and Ipswich, men of "landed estates" enjoyed almost a monopoly of local power. In fact, since Salem was a port with other sources of wealth and prestige, the control of the large landowners was not as complete there as in many other towns.[5] These alternate possibilities had been among the causes of Salem's instability in the early 1630s. Fishermen and merchants, like Holgrave and Bartholomew, who in 1638 held 61 acres and one half an acre respectively, became leaders. Yet, as table 4 shows, such success was unusual before 1650.

The Salem ruling class had other peculiarities, the most striking of which was its large size. Almost one landed family in five held this status during the winter of 1636-37. In Andover, forty men held house lots before 1662, and of that forty only two seem

[5] Emery Battis, *Saints and Sectaries* (Chapel Hill, N.C., 1962), pp. 96-97; Kenneth A. Lockridge, *A New England Town: The First Hundred Years; Dedham, Massachusetts, 1636-1736* (New York, 1970), pp. 10-11; Perzel, p. 322.

comparable in power and prestige to Salem's great men and only two more seem close enough to rank with Salem's lesser leaders. Thus Andover's leading families comprised but 10 percent of the town's landholding families. This percentage seems to have prevailed in Sudbury and Ipswich as well.[6]

Salem's large ruling class resulted from the town's unique history before 1636. A large number of families, mostly West Countrymen, held claims, usually of 200 acres, from the defunct New England Company. These claims were honored in the land division of 1636. Table 5 illustrates this situation by comparing the English origins of Salem's large landowners, the rest of Salem's settlers, and the Massachusetts population at large. Since 1637 was another year of East Anglian migration, the newcomers of that year made the disparity between the West Country character of the large landholders and the East Anglian complexion of the small landowners even greater.

Table 5. Regional origins of Salem and Massachusetts landholders

Area	Salem (100 + acres)		Salem (10-99 acres)		General Massachusetts
	No.	%	No.	%	%
East Anglia, Essex Co.	7	27	49	55	20.5
West Country	11	42	11	13	19.0
London, home counties	5	19	17	19	18.5
Southern counties	1	4	1	1	8.0
Midlands	2	8	5	6	18.0
North Country	0	0	5	6	10.0
Total Known	26	100	88	100	
Unknown	3		46		

Sources: for Salem, *Town Recs.*, I, 18-27; for Massachusetts, Carl Bridenbaugh, *Vexed and Troubled Englishmen, 1590-1642* (New York, 1968), p. 465.

All the West Country large landholders arrived in Salem before the Winthrop migration of 1630. Twenty-one of the twenty-nine families holding at least 100 acres are known to have settled in the town before the East Anglian immigration reached its peak in 1635. Since Salem, unlike most New England towns, took about a decade to settle, early arrivals were more likely to get larger grants, and of course, the earliest settlers were West Countrymen. In this

[6]Philip J. Greven, Jr., *Four Generations: Population, Land, and Family in Colonial Andover, Massachusetts* (Ithaca, N.Y., 1970), chap. 2; Sumner Chilton Powell, *Puritan Village: The Formation of a New England Town* (Middleton, Conn., 1963), app. 6; Thomas Franklin Waters, *Ipswich in the Massachusetts Bay Colony, 1633-1700* (Ipswich, 1905), pp. 86-106.

way both the West Country leadership and their original followers benefited. Of the eleven known West Country families who were granted less than 100 acres, seven were given more than 30 acres. The average East Anglian grant was 20 acres in 1636 and considerably less afterwards.

Gradually the disparity was lessened, but not eliminated. The 1636 distribution was Salem's only large-scale land division. In Andover, where the population growth was slower, and in Ipswich, where there was need to attract new settlers, the leaders divided up large tracts to increase the holdings of inhabitants. In Salem the opposite was the case. After Conant and his fellow West Country "layers out of lots" divided a tract of marsh and meadow into strips of between half and one acre in December 1637, there were no more mass grants. For the next twenty years grants were made to individuals and small groups. The greatest increase in numbers of landowners occurred at the bottom of the scale, gradually lowering the proportion of large holders in the town's population.[7]

This trend is apparent in table 6, which combines the land information in Fogg's and Conant's lists and includes all the grants

Table 6. Basic land system by March 1638

Acres		Landholders	
		No.	%
300+		6	3
100-299		24	10
60-99		16	6
30-59		42	19
10-29		67	28
½-9	(F)	22	8
	(C)	57	24
0		4	2
Total		238	100

Source: *Town Recs.*, I, 18-56, 101-4.
F: Fogg's list. C: Conant's list.

made up to March 1638. Because of the incompleteness of Fogg's list in particular, the number of families holding less than ten acres is exaggerated. Therefore a distinction is drawn between those holding less than ten acres who appear on Fogg's list (*F*) and those with the same acreage who first appear on Conant's (*C*). It is likely that most of the families holding less than ten acres on Fogg's list were granted at least ten more acres than the acreage he credited

[7]Greven, pp. 45-46; Perzel, p. 320; *Town Recs.*, I, 101-4.

to them. These families generally arrived before the policy granting each immigrant family ten acres was abrogated. Those who first appear in Conant's division were not as fortunate. By March 1638, when the immigration to Salem had slowed to a trickle, the percentage of large landholders in the town's population had dropped from 18 percent to 13 percent. The proportion of "the better sort" to the rest of the town had become more analogous to that of other towns, but its West Country cast was generally unchanged.

This landed class comprised the unquestioned leadership of Salem society until the 1650s. Even most of the town's early merchants like Edmund Batter and William Hathorne were among this landed elite. Their behavior gives the impression that they viewed commerce as just one more of their prerogatives and responsibilities within the communal system of the town. None of these original landed merchants applied themselves exclusively enough to commerce to amass the kind of fortune that other Salem merchants of less land and more commercial dedication accumulated. When Hathorne died in 1681 he left an estate of £754, while his contemporary George Corwin, who began with twenty acres in 1638, had amassed a fortune of nearly £6,000 by the time of his death in 1685.[8] It was the meteoric rise of mercantile-minded men like Corwin that helped confuse the status system of the town after 1650. But until then the older landed leadership held undisputed sway.

In order to maintain a comparatively lavish standard of living and at the same time have the necessary leisure in the seventeenth-century sense to devote to civil and ecclesiastical affairs, "the better sort" needed a reliable labor force to support their households and their activities. In the seventeenth-century the household itself was the basic economic as well as social unit. Families ran the farms and the artisans' shops. Even in commerce, family connections provided vital contacts for trade among distant points. Although the families varied greatly in size and occasionally included an aged grandparent, an unmarried relative or lodgers, they resembled modern nuclear families. As might be expected, the landed leaders tended to be older men who had the larger families necessary for their support.[9] In his list Conant wrote the sizes of 206 families, and from genealogical sources the

---

[8] *Probate Record of Essex County, Massachusetts,* ed. George F. Dow, 3 vols. (Salem, 1916-20), III, 423-24 (hereafter cited as *Pro Recs.*).

[9] Greven, pp. 30-31; Edmund S. Morgan, *The Puritan Family: Religion and Domestic Relations in Seventeenth Century New England* (New York, 1956), pp. 19-20, 26-28.

ages of sixty-five of the heads of these families in 1637 can be ascertained (table 7).

Table 7. Age of family head and family size in 1637

Acreage	Average age	Average family size
100-300	42.3	6.8
60-99	35.0	5.7
30-59	32.1	5.0
10-29	29.2	3.8
½-9	24.7	2.7
Total	30.1	3.9

Sources: *Town Recs.*, I, 101-4; Sidney J. Perley, *The History of Salem, Massachusetts*, 3 vols. (Salem, 1924-27), I, biographical footnotes.

One of the most valuable economic assets a man might command in early Massachusetts was the labor of his sons. Since the fathers controlled the land and were often quite reluctant to part with it, they were frequently able to keep their sons dependent upon them even after the sons married. Large land-owners, like Thomas Gardner, were often able to settle their sons in semiseparate households on or near the farm and maintain control of their labor.[10] In Salem the fishing and maritime men of the period took their sons to sea much as the farmers relied on their sons in the fields.

Some large landholders, not so fortunate as to have a brood of sons, had to use servants. With a large estate and a multitude of responsibilities, Endecott had but two sons, both born in the 1630s. Consequently in 1637 he had five servants counted among his household on Conant's list. As might be expected, the number of servants in a family varied proportionately to the labor needed to maintain farm, shop, or vessels and inversely to the number of sons. Servants were a less satisfactory labor force than sons largely because personal ties were not as easily forged. Although there were a large number of apprentices, quite a few of the servants, especially after immigration slowed, were hired, and their compensation, beyond room and board, was strictly financial, up to £6-£10 a year. Hired men who did not like their treatment or wages could quit and usually find other work easily. In the labor-starved economy, masters, on the other hand, often were not able to hire another servant.[11]

[10]Greven, chaps. 4, 6.
[11]*Winthrop Papers*, 7 vols. (Boston, 1929-47), IV, 43, 47-48; John Demos, *A Little Commonwealth: Family Life in Plymouth Colony* (New York, 1970), p. 108.

Despite attempts at wage and price control, wage earners were in an excellent position to accumulate capital, not necessarily money but items of value, in exchange for their labor. Since accumulation of wealth was one sign of status, confusion soon set in. In 1645 John Winthrop related an ironic anecdote of the relations between master and servant: "I may upon this occasion report a passage between one of Rowley and his servant. The master, being forced to sell a pair of his oxen to pay his servant his wages, told his servant he could keep him no longer, not knowing how to pay him the next year. The servant answered him, he would serve him for more of his cattle. But how shall I do (saith the master) when all my cattle are gone? The servant replied, you shall then serve me, and so you may have your cattle again."[12]

As the story implies, the threat was to the status of small landholders. The large landowners, despite what a number of them like Winthrop considered extortion by their servants, were hardly vulnerable. Their lack of interest in accumulating more land stands as testimony to their sense of security. Land for men like Conant was not a commodity but an estate. Clearing and developing a farm of 200 acres was task enough for him for forty years. Of the original large landowners in Salem, only two sought more land (see table 10).

In composite, the smaller landholders, those holding less than 100 acres, were a much less secure group. In origins they were largely East Anglians and relative newcomers to the town. In occupation they varied as widely as had the landed elite when they first came to Salem. A major difference between them and "the better sort" was that the smaller holders were less likely to abandon their original trades. Although comprising over 80 percent of the town's population by 1637, they were unlikely to find themselves in positions of appreciable civil or ecclesiastical authority. The two deacons, Charles Gott and John Horne, belonged to the upper reaches of the small landholding class with 75 acres each. But the minister and the ruling elder each held over 300. Before 1650 the more land a person held, the more likely he was to be a member of the church. The men mentioned in the town's land records by March 1638 were more likely to join the Elect than those who came later (table 8).

Given the oligarchic reputation of Puritan churches, the fact that about 53 percent of the original landholders joined the church before 1650 may seem unusual. Yet the percentages in several of

---

[12]*Winthrop's Journal, 1630-1649* (1649; 2 vols., ed. James K. Hosmer, New York, 1908), II, 219-20.

Table 8. Church membership of original landholders to 1650

Acreage	No. of landholders	No. in church	% in church
100-300	30	25	83.3
60-99	16	13	81.3
30-59	42	32	75.1
10-29	67	28	41.7
½-9	79	29	35.4
0	4	1	25.0
Total	238	127	53.4

Sources: for church membership, James Duncan Phillips, *Salem in the Seventeenth Century* (Boston, 1933), pp. 350-55; for landholders, *Town Recs.*, I, 18-56, 101-4.

the inland towns like Dedham were even larger, mainly because the population was stable and there was time to bring people into the church. In Salem the stream of immigrants created a constantly changing population. The church, under the vigorous leadership of Hugh Peter, was much more successful with the original landholders than with those who came later; yet from 1638 to 1641 the church was able to include thirty-four family heads who were newly arrived. But after Peter left, admissions, especially of newcomers, fell off precipitously. During the rest of the decade only twenty-two of the late arrivals joined. In all, only 56 of the known 147 families that came to Salem between March 1638 and 1650 were represented in church before the latter date. The remainder of the new admissions were older residents or their children.

The same rule generally applied to political power. The more land a man held, the more likely he was to hold civil offices. Also the larger landholders tended to hold the more powerful positions and for a longer period of time.

Table 9 shows clearly the hierarchical pattern of Salem politics,

Table 9. Civil offices and tenure of landholders to 1650

Acreage	Deputy		Selectman		Constable		Juries	
	No.	Average tenure	No.	Average tenure	No.	Average tenure	No.	Average tenure
100-300+	16	2.9	24	2.1	3	1	20	4.6
60-99	3	1.3	5	1.8	5	1	11	2.8
30-59	–	–	–	–	3	1	6	2.0
10-29	–	–	–	–	2	1	7	1.1
½-9	–	–	–	–	–	–	–	–
Unknown	–	–	–	–	2	1	1	2.0

Sources: Sidney J. Perley, *The History of Salem, Massachusetts*, 3 vols. (Salem, 1924-27), I, 317- 19, II, 8-11; James Duncan Phillips, *Salem in the Seventeenth Century* (Boston, 1933), pp. 358-62; *Town Recs.*, I, 18-56, 101-4.

a pattern quite common throughout early Massachus[e] unusual feature is the relative lack of accumulated experience among the deputies and selectmen.[13] What dis averages is the rapid turnover in office during the crisi from 1634 to 1637. After 1637 the town's political life st..........d under the new covenant and a much smaller leadership emerged, gathering ever greater experience and power. Hathorne, for example, was five times elected selectman and twelve times deputy before 1650.

Up to 1650 the Salem social hierarchy was rather clearly defined. Landholding, church membership, and political leadership all correlated in accordance with the non-Separatist ideal of clear status relationships. Even the geographic pattern reflected the hierarchy. The land division of 1636 defined trends that dated at least from 1634 and blocked the town's lands out into three major segments: peninsula, fields, and farms. The first segment and the core of the town was the peninsula that jutted into Salem harbor and was bounded by the North and South Rivers. The peninsula was the central village of an open-field system. Here were the one- and two-acre house lots which comprised the bulk of the town's housing and, of course, the meetinghouse. Although no record of the original layout of the village is extant, it is conjectured that there were also two large commons. One of these areas may have been the marsh that Conant divided in 1637.[14]

Each working day the open-field farmers of Salem walked to the North and South Fields, which were originally fields of ten-acre lots or strips. Although these fields were across the North and South Rivers they were easily accessible. Farmlands on the other side of the harbor were more difficult to reach, and consequently grants in the Ryal Side and Cape Ann Side tended to be larger, twenty acres or more. Since during this early period the men who farmed that area lived on the peninsula, the town contracted with various men to run a ferry for both people and cattle.

Up the creeks and rivers that empty into Salem harbor and beyond the ring of small landholdings were the farms of the large landowners. Since "the better sort" had town lots in addition to their farms, it is impossible to determine whether or not most of them lived on their estates or in the village. Some, like Emanuel Downing, who had tenants on his land, spent most of their time in

---

[13]Lockridge, pp. 42-44; Darrett B. Rutman, *Winthrop's Boston: Portrait of a Puritan Town, 1630-1649* (Chapel Hill, N.C., 1965), pp. 46-47, 81.
[14]Sidney Perley, *History of Salem, Massachusetts*, 3 vols. (Salem, 1924-27), I, 311-17; James Duncan Phillips, *Salem in the Seventeenth Century* (Boston, 1933), p. 172.

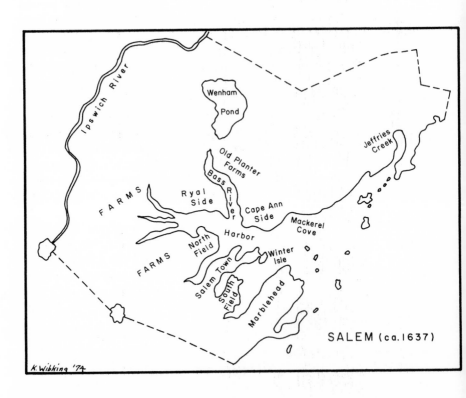

SALEM (ca. 1637)

K. Wibking '74

the village. But before 1650 the general trend among the landed elite, as well as among the smaller landowners whose acreage was far from the village, was to move out to their lands. They came to the peninsula for public occasions or to do business. Hathorne's children, for example, were born on his farm in what is now Danvers. The Old Planter leadership—Conant, Woodbury, John Balch, and Peter Palfrey—also tended to stay on their lands.[15]

This basic system of village, fields, and outlying farms was common in early Massachusetts. Both Ipswich and Boston were settled similarly. To some extent it was also a reproduction of the English parish system. Yet Salem's land pattern had some unusual features engendered by the town's geography and the diversity of its population. The most important geographic feature was, of course, the main Salem harbor, which not only destined the town for commerce but also split it into relatively discreet areas that tended to fragment its sense of community as well as its geographic identity.

Commuting across the harbor was inconvenient, time-consuming, and at times even dangerous. Consequently the men who held land there began in the late 1630s to move their homes out to their lands, at first temporarily in the busiest seasons of planting and harvesting and then more permanently. Boston, which also had a large bay in the midst of its territory, went through a similar process. The tendency of farmers to move out to the outlying lots and gradually to consolidate their holdings became common in the older towns immediately after the Pequot War removed the Indian menace in 1637.[16] In Salem, however, the movement began before the war. Its effect was to give geographic reinforcement to the division between East Anglians and West Countrymen. Most of the West Countrymen held land on Cape Ann Side and along the Bass River. As early as February 1636 West Country small landholders were settling "to the waterside, by that place where the Old Planters do move for," that is, across the harbor. The agricultural tradition of the West Country, scattered farms of all sizes, was reproduced as rapidly as possible. The East Anglians, on the other hand, organized the peninsula and the North and South Fields for open-field farming. So tenacious was the open-field tradition that traces of it remained in the Fields until after 1700, despite the development of the peninsula as a port.[17]

[15]Perley, II, 19-21; Vernon Loggins, *The Hawthornes: The Story of Seven Generations of an American Family* (New York, 1951), pp. 34-35.

[16]Edna Scofield, "The Origins of Settlement Patterns in Rural New England," *Geographical Review* 28 (1938): 657; Rutman, pp. 93-96.

[17]*Town Recs.*, I, 15; Phillips, pp. 363-70.

This geographic separation between West Countrymen and the rest of the townsmen also affected the large landowners. The West Country "better sort," with the exception of Endecott and the Gardners, concentrated in the region east of Bass River. The other large landholders, men like Hathorne, Downing, Batter, and Sharp, had farms north and west of the peninsula. It may be that this geographic separation of the West Countrymen of all classes from the East Anglians was one of the adjustments deliberately made to prevent future clashes within the town.

Two smaller harbors, Marblehead and Jeffries Creek, at either end of the town's long shoreline further encouraged fragmentation. Villages whose inhabitants combined farming with fishing quickly grew up at both sites. Both became separate towns: Jeffries Creek was renamed Manchester and became a town in 1645, and Marblehead was declared officially separate in 1648. Both of these communities were West Country.

Marblehead was larger, older, and more notorious than Manchester. As a settlement it was nearly as old as Salem itself, with fishermen resident there as early as 1630. By January 1638 Salem listed twenty-four families on Marblehead, and when it became a town in 1648 there were at least forty. The people of Marblehead had an unsavory reputation for "prophaness." As late as 1644 not a single inhabitant could claim the freedom of the commonwealth. But their economic value to the colony could hardly be questioned. In 1647 £4,000 worth of fish was brought into its harbor.[18]

From the beginning Salem's relationship to Marblehead was peculiar, and it illustrates well the problems such a community posed for Puritans. Despite its relative proximity to the peninsula, Marblehead was always considered somewhat independent of Salem. During the 1630s the colonial tax was assessed as if Marblehead were a separate town, a procedure justified by its wealth. In 1641 Salem allowed the inhabitants "to lay out their own lands." Yet Salem kept a close watch on its rambunctious precinct, appointing constables for just that area as early as 1637. Moses Maverick, one of Marblehead's most substantial citizens, was a quasi-magistrate empowered to hear small causes and was invariably on the grand jury. Even after Marblehead became a separate town, Salem maintained some responsibility for the people and morals of the settlement, for the inhabitants were required to attend the Salem church until their own was formed in 1684.[19]

[18]Perley, II, 196; Bernard Bailyn, *The New England Merchants in the Seventeenth Century* (paperback ed., New York, 1964), p. 78; *Town Recs.*, I, 63.
[19]*Town Recs.*, I, 111, 127; Perley, II, 202.

Before 1650 another town, Wenham, was formed out of Salem land. It represented an entirely different strand of Salem life. It was an East Anglian farming village created in the region north and east of the Old Planters' farms near Wenham Pond. In December 1638 the Salem town meeting "agreed and voted that there should be a Village granted to Mr. Phillips and his company upon such conditions as the seven men appointed for the town affairs should agree on." The undoubted leader of the twelve families, most of whom derived from Wrentham, Suffolk, and came together in the same ship in 1638, was John Phillips, the nonconformist rector of the Wrentham church who was removed from that position in August 1638. Salem granted the newcomers lots ranging from twenty to fifty acres on condition that the grantees remain in the plantation and use the premises.[20]

The conditions imposed by the Salem selectmen point to some of the problems of assimilation. Salem's officers felt that the newly arrived group was too coherent and that their strong commitment to each other and lack of roots in Salem could lead them to further migrations. Having their own pastor, they proved difficult to incorporate into Salem society. The worst of these fears were exaggerated, for in November 1640 Phillips moved to Dedham. The rest of the group stayed on their lands and were soon joined by other settlers, who must have diluted their group identity. Yet Wenham was never fully absorbed into Salem, and in 1643 the General Court ordered, "Wenham is granted to be a town and hath liberty to send a deputy."[21]

Part of the problem of assimilating the people of Wenham was religious. A small meetinghouse was built in 1641, but a church was not immediately gathered. Early in 1644 an attempt to form a church failed because "the magistrates and elders present [from various Massachusetts churches], finding upon trial, that the persons appointed were not fit for foundation stones, they advised them not to proceed, which they obeyed." Within a few months, Salem's former assistant minister, John Fiske, and his brother William went to Wenham to be pastor and magistrate respectively. They were successful, for a church was formed on October 10, 1644.[22]

The three towns of Wenham, Manchester, and Marblehead were the only ones to be formed out of Salem territory until Beverly was incorporated in 1667. To some extent all three of the new towns represented disquieting elements in Salem's social structure. This fragmentation was partly an attempt to preserve the tenuous

[20]Perley., II, 147-49; *Town Recs.,* I, 77, 98.
[21]Perley, II, 153-53.
[22]Winthrop, II, 177.

peace gained during the late 1630s and to maintain the power relationships and adjustments upon which that peace rested. The West Countrymen of the Bass River region, although not entirely comfortable with their fellow townsmen, constituted an integral part of the community. Not until 1667 was their separateness aggravated enough by economic change to necessitate the formation of a new town.

Although the creation of the first three new towns was a reasonable attempt to cope with pluralism and population growth, it was hardly a complete solution. In fact, the loss of so much land may have aggravated the problem by reducing the amount of acreage Salem had left. Yet the land system was not rigid before 1650; Salem's inhabitants and newcomers were usually accommodated with at least some acreage. The status system was maintained, but that did not preclude social mobility.

Salem's original landholders, those who held land before March 1638, could accumulate more land, but only seventy-six of them did. Table 10 shows comparative land accumulation by the original classes and the general size of the increases. It indicates something of the economic mobility of the original holders and testifies to the stability of the social hierarchy. Only thirteen men passed over the gulf between the small and large landholders.

Table 10. Land accumulation by original holders to 1650

Acres held in 1637	Additional acres acquired					
	½-9	10-29	30-59	60-99	100-299	300+
300+	—	—	1	—	1	—
100-299	3	2	3	1	—	—
60-99	2	3	3	—	2	—
30-59	3	2	7	2	1	—
10-29	6	10	5	6	1	2
½-9	2	4	3	—	1	—

Source: *Town Recs.*, I.

Generally the success of these men followed the pattern expected in a Puritan community. They proved themselves by joining the church and by participating in the town's political life as minor officeholders. Then they were granted more land as a reward and an affirmation of status earned in noneconomic pursuits. The careers of Richard Bishop and Thomas Browning are typical. Richard Bishop, his wife, and four children were given a 20-acre lot in the North Field in 1637. In 1639 he joined the church, and that same year the town granted him a 150-acre farm. The town's trust was not misplaced, for he served three terms on each jury before 1650 and as constable in 1644. Thomas Browning, a substantial family man of fifty years of age in 1637, was given 40 acres that year. Soon afterwards he was among the Elect and was on the grand jury. The town then gave him 80 acres more. A careful farmer, Browning died in 1671 with an estate of £378.

Another way to earn a large land grant before 1650 was to be a political and social leader of a significant interest group. John Holgrave, fisherman and tavern keeper on Winter Isle, was a respected East Anglian church member since 1636 and influential among the fishermen. He was given 100 acres in 1638 and twice served as selectman. Henry Bartholomew, the twenty-year-old unmarried East Anglian merchant who had imprudently supported Roger Williams, was given only a half acre in 1637. But later in that year he returned to the church. In 1639 he was given 150 acres. He began serving a total of thirteen terms on both juries that year. In 1642 he was given an additional 110 acres. The next year the town elected him selectman and two years later deputy. He was chosen either selectman or deputy practically every year from 1643 to 1684. Although Bartholomew was a prominent leader of the mercantile element that eventually made the non-Separatist ideal unworkable in Salem, he had conformed well, after his initial lapse, to the expected pattern of service, piety, and subsequent reward.

Four of the thirteen did not fit into the system so easily because of their difficulty in joining the church. Only one of the four, John Hardy, ever became a member, in 1648. But he and two of the others proved their worth to the town by being among the few unchurched townsmen to serve on the juries or town committees. Hardy was once even elected selectman before the joining the Elect, one of only three men to achieve that distinction before 1650. Two of the four, Richard Ingersoll and William Dodge, and probably Hardy as well, were West Countrymen. For this reason, their failure to fit all the specifications of the status system did not signify its demise, since the West Country position rested more firmly on other qualities besides church activities.

However, the career of the fourth man, Robert Goodale, an East Anglian farmer, was a harbinger of the troubles to come. He never joined the church or participated actively in the political life of Salem. Yet by 1650 he had parlayed his original 20 acres into a vast estate of 504 acres by purchase from no less than fifteen original grantees during the 1640s. The lots generally ranged from 30 to 50 acres apiece and were located near the Ipswich River, fairly far from the peninsula and in the area that would later become Salem Village. The known sellers included a shipwright, a tanner, a shopkeeper, a tailor, a weaver, a cooper, and a mariner. Three of the original grantees apparently became tenants of Goodale. This land transfer was a forerunner of trends that in the 1650s and 1660s fragmented the town in much more fundamental ways than had the separation of the three new towns. The rise of men like Goodale to wealth shattered the close correlation of the various signs of status. The decision to sell to him also marked the tendency toward growing economic specialization and concentration of trades in the town core.

Before 1650 such occurrences were rare. The only occupations that were strongly specialized were fishing and farming, and even fishermen usually had gardens at least. Most of the town's artisans, merchants, and mariners were also landowners who tended their lots along with their trades. The status system, especially the upper segment, remained relatively stable. Man gained land by service to church and state. Newcomers were carefully scrutinized and then were given "accommodation" in proportion to the town's estimate of their worth to the community. Table 11 shows the grants given new holders between 1638 and 1650. The town was maintaining the rough proportions among the various classes by landholding. The large majority, 102 out of 146, received the ten acres or more that would support an agricultural style of life. Generally the same high standards of potential service, wealth, birth, and piety that pertained to the original large landholders were applied to the newcomers. Emanuel Downing, John Winthrop's brother-in-law, arrived in Salem in 1638, joined the church that year, and served three terms as selectman and five as deputy. He was given over 300 acres. Edward Norris, who replaced Hugh Peter as minister, also received a large grant. Other

Table 11. Land grants to new holders, 1638-50

Year	Acreage						
	0	½-9	10-29	30-59	60-99	100-299	300+
1638	2	8	14	1	–	1	1
1639	6	15	16	4	6	1	–
1640	1	2	5	–	1	1	–
1641	–	1	3	2	–	1	–
1642	–	1	15	1	–	–	–
1643	2	2	8	1	1	–	–
1646	–	–	–	1	1	–	–
1649	1	1	2	9	–	2	–
1650	–	2	1	4	–	–	–
Total	12	32	64	23	8	6	1

Source: *Town Recs.*, I.

newcomers gradually earned farms according to the established pattern of joining the church and working in minor offices.

Yet during the 1640s a number of the new recruits to the leadership class were primarily merchants who were given land rather than farmers who indulged in trade as a sideline. For example, Walter Price, an unmarried youth of twenty-six, arrived in Salem during the spring of 1641 from Bristol, England. In 1642 he joined the church and married into a small-time merchant and mariner family, the Gerrishes. Then he served on the juries and a year as constable in 1646. In 1649 the town granted him 110 acres, and Price began serving a total of sixteen years as selectman. During his long service to the town he had not neglected his calling, for when he died in 1674 he was worth nearly £2,060. Although Price fit the behavioral pattern expected of potential leaders in Salem during the 1630s and 1640s, his career also represents a shift of emphasis from agriculture to commerce as an economic means of gaining status. Later a number of merchants rose to power who did not join the church or serve politically, and the whole system of status and expected behavior had to adapt.

At the opposite end of the scale from the large landowners were twelve men who were received as inhabitants but not given any land. Only two of the twelve were ever able to meet the town's standards of success. Thomas Oliver and James Underwood were able to join the church, purchase ten-acre lots, and serve on the juries. Underwood even became a constable in 1657 and, in his old age, owned half of the ketch *Dolphin*. Oliver died in 1679 with a fairly substantial estate of £100. Almost nothing is known about the other ten men except that five of them were artisans and that one left immediately for Connecticut. There is no way to know what happened to these men. Perhaps they followed their trades, leased land without appearing in the records, or quietly moved on.

That these ten landless inhabitants were an early contingent of the perenially poor is highly unlikely. In the labor-starved economy of New England there was enough essential work to make the Puritan proscription against idleness less ironic than such injunctions have been in other times and places. Poverty was not yet a serious problem. As Thomas Lechford remarked, "Prophane swearing, drunkenness, and beggars, are but rare in the compass of this patent, through the circumspection of the Magistrates, and the providence of God hitherto, the poor there living by their labours, and great wages, proportionably, better than the rich, by their stock, which without exceeding great care, quickly waste." [23]

[23] Lechford, *Plain Dealing; or, News from New England* (1642; ed. J. Hammond Trumbull, Boston, 1867), p. 69.

As Lechford noted and Winthrop lamented, there was more economic upward mobility than seemed normal to seventeenth-century Englishmen. But during the first half of the century this movement did not threaten the ideal hierarchy of Puritan hope. In fact, it was an economic fulfillment of the vision that men like Francis Higginson held of New World opportunity.

The people of Salem were attempting to make actual a traditional English ideal, a flawless peasant community. The term *peasant* describes not an economic or social status but rather a state of mind that exults in the land, family, and the organic web of families that make a community. Its values, often inarticulate, can be summarized, according to Darrett Rutman, "in the familiar words unity, order, the family structure of society, diligence, and a subsuming of self to the good of the whole." [24]

These values largely determined the social structure and the land adjustments of the period. Unity meant approximate homogeneity, and for that reason Salem allowed new towns to be formed from its lands and the remaining West Countrymen to concentrate along the Bass River. Order meant a stable hierarchy of status and power. The various sizes of the land grants were designed to meet this need. In law and custom the patriarchal family and the ideals of diligence for the communal good were embodied. The problem was that even though almost everyone shared these ideals, the degree of commitment to any one or all of them varied from person to person. In Salem consensus over the proper means of implementing and expressing these ideals had to be renewed constantly.

[24] Rutman, *American Puritanism: Faith and Practice* (New York, 1970), pp. 77-78.

Chapter V

Communal Society
and Patterns of Dissent
1638-1650

The late 1630s and 1640s were a period of relative internal calm for Salem. In pursuing "peace and unity" the town stressed accommodation to maintain a stable hierarchical society. All the community's institutions were geared to that end. There was, however, some dissent. A small number of individuals could not adjust easily to the system. But mild dissent was not a sign of flaws in the social order. In manageable quantities, dissent and the efforts to control it provided means of continually clarifying and strengthening the system.

The basis of Salem's political life during the 1630s and 1640s was the town's communal sense of identity. The daily business of civil and ecclesiastical government was to apply the general principles of the 1636 covenant to specific cases and problems. This agricultural society's basic resource was, of course, the land. Disagreement over its proper distribution and use could involve most of the townsmen and lead to irreparable "breaches among men." The town's response was usually a combination of regulation and accommodation of the various interests and needs of the community. The bulk of the business conducted by the town meeting and the board of selectmen concerned this process. Typical was this 1644 decision by the town meeting: "It is ordered that the highway from Francis Lawes his ten acre lot may be viewed by Jeffrey Massey and Peter Palfrey and laid out most conveniently for him."[1] The two viewers, both substantial West Countrymen, were to mediate between the public interest in the roadway and the rights of the lot owner, using accommodation to the lot owner's wishes as the criterion for a settlement.

Once the lots and roads were laid out, elected town officials, surveyors of the highway, fence viewers, and occasional committees were responsible for insuring that the boundaries were understood and maintained in order to prevent the confusion and "encroachments" that bred dissension. These officers, particularly the surveyors, who were empowered to raise and oversee labor from the townsmen to repair the roads, had great influence upon the daily lives of the people. As a result the surveyors were

[1] *Town Recs.*, I, 133.

prestigious men in the hierarchy. Eight surveyors are known to have been elected before 1650 to serve terms of approximately seven years, including such prominent leaders as Conant, Batter, Downing, and Gardner. They all held over sixty acres and averaged about two hundred acres. The more numerous fence viewers, not having the power to raise communal labor but only to order landowners to repair their fences, were a less prestigious group. The twenty-five different men elected to the post were substantial landholders, averaging eighty-seven acres. Although a few of the town's prominent leaders, like Henry Bartholomew, served the approximate four-year term as fence viewer, the group was largely composed of farmer and artisan church members, the kinds of men who often served on juries. Both the surveyors of the highways and the fence viewers must have been men who could command the respect and gain the consent of their fellow townsmen with the least possible difficulty.

Town government affected the daily economic life of the citizens in myriad ways besides land regulation. The town hired communal herdsmen. There were extensive regulations on such matters as ringing swine in the summer to protect crops. Since a family needed about fifteen cords of wood a winter, or about three-fifths of an acre of standing timber for firewood, timber regulation began early in the history of most New England towns. Salem, desiring to encourage shipbuilding, had additional incentive. On occasion the town meeting even determined local produce prices by fixing monetary equivalents of bushels of wheat, barley, rye, and Indian corn for tax and welfare purposes.[2]

As Salem's commerce began to increase after the depression the colony had suffered in the early 1640s, the town government not only regulated trade but also actively participated in it for the common good. On occasion this participation took the form of subsidies. For example, the town meeting raised forty shillings to purchase cloth for a poor tailor in 1644. A year later it authorized the deputies to buy sheep in Boston "at 40[s.] a head" for the town's use. For several years the town held shares in a bark whose construction it had subsidized under the encouragement of Hugh Peter. Usually each voyage brought in profits of £7 to £10 for the town. In January 1646 the agenda for the town meeting included the purchase of "a Town Stock of Cotton Wool," encouragement to Salem farmers "to sow hemp and flax," and even the possibility of having "an agent at Barbados." Besides these rather ambitious examples of communal enterprise, the town was also concerned with the more mundane business of licensing ferries, forming

[2] Ibid., I, 112, 130, 132.

incipient housing codes, letting out contracts for bridge and meetinghouse repairs, and contracting with individuals to care for welfare cases.[3]

One of the most intriguing aspects of Salem politics between 1638 and 1650 was the high degree of unanimity the town maintained on many crucial issues, particularly economic questions. No segment of the population questioned the need to encourage commerce. Land distribution after 1637, admissions of new inhabitants, and welfare decisions were made easily, and the communal assumptions that governed these actions went largely unchallenged. This "peace and unity" was not accidental but carefully cultivated by a process of adjustment and regulation forged in open meetings. The 1637 rule governing behavior in the Salem church applied to the town meeting as well: "Members are not to reason between themselves before the Church by way of opposition, but members must speak their case to the Church."[4] All dissension was to be brought immediately into the open so that it could be dealt with swiftly, preventing the formation of cliques or the spread of bad feeling.

Yet consensus on many issues and the relative success of the hierarchical ideal did not prevent all dissent. A number of people were unable to fit themselves into the communal system of the town. Generally they showed their discomfort by violation of the town's social or economic mores or, most seriously, through heresy.

After the suppression of Separatism and before the Quaker movement of the 1650s, religious dissent in Salem was sporadic, infrequent, and various in its character. There were Anabaptists, Familiarists, and Gortonists. Others seem to have held no definite doctrinal position but only a deep dislike for the Salem church. Typical of the latter attitude was William Gault, who was tried in December 1642 by the Quarterly Court "for reproachful and unseemly speeches against the rule of the Church."[5] Gault had been a church member since 1639. He joined while Hugh Peter was pastor and apparently had difficulty relating to the new minister, Edward Norris, who took up the pastorate a few months before Gault's trial. After this clash Gault seems never to have strayed again from "the rule of the Church."

[3] Ibid., I, 127, 133, 135-36, 140, 142, 147, 148, 150.

[4] Daniel A. White, *New England Congregationalism in Its Origin and Purity, Illustrated by the Foundation and Early Records of the First Church of Salem* (Salem, 1861), p. 31.

[5] *Records and Files of the Quarterly Courts of Essex County, Massachusetts, 1636-1692*, ed. George F. Dow, 8 vols. (Salem, 1911-21), I, 49 (hereafter cited as *Q.C.R.*)

Between 1638 and 1650 only nine people from Salem held obstinately enough to a heretical opinion or behaved badly enough in church affairs to find themselves before the Quarterly Court. Undoubtedly there were many other persons who were uncomfortable within the town's religious system. But most cases were dealt with within the church's own machinery, which, after all, was designed to cope with doubters.[6] One of the major functions of pastors and ruling elders was to detect and solve such difficulties. Under congregational polity, made explicit by the 1636 covenant, members were to watch over the townsmen's spiritual estate. The most effective of these efforts were likely to be intimate and informal, leaving no trace for the historian. The psychology of village life militated against overt expression of dissent. Further, the civil authorities were reluctant to cope with doubters in an official capacity. On occasion cases were passed back to the church even after presentment to the court.[7] Those who were tried by the Quarterly Court were either the most persistent and uncompromising or, as in the case of Gault, the most spectacularly overt in their behavior.

Although opinion, behavior, and the degree of persistence varied tremendously, the dissenters revealed a number of traits which show some of the limits of the town's unanimity in the period. Five of the nine were women. Most of their cases were more threatening to the established order, largely because they involved serious doctrinal issues. Of the four men only one was tried on a doctrinal point, John Wood, who was "presented for holding the doctrine of anabaptism and withholding his children from the ordinance." The other three men were presented for violating church mores. All four were church members. Gault's case has been mentioned. William Robinson, a fisherman, was tried for absence from church and for "fowling" on the Sabbath. John Holgrave, the tavern keeper and political leader of the fishermen, was "admonished for perjury and for affirming untruths before the Church of Salem." These cases show little sign of serious dissonance. Although we know no further details of Holgrave's disagreement, it seems safe to assume that only Wood's Anabaptism represented a fundamental incapacity to accept the social and religious structure of the community.[8]

It was otherwise in the women's cases. Two of the women, both

---

[6] Emil Oberholzer, Jr., "The Church in New England Society," in *Seventeenth-Century America*, ed. James Morton Smith (Chapel Hill, N.C., 1959), pp. 143-65.

[7] *Q.C.R.*, I, 10, for example.

[8] Ibid., I, 50, 51, 92.

church members, were Anabaptists. One of these women, Lady Deborah Moody, enjoyed great wealth, a high social standing, and a reputation, according to Winthrop, as "a wise and anciently religious woman." A member of the Salem church since 1640, she was presented by a grand juryman of Lynn for Anabaptism in December 1642. However, "she did not appear, report being that she was in a way of conviction before the elders." She did not recant and instead moved to Long Island. Despite her removal she continued to communicate with the leaders of Massachusetts and their wives about Anabaptism and her desire to return to the Bay Colony. Her social position magnified the danger of her opinions, and her case probably added incentive to the magistrates' suggestion in 1644 for a law against Anabaptists, "banishing such as continued obstinate after due conviction."[9]

By asserting that infants should not be baptized, Anabaptists were questioning basic non-Separatist assumptions, especially its organicism. For Puritans infant baptism was a seal of the children's provisional membership among the Chosen People. It implied the continuity and communalism essential to non-Separatist ideals. Anabaptism suggested Separatism, which the authorities were determined to suppress.

Another form of religious dissent implying Separatism was named after Samuel Gorton, who was tried in Boston, jailed, and eventually sent to Rhode Island. His beliefs were highly individualistic, rejecting the authority of both church and Bible. He stressed private judgment and natural theology in contrast to Trinitarian and Calvinist tenets on the corruption of man and the need for Grace. In mood Gortonism seems to have been a clear precursor of Quakerism.[10]

There was some Gortonist opinion in Salem, but only one woman, Eleanor Truslar, a church member and wife of a farmer, remained "obstinate" enough to appear in court. In April 1644, before Mrs. Truslar's July trial, Endecott wrote to Winthrop "to advise with you whether it were not best to bind the party over to Boston Court, to make such a one exemplary, that others might fear." Apparently Winthrop suggested leniency, for the trial record concludes "Mr. Endecott forgave her" after fining her twenty marks. Yet the testimony reveals that Mrs. Truslar's criticism of

[9]James Duncan Phillips, *Salem in the Seventeenth Century* (Boston, 1933), pp. 130-31; *Q.C.R.*, I, 48; *Winthrop Papers*, 7 vols. (Boston, 1929-47), IV, 45; John Winthrop, *Winthrop's Journal, 1630-1649* (1649; 2 vols., ed. James K. Hosmer, New York, 1908), II, 174.

[10]Nathaniel Morton, *New Englands Memorial* (1669; facsimile ed., Boston, 1903), pp. 205-6.

Salem and its leadership was both broad and severe. Specifically she was fined "for saying that their teacher Mr. Norris taught the people lies and that Mr. Norris and Mr. Endecott were the foundation of their church and they were unfaithful." [11]

She was asserting that the church was a wholly secular institution and that even as such it was not functioning well. Witnesses "testified that Goody Truslar said there was no love in the church and that they were biters and devourers." She went further and said that the Puritan system of rewards for piety and good behavior was cynical, claiming "that Mr. Norris said that men would change their judgment for a dish of meat." Somewhat redundantly, one witness said that "she did question the government ever since she came." Mrs. Truslar's defense involved a partial but significant recantation; "she said that before she came to New England, she knew that men were not the foundation of the Church." It sufficed.

The main witnesses in the case, Lawrence and Cassandra Southwick, provide an ironic footnote to the trial. They, along with Mrs. Truslar's husband and children, eventually became Quakers and expressed similar indictments against Salem society. They suffered more severely at the hands of magistrates Endecott and Hathorne than did Mrs. Truslar a dozen years before. Although couched in colorful and personal invective, her criticisms were a trenchant questioning of the assumptions that governed the town's attempt to form a godly community.

The pathetic case of Dorothy Talby, on the other hand, reveals a danger the system posed to some who accepted its premises but could not cope with the terrifying ramifications of Puritan doctrine. In December 1638 she "was hanged at Boston for murdering her own daughter, a child of three years old" with the haunting name "Difficult." She had worked hard to fulfill Puritan expectations for "she had been a member of the church of Salem, and of good esteem for godliness." But she and her husband, also a member, had failed to create a family that approximated Puritan ideals. That failure drove her insane; "falling at difference with her husband, through melancholy or spiritual delusions, she sometimes attempted to kill him, and her children, and herself, by refusing meat, saying it was so revealed to her." [12]

The community employed its usual means of discipline with disastrous results. "After much patience, and diverse admonitions not prevailing, the church cast her out. Whereupon she grew worse; so as the magistrate caused her to be whipped. Whereupon

[11] *Winthrop Papers*, IV, 456; *Q.C.R.*, I, 68.
[12] Winthrop, *Journal*, I, 279.

she was reformed for a time, and carried herself more dutifully to her husband." But the sentence of excommunication provoked a severe reaction. Apparently she became convinced that she and her daughter were damned in this and perhaps the next life, for she killed young Difficult "that she might free it from future misery." The disaster also resulted in John Talby's excommunication "for much pride, and unnaturalness to his wife." Dorothy Talby seems to have been one of those who become "deviants," in Kai T. Erikson's words, "because they clumsily violate a norm in their very eagerness to abide by it."[13]

The case of Mary Oliver, the most persistent "heretic" of the period, illustrates another source of deviance. She was the wife of Thomas Oliver, whose gradual rise from landlessness to relative respectability was mentioned in the previous chapter. Her problem resembled that of the East Anglian Separatists, that is, an inability to reconcile her own sense of worth with the lower assessment made by the community. It is an interesting commentary on the changes in the Salem church since 1633 that Mrs. Oliver, who was not a church member, was treated as a heretic for arguing in favor of the implicit system of inclusiveness. Having emigrated from England in 1638, after Salem had passed through the crisis of the implicit covenant, she never understood the rationale behind the more explicit criteria for membership. "She took offence at this, that she might not be admitted to the Lord's Supper without giving public satisfaction to the church of her faith, etc., and covenanting or professing to walk with them according to the rule of gospel." She would have met the earlier standards. Comparing her with Anne Hutchinson, Winthrop wrote, "She was (for ability of speech, and appearance of zeal and devotion) far before Mrs. Hutchinson, and so the fitter instrument to have done hurt, but that she was poor and had little acquaintance."[14]

To press her claim to the sacraments she interrupted a church service. She was arrested by Endecott and sent to Boston jail to await trial before the General Court, which had sole jurisdiction over the serious offense of disturbing worship. On December 4, 1638, she was examined before the court, and "there she gave such peremptory answers, as she was committed till she should find sureties for her good behavior."[15]

---

[13] Sidney Perley, *History of Salem, Massachusetts*, 3 vols. (Salem, 1924-27), I, 272; Erikson, *Wayward Puritans: A Study in the Sociology of Deviance* (New York, 1966), p. 20.

[14] *Journal*, I, 281-82.

[15] Vernon Loggins, *The Hawthornes: The Story of Seven Generations of an American Family* (New York, 1951), pp. 49-51.

Drastic as this experience must have been, it only temporarily quieted her. She soon began to articulate a more rounded critique of the church, in which she persisted for almost twelve years. Before coming to America, Mrs. Oliver "had suffered somewhat" in her native town of Norwich "for refusing to bow at the name of Jesus." This refusal to accept a "popish" rite was her only quarrel with the established church; "otherwise she was conformable to all their orders." Her criticisms of Salem sound Anglican, or more accurately, Presbyterian. She insisted on the parish ideal, "that all that dwell in the same town, and will profess their faith in Christ Jesus, ought to be received to the sacraments there." Further she felt that power in the church should not rest with the congregation, but "that the church is the heads of the people, both magistrates and ministers, met together, and that these have power to ordain ministers, etc."[16]

Despite relative impotence stemming from her low social status and the stigma of her first encounter with the General Court, Mrs. Oliver mounted a continuous campaign to change the standing order. In January 1641 she was "admonished" by the Quarterly Court and ordered "to humble herself to Mr. Norris." Shortly her opposition turned bitter. The court sentenced her to stand tied to the whipping post for a couple of hours with a split stick on her tongue for saying, "All the ministers in this country are blood-thirsty men," and for daring the magistrates to persecute her by remarking, "My blood is too thin for them to draw it out."[17]

During the 1640s Mrs. Oliver was in and out of court for "uttering diverse mutinous speeches" including, "You in New England are thieves and robbers." Once she addressed a group of nonmembers with "Lift up your heads! Your redemption draweth nigh!" Of Hathorne, one of the judges and the emerging political spokesman of the laity, she said, "I do hope to live and tear his flesh in pieces, and all such as he." That particular remark landed her once again in the stocks. By 1651 she had been presented at various times for defamation, petty theft, and living apart from her husband, who had temporarily returned to England. She in turn made countercharges against others for similar offenses. Finally in the spring of 1651 Mrs. Oliver, continually harassed and harassing at law, was ordered to return to England. She died shortly after arriving home. A year later her husband came back to Salem and married a more orthodox woman.[18]

[16] Winthrop, *Journal,* I, 282.
[17] *Q.C.R.* I, 34.
[18] Loggins, pp. 52-53.

Not only was Mary Oliver persistent in her dissent but the authorities were tolerant toward her compared with their behavior toward others. Their patience was based on the assumption that her behavior was not a serious threat. She was "poor and of little acquaintance," in sharp contrast to Lady Deborah Moody, for example. She was not a church member, the only non-Elect dissenter of the period. After all, behavioral standards were not set as high for the unregenerate as for the Elect, who were supposedly on their way to sanctification.

These few episodes reveal the kind of religious dissent that the community considered egregious enough to warrant formal sanctions. The theoretical questions of some of the dissenters, most impressively Mrs. Truslar, served as a means of defining orthodoxy, albeit negatively. Also, the religious issues encompassed social and political problems. Mrs. Oliver and Mrs. Truslar were social as well as religious critics. Dorothy Talby's problems arose more from the standards of Puritan family life than from religious ideology, narrowly defined. Anabaptism, of course, posited a radically different concept of the good society than that of non-Separatist Puritanism.[19]

The prevalence of women among the dissenters seems a sharp challenge to the Puritan conception of the role of women. A woman's calling was, to quote Winthrop, "her household affairs," not theoretical issues "as are proper to men."[20] Yet in Salem there was some confusion or ambivalence on the role of women. Perhaps the contradiction between the requirement of veils and the right to speak had something to do with the number and intensity of female dissenters, and perhaps these challenges helped the community to clarify the place of women in Salem.

The occasional economic challenges to the communal ideal were treated in the same way as religious dissent. The authorities defined an economic orthodoxy through covenant and enforcement just as they defined a religious one. The ideal of the just price, the quality of workmanship, and the strictures against idleness all came into the purview of the courts. The method of enforcing the economic standards was identical to that used in religious matters; education of both the offender and the populous was most important. Attitude and motive of the offender had as much to do with the reaction of judges, selectmen, elders, and so on as did the act committed. The process went from admonition to private conference and, if necessary, to public examination in

[19]Erikson, p. 13.
[20]Ibid., p. 82.

church or court in the atmosphere of informality and intimacy that one would expect in a communal society.[21]

In the Puritan hierarchical organization the magistrates and elders wielded great responsibility not only for the stability of society but also for the spiritual estate of the people. A biographer of William Hathorne has described well his subject's place in the enforcement of Salem's values. "Captain Hathorne, endowed with the power of magistrate in Essex County, was much more than a trial judge. He was an arbiter of conduct, a moral adviser, a confessor, and a conciliator." He also functioned as a modern-day police chief, since he directed the constables, and as, "above all, prosecutor." The other magistrates, Endecott and Downing, exercised the same power, as did the ruling elder, Sharp, and the ministers in their sphere. These men were at the pinnacle of the value system in the eyes of most of the population. From their probing questions nothing should be hidden, and from their decisions no practical appeal should be made.[22]

This system kept the communal order remarkably stable until around 1650. Ironically the method of coping with dissenters proved so effective these harbingers of the troubles to come went unheeded. For example, the heresy cases, especially those of Mary Oliver and Eleanor Truslar, implied strongly that something was wrong with the way the church was fulfilling its role in society. The fact that so many of the dissenters were themselves church members may have indicated internal problems as well.

In the summer of 1641 the Massachusetts government sent Hugh Peter to England to act as agent for the colony. Edward Norris, who had been ordained teacher of the Salem church in March 1640, became sole minister and remained in his pulpit for eighteen years. Norris, unlike Peter, was rigorous in applying the test of conversion to prospective members. The test, which had become an increasingly important part of the New England Way by the time of Norris's ordination, meant giving a detailed narration of one's conversion first before the minister and elders and then before the whole congregation. The auditors were allowed to ask questions and then attempted to judge the validity of the conversion. Under this requirement, new membership fell off. In 1640 and 1641, while Peter was still pastor, seventy-seven people joined the church (table 12). In 1642 the number dropped to fifteen. The church seemed to be turning inward and becoming "tribal."[23] Not only were fewer people joining the Elect, but

[21] *Q.C.R.*, I, 15, 21, 50-51.   [22] Loggins, p. 40.

[23] Darrett B. Rutman, *Winthrop's Boston: Portrait of a Puritan Town, 1630-1649* (Chapel Hill, N.C., 1965), pp. 148-54; Robert G. Pope, *The Half-Way Covenant: Church Membership in Puritan New England* (Princeton, N.J., 1969), p. 13.

fewer representatives of unchurched families were being included. Spouses and children of old members were more likely to join.

Table 12. Church admissions, 1640-50

Year	Number	Men	Women	Spouses and children	New families
1640	39	14	25	12	27
1641	38	18	20	14	24
1642	15	11	4	9	6
1643	16	9	7	11	5
1644	4	2	2	3	1
1645	4	1	3	3	1
1646	5	3	2	3	2
1647	15	6	9	11	4
1648	29	13	16	20	9
1649	8	2	6	8	0
1650	22	9	13	19	3

Sources: James Duncan Phillips, *Salem in the Seventeenth Century* (Boston, 1933), pp. 353-56; Sidney J. Perley, *The History of Salem, Massachusetts*, 3 vols. (Salem, 1924-27), I, II, genealogical footnotes.

Once immigration into Salem slowed after 1638 there were fewer new families to bring into the church. But the town did not lack for candidates. Before 1650 some eighty families out of 238 that held land were not represented within the church. This does not mean that the church was consciously turning its back on the ideal of inclusiveness. Complacency engendered by relative success was another possible reason. If not all, then certainly most of the town's people of influence or power, roughly those holding more than thirty acres, were officially among the Elect. In view of the high proportion of people in the church and the relative calm in Salem's spiritual life after 1638, Norris and the other officers may have felt that stricter criteria for membership would raise the quality of the church's life and that, if all went well, many of the townsmen would still be able to join. Towns like Sudbury had proved successful in combining rigorous conversion tests with near universal membership.[24]

There were other signs of difficulty for the church. Attendance at services had to be enforced by the mid-1640s. In July 1644 the town meeting "ordered that two be appointed every Lord's day to walk forth in the time of God's worship, to take notice of such as either lie about the meetinghouse without attending to the word or ordinances, or that lie at home or in the fields, without giving

[24] Sumner Chilton Powell, *Puritan Village: The Formation of a New England Town* (Middleton, Conn., 1963), p. 144.

good account thereof, and to take the names of such persons and to present them to the Magistrate."[25]

The church began to experience financial problems as well. Since 1639, and probably before, "there was a voluntary town contribution toward the maintenance of the ministry, quarterly to be paid" to the deacons. But in December 1645 the town meeting "ordered and agreed that the nonmembers of this congregation shall be rated for the helping and supporting of some of the public ordinances in the Church: as namely the preaching of the word." [26] Voluntarism had failed and town had to impose a tax explicitly including the nonmembers. The change may reflect indifference or, more probably, judging from Mrs. Oliver's exhortation to nonmembers to "Lift up your heads," a sense of despair among them at ever joining the Elect.

The character of church life changed under Norris's pastorate. Norris, while competent, did not have the vast experience, wit, and energy of Hugh Peter. Emanuel Downing, magistrate and Winthrop's brother-in-law, had been lavish in his praise of Peter, describing him as "constant to his daily charge, so that all his friends are resolved to leave him to his own way, yet blessed be God his preaching is very profitable and comfortable to all." Downing's attitude toward Norris, however, was much more restrained: "Mr. Norris preached here last Sabbath to the well liking of most. Some few only found fault with the weakness of his voice." When the possibility of sending Peter to England was first broached, Endecott, who knew both Peter and Norris intimately, was strongly opposed to losing the former.[27] It is obvious that many townsmen and some of the leadership regretted the change. In such a small, personal, and church-centered society, a change in ministers was bound to effect subtly the community's sense of itself.

The more overt and formal transition to proof of conversion that Norris began to implement in Salem was part of a shifting view of the church spreading across New England wherever pastors rigorously implemented the new criteria for church membership. The pastors' assumption that they could almost infallibly identify the Elect, show no serious evangelical interest in those who were not members, and still maintain the centrality and power of the churches was not merely optimistic; it was arrogant as well.[28] In a

[25] *Town Recs.*, I, 131-32.
[26] Ibid., I, 93, 140.
[27] *Winthrop Papers*, IV, 111, 314-15, 502.
[28] Edmund S. Morgan, *Visible Saints: The History of a Puritan Idea* (New York, 1963), pp. 120-24.

sense the conversion test and the assumptions upon which it rested were the ultimate institutional statement of Puritan utopian hopes.

In Salem this extravagant optimism was not altogether ground-less, despite the warning signals. During the late 1630s and 1640s Salem came as close as it ever would to fulfilling the hopes embodied in the 1636 covenant. In their more carefully delineated institutions the townsmen found effective means of adjusting their various interests. It seemed that finally "peace and unity" might emerge. Even the diffuse dissent served the community by clarifying standards of behavior and belief. Salem's tenuous internal peace allowed the town's leadership to play an expansive role in the colony's politics, a role that reflected their ambitions for themselves, their town and, indeed, for the Puritan experiment.

Chapter VI

Communal Identity: Salem
in Colonial Politics, 1636-1647

Through the reforms of the late 1630s the leadership of Salem and the Bay Colony successfully coped with the problems of Separatism and religious disruption. The question of who held power in the town and what values were dominant was temporarily resolved. But a related political issue was not laid to rest so easily. The problem was whether the towns or the magistrates in the Court of Assistants would be the proper center of power and authority in the colony. The leaders of Salem, their confidence blossoming, took significant roles in the controversy and thereby reflected and reinforced the community's intense sense of identity.

The issue was not a new one. Roger Williams and the Salem Separatists had raised emphatically the notion of local autonomy. William Hathorne and Edward Norris, two of Salem's particularist leaders of the 1640s, revived many of the arguments and emotions of the earlier movement. A good part of those arguments and emotions were rooted, as before, in suspicion and jealousy of the political, economic, and ecclesiastical power of Boston and its surrounding towns. Even Endecott, who was not a supporter of this town-centered movement, could not help complaining to Winthrop that "all the news comes to your parts first."[1]

As late as 1646 Norris refused to heed the General Court's call to the Cambridge Synod to consider standardizing the organization and practices of Massachusetts churches on roughly the same grounds that Roger Williams had used to oppose the Bay ministers' fortnightly meetings, arguing "that they should betray the liberty of the churches, if they should consent to such a synod."[2] Ironically the Boston church was the only one to concur in this judgment. By 1646 both churches and their respective towns had ample reason to fear each other's power as well as the unpredict-

---

[1] Darrett B. Rutman, *Winthrop's Boston: Portrait of a Puritan Town, 1630-1649* (Chapel Hill, N.C., 1965), p. 250; *Winthrop Papers*, 7 vols. (Boston, 1929-47), IV, 312.

[2] John Winthrop, *Winthrop's Journal 1630-1649* (1649; 2 vols., ed. James K. Hosmer, New York, 1908), II, 269.

able perversity of the small, inland towns who were developing some hostility to the commercial centers, Boston in particular.

Although Salem's rivalry with Boston dated from the 1630s, Salem's political situation was internally more stable and externally more potent from 1639 on. In 1635-36 the Salem church had stood alone, advocating an untenable Separatism, while its spiritual leader undercut his own position by alienating not only the colonial authorities but his fellow townsmen as well. The leaders of the particularist movement in the 1640s were incomparably shrewder and much less scrupulous than Roger Williams. Although engaged in sharp power struggles both within the town and the colony, they sought consensus, not permanent alienation; in short, their method was impeccably non-Separatist. Also, by the 1640s, enough of the other smaller, agricultural towns were suspicious of Boston to make political coalition feasible.

Hathorne, in particular, was an ingenious coalition builder who appealed carefully to the varied interests that made up the town and the colony. This talent led him into remarkable inconsistencies that occasionally seem cynical. For example, he was a strong advocate of harsh measures against all dissenters except those of "the better sort." This inconsistency has led some to paint him as a liberal tolerationist serving the interests of the mercantile community, while others have seen him as the very spirit of persecution. Actually he was both and therefore really neither. He was just satisfying different constituencies. More enlightening is Lawrence S. Mayo's assessment of Hathorne: "He was an assertive, belligerent hustler, who enjoyed politics and made the most of every opportunity for his own advancement in that field."[3] Yet, like many another political "hustler," Hathorne, in his scramble for power for himself and his town, helped to solidify his community's sense of identity and purpose in a period when the English civil war fomented serious doubts about Massachusetts's sense of mission as defined by Winthrop in 1630. The best way to understand what Salem thought of itself and its destiny in the 1640s is to trace the steps of Hathorne and his allies.

In the 1640s Salem was not alone in its opposition to the power of Boston and the Court of Assistants. A coalition was formed with other towns in what became Essex County, most notably Ipswich. After 1641 the rich agricultural sections inland filled

[3] Bernard Bailyn, *The New England Merchants in the Seventeenth Century* (paperback ed., New York, 1964), pp. 107-8; Vernon Loggins, *The Hawthornes: The Story of Seven Generations of an American Family* (New York, 1951), pp. 40-41; Mayo, *John Endecott: A Biography* (Cambridge, Mass., 1936), p. 151.

with people and the formation of towns proceeded apace. In 1643 Salem was designated the county seat, making formal a power and influence that the town had exercised for several years. The combination was concerted enough to be recognized by Winthrop as a faction which he labeled "those of Essex."[4] Ipswich contributed its irascible pastor, Nathaniel Ward, and a young assistant, Richard Saltonstall, Jr. From other parts of Essex came Richard Bellingham, a frequent assistant, and Simon Bradstreet, the leading man of Andover.

The faction was a loose alliance of influential men. Although Hathorne has often been cast as the dominant character, it is difficult to identify a single leader for the group. Rather its leadership seems to have been fragmented by the colony's institutional structure, much as modern political parties are divided into state, congressional, and presidential wings. Hathorne was the leader of the Essex faction among the deputies, a highly strategic position made even stronger after the separation of the General Court into two houses in 1644. Hathorne then became the first Speaker of the lower house. Edward Norris and Ward provided strong clerical support. Saltonstall and Bellingham, with occasional help from Bradstreet, made up the faction's contingent among the assistants.

In the quest for power, the Essex faction raised issues that were chiefly constitutional, centering on the power of the assistants.[5] The first issue, brought up in May 1639, was the question of life tenure for the colony's highest officers. Emphatically opposing an informal suggestion that the governor "ought to be for his life," a majority of the deputies seized the opportunity to attack the colony's only institution that involved life tenure, the standing council, set up in 1636. In theory the law was not clear on whether or not the counselors were to continue to exercise the power of magistracy after their annual term as magistrates expired. The law read, "The General Court . . . shall elect a certain number of magistrates for the term of their lives, as a standing council."[6] In practice the distinction between magistrates and counselors was almost meaningless, given the prestige of the men who had been selected for the standing council, Winthrop, Dudley, and

[4] James Duncan Phillips, *Salem in the Seventeenth Century* (Boston, 1933), p. 160; Rutman, p. 250n.

[5] For good discussions of the issues at stake, see Ellen E. Brennan, "The Massachusetts Council of Magistrates," *New England Quarterly* 4 (1931): 54-93; Mark DeWolfe Howe and Louis F. Eaton, Jr., "The Supreme Judicial Power in the Colony of Massachusetts Bay," ibid., 20 (1947): 291-316.

[6] Winthrop, *Journal*, I, 299-300; Brennan, pp. 62, 65-66.

Endecott. The deputies now challenged their power. In turn, Winthrop insisted that the 1636 law made members of the council magistrates for life; "till this court those of the council, viz. Mr. Endecott, had stood and executed as a magistrate, without any annual election, and so they had been reputed by the elders and all the people till this present." The deputies then proposed a clarification of the law: "No person, chosen a counselor for life, should have any authority as a magistrate, except he were chosen in the elections to one of the said places of magistracy established by the patent."[7]

Through adroit maneuvering, Winthrop gained a compromise that did not settle the question of annual elections. The law as passed in 1639 simply held that counselors when acting as magistrates "shall do such things as magistrates, and not as counselors." The standing council with its three members survived as an institution until 1644, and the three leaders continued to act as magistrates. Yet no further powers were conferred upon the council by the General Court, and, having been questioned, it fell into disuse. Its survival in a weakened condition continued to provide the faction with a convenient issue for several years. In 1642, for example, Richard Saltonstall wrote a tract denouncing the standing council as "a sinful innovation." The pamphlet became the subject of a heated contest in the General Court lasting several days.[8]

Although partially motivated by fear of tyranny, the deputies were engaged in a power play whose real focus was Salem and the surrounding area. The chief target, according to Winthrop, was Endecott, since he, unlike Winthrop and Dudley, did not enjoy the security of frequent election as governor or deputy governor. By 1639 Hathorne had only two strong rivals for local power in Salem, Endecott and Emanuel Downing. For several years the town had been electing Hathorne not only deputy but also commissioner to aid Endecott on the Quarterly Court. Hathorne may have thought that his popular standing, ever increasing since his emergence as a compromise figure between the East Anglians and the West Countrymen, was more secure than Endecott's. Endecott, after all, apparently had been wielding local power without benefit of a vote and was also still suffering under the stigma of the Williams episode. Neither Saltonstall nor Bellingham would have been adverse to seeing Endecott's power curbed or eliminated in the region. If that was their intent, they failed in 1639.

[7]Winthrop, *Journal*, I, 302.
[8]*Mass. Recs.*, I, 264; Winthrop, *Journal*, II, 64-65.

Significantly, a simultaneous move was made against Downing's rising influence. In order to fill vacancies among the assistants, Winthrop and "other magistrates" suggested Downing along with two others for the posts. But "some jealousies arose." It was argued that Downing, as Winthrop's brother-in-law, would only strengthen Winthrop's "party"; "therefore, though he were known to be a very able man, etc., and one who had done many good offices for the country for these ten years, yet the people would not choose him."[9] Yet Downing retained strong influence within the town and colony perhaps because of his excellent connections in Boston and in the English mercantile community. He was often elected a commissioner to the Quarterly Court. During the early years of the faction, 1639 to 1641, he served as a deputy, which may have made him something of a thorn in its side. He was also elected during two other peak periods of controversy, 1644 and 1648.

In 1641 the faction picked up another strong issue involving the on-going attempt to curb the discretionary powers of the magistrates. As early as 1635 the deputies had called attention to the need for a printed code of laws, and in 1636, at the suggestion of Hugh Peter, John Cotton had been asked to assist the magistrates in compiling a body of fundamentals. The result, "Moses, his Judicials," was not enacted. In 1639 Cotton and Nathaniel Ward, who besides being a minister had also been a common law attorney, were each assigned the task of framing a model for consideration by the General Court. Ward's version was accepted. After three weeks of debate, it was reduced to one hundred clauses and adopted by the court. They were published as the Body of Liberties in 1641.[10]

The Body of Liberties was not a faction measure, but it was definitely a product of their geographic area. After the new code passed the General Court, it was voted that nineteen copies be made, probably for circulation among the towns. Presumably to prevent the distribution of faulty versions, the court declared that each copy was valid only if signed by Endecott, Downing, and Hathorne, thus implying that the three Salem leaders were the men most familiar with the product begun by their Ipswich neighbor Ward. Not only had these locally antagonistic leaders been able to ally on this matter, but they also seem to have merged their interests in the election of that year. On June 2, 1641, a man from their area, Richard Bellingham, was elected

---

[9] Winthrop, *Journal*, I, 300.

[10] I. M. Calder, " 'Moses, his Judicials,' " *New England Quarterly* 3 (1930): 82-94; *Mass. Recs.*, I, 346; Winthrop, Journal, II, 49.

governor for the first time, although he had previously served twice as deputy governor. Endecott was elected deputy governor for the first time.

The coalition soon collapsed. The finished Body of Liberties was a compromise that disappointed Hathorne and some others of the faction. In the December meeting of the General Court, "Mr. Hathorne and some others were very earnest to have some certain penalty set upon lying, swearing, etc." A majority of the magistrates, most vociferously Endecott, opposed the suggestion, arguing that although there should be laws against such offenses, the punishment in each case should fit the spiritual state of the offender. In Puritan theory Endecott was on excellent ground. Yet Hathorne too had a valid point. According to Winthrop's brief and hostile account, Hathorne charged Endecott "with seeking to have the government arbitrary, etc." Hathorne was calling for a stricter, more impersonal system of justice. His demand for more stringent sanctions may not have been practical in a frontier society based largely on consent, but the notion of impersonal justice was a reasonable response to the problem of legal control over a large, dispersed population. In factional squabbles, however, principle and personal antagonisms were hard to separate. Both Endecott and Hathorne took their disagreement personally, "and the matter grew to some heat, for [Endecott] was a wise and a stout gentleman, and knew Mr. Hathorne, his neighbor well." As Winthrop broadly hinted, Hathorne may well have been using the issue as a stick with which to beat his rival. In any case Hathorne lost this battle too.[11]

At the same session Hathorne and Bellingham engaged in a less laudable attack on Endecott and Winthrop. Bellingham took umbrage at the fact that he was the first Massachusetts governor not elected to the standing council. It was to this "evil spirit of emulation and jealousy" that Winthrop attributed Bellingham's unflagging opposition to the other magistrates, "which did much retard all business." More important, the governor backed Hathorne's attempt to throw both Winthrop and Endecott out of the magistracy "because they were grown poor." This bitter move brought the eminent John Cotton into the fray. On the next lecture day Cotton appealed to the Fifth Commandment and "told the country" that "such as were decayed in their estates by attending the service of the country ought to be maintained by the country, and not set aside for their poverty being otherwise so well gifted, and approved by long experience to be faithful." The sermon effectively squelched the move.[12]

[11] Winthrop, *Journal*, II, 55-56

Hathorne's and Bellingham's manuever was petty and factional; yet once again Hathorne had touched upon an emerging problem in the commonwealth. The hierarchical ideal depended on the correlation of all signs of status. The argument was already heard, especially in mercantile quarters, that men who were not profiting financially did not have the blessing of God. Nonetheless, it was an unsavory and, indeed, inept political move. This attack along with other factional bickering cost the Essex group the next election. In May 1642 Winthrop was once again elected governor and Endecott deputy governor.

The argument over the fitness of the magistrates did yield one temporary concession. In June the General Court ordered that each town in the colony send one or two freemen to a meeting in Salem to nominate "a certain number of the most able and fit men" for the Court of Assistants; no others were to be eligible. This new method of nomination led to no changes in personnel. The next year the order was rescinded, and once again "all the freemen" were allowed to "propound names" "at the preliminary nominations in town meetings."[13]

Despite setbacks, the Essex faction was still strong. During the mid-1640s Hathorne and his allies began making gains. In 1643 the colony was formally divided into shires, or counties. This action was primarily an administrative reform, a logical extension of the 1636 creation of the Quarterly Court system. However, it soon developed immense political significance. As Lawrence Mayo has put it: "Essex County, from the time of Nathaniel Ward through the era of Henry Cabot Lodge, has possessed and displayed a genius for politics. The setting apart of that region as a unit strengthened a natural tendency, and it was not long before it produced interesting developments."[14]

The faction quickly grasped the political importance of the new govermental units. In fact, the idea of counties may have been theirs. They had already evinced concern over the problem of governing the dispersed towns, and certainly they knew that the people of the inland areas were potential allies. In any case, they wasted little time in exploiting the possibilities. During the final session of the General Court under Winthrop's latest administration (1642-43), "those of Essex . . . procured . . . that the deputies of the several shires should meet . . . to prepare business, etc." The

---

[12] Ibid.

[13] William H. Whitmore, *The Massachusetts Civil List for the Colonial and Provincial Periods, 1630-1774* (rept. Baltimore, 1969), p. 13.

[14] P. 172.

Essex Caucus was born. Neither Downing nor Endecott attended the meetings held in the spring of 1644. Endecott had been elected governor in May 1644, and Downing had been replaced by Hathorne's chief Salem ally, Edmund Batter, as Salem's other deputy. In their caucus the faction hammered out a legislative program whose "chief intent was to advantage their own shire."[15]

The program was bold, expressing the full ambition of the faction. First they sought to have Salem made the capital, with the full panoply of courts and treasury. They argued that since the colony was expanding north and not south, Salem was much nearer the geographic center and more convenient for most settlers than Boston. Also the election of Endecott, albeit not one of their own, as governor and the control enjoyed by Essex men in the newly independent lower house convinced the faction that the days of Boston's hegemony had passed. In 1644 and 1645 deputies from Essex held three offices, twenty-two committee posts, and thirteen minor posts, compared to Suffolk's two offices, sixteen major posts, and twenty-four minor ones. Salem and Ipswich controlled the speakership and ten major and five minor committee posts. Boston and Charlestown, in sharp contrast, held no offices and only two major and ten minor posts.[16] But men from Suffolk County still dominated the Court of Assistants. To cope with this fact the Essex faction had another suggestion. They sought to join three Essex deputies and Nathaniel Ward with three magistrates in order to create a special council "to order all affairs of the commonwealth" when the General Court was not in session.[17] This was an effort to supplant the Court of Assistants, controlled by Boston and the Bay towns, that usually handled business between sessions of the General Court.

In pursuit of their program during June 1644, "they had made so strong a party among the deputies of the smaller towns (being most of them mean men, and such as had small understanding in affairs of state) as they easily carried all these among the deputies."[18] The faction's voting allies may have been as naive as Winthrop said. But it is equally probable that the deputies from "the smaller towns" were already feeling the suspicion of Boston that would dominate Massachusetts politics into the twentieth century. Boston by 1644 had failed as a Puritan utopia. Salem, on the other hand, still closely resembled the functioning "collective

[15] Winthrop, *Journal*, II, 167-69; Mayo, pp. 173-74.
[16] Rutman, p. 250n.
[17] Winthrop, *Journal*, II, 170.   [18] Ibid., II, 170.

hierarchies" from which these deputies came. Hathorne and especially Ward, had a sympathetic audience when they expressed their hopes, fears, and prejudices.[19] More directly, their program appealed strongly to almost every interest in Salem, with the exception of those persons who were closely tied to Winthrop and to the magisterial party, like Endecott and Downing. Its success certainly would have meant new wealth and prestige for the town.

A majority of the deputies concurred in the Essex faction's proposals, but not the Court of Assistants, who, "finding them hurtful to the commonwealth, refused to pass them." The result was a conference of both houses. In the course of the conference the deputies particularly stressed the formation of the special council, on which the faction would have at least a four-to-three majority. The magistrates argued that such a council threatened the liberties of the freemen and gratuitously insulted the magistrates who would have to be removed from the Court of Assistants to make room for the faction in the refurbished upper house. The deputies argued their corporate privilege, saying "that the governor and assistants had no power out of court but what was given them by the general court," so the whole General Court could create or abolish offices at will. Several compromises put forward by the deputies failed, including prolonging the General Court session until the elders of the colony churches could be consulted. As a desperate last hope, the deputies requested that the Court of Assistants "would consent that nothing be done till the court met again." The magistrates refused, and Hathorne angrily replied, "You will not be obeyed."[20]

After tempers cooled and the possibility of Indian troubles arose the deputies agreed to acquiesce temporarily in the exercise of magisterial power. In reaching agreement late in June 1644, the deputies and magistrates exchanged position papers defining their differences. Although some participants on both sides wished to publish the statements, the majority of both houses was opposed, because, as Winthrop explained, it "would cause a public breach throughout the country: and if it should come to that, that people would fall into factions, and the non-members would certainly take part with the magistrates, (we should not be able to avoid it), and this would make us and our course, though never so just, obnoxious to the common sort of freemen, the issues whereof must needs have been very doubtful."[21] Winthrop feared that the

[19] Perry Miller and Thomas H. Johnson, eds., *The Puritans: A Sourcebook of Their Writings* (paperback ed., 2 vols., New York, 1963), I, 225-36; Bailyn, pp. 103-4.

[20] Winthrop, *Journal*, II, 170-72.

[21] Ibid., II, 174.

nonmembers, who were voteless in colonial affairs but who helped form public opinion and had some influence in the towns, would use support for the magistrates to bid for more political power.

In the conference and their position paper, the faction chose to stress the creation of the council rather than the moving of the capital, apparently because such a change in the governmental structure would give them power to gain the whole program, since the faction would then control both houses. Another reason arose from the fact that the core of the faction's support was "the common sort of freemen," church members, especially those from rural towns, who were strongly in favor of placing spokesmen like Ward into positions of power. It was this half of the loaf for which there was most support.

In July, Governor Endecott began the customary process that he hoped would lead to a "thorough reconciliation." In a speech he reversed his policy of no compromise and suggested that "the way to redress hereof was, that the place and power of magistrates and deputies might be known; and so the elders were desired (which they willingly assented) to be mediators." Winthrop had qualms about this proposal, for the elders, after all, were also spokesmen for the church members. Moreover, he wrote, "some of the elders had done no good offices in this matter, through their misapprehension both of the intentions of the magistrates, and also of the matters themselves, being affairs of state, which did not belong to their calling."[22]

The elders, however, were as disturbed as the magistrates by the explosive potential of extended controversy. They decided, with "not one dissentient," that the magistrates as constituted in the Court of Assistants had, authority "in the vacancy of the general court." At the same time, in clarifying the role of the magistracy, the elders adopted some of the faction's ideas. They decided that the magistrates' authority was subject to instruction from the whole General Court. The old standing council was abolished, making all magistrates clearly selected by annual colonywide election. Finally, deputies had the right to become judges on the Quarterly Courts rather than merely subordinate commissioners, a minor point involving the prestige of the town-elected members of the courts.[23]

The magistrates continued after 1644 to be effective political leaders and to exercise the vast power that was theirs as judges of the Quarterly courts and as assistants. The majority of the

[22] Ibid., II, 185-86.
[23] Brennan, pp. 90-93; Winthrop, *Journal*, II, 204-9.

deputies "were now well satisfied concerning the authority of the magistrates," but the leaders of the faction were disappointed. Richard Saltonstall was angry enough to refuse to stand at the next election. In a society where "the better sort," as well as the commonalty, had obligations to act communally, his decision "gave great offense throughout the country." He reconsidered and continued as an assistant until 1650.[24]

The faction managed to win a number of victories besides the defining of magisterial power. During the summer of 1644 the General Court held its sessions in Salem, a definite salve to the town's pride. But of more lasting effect was their success in appointing commissioners to the newly formed United Colonies. When the alliance was formed in 1643, Winthrop and Dudley were elected to represent Massachusetts. Soon thereafter, Winthrop made a foreign policy blunder in his handling of the La Tour–D'Aulnay controversy over the control of French Acadia.[25] The court of Louis XIII had commissioned both men as governor over the region, and the two fought a small war that occasionally spilled over into English fishing villages on the Maine Coast. In 1641 and again in 1643 La Tour asked for aid from Massachusetts. Winthrop was understandably cautious. But in 1643, after remarking that the other members of the confederation must be consulted before official help could be granted, he and the assistants who lived near Boston allowed La Tour to employ men and hire ships to enforce his claim. Within a month La Tour hired four ships and recruited seventy fighting men, all from Boston.

The reaction, particularly in Essex County, was swift and crossed factional lines. Endecott, who was not among the assistants consulted by Winthrop, wrote a mildly rebuking letter, reminding Winthrop that forces of both sides had pillaged Massachusetts fishermen and that it would be better if Massachusetts remained impeccably neutral. Much sharper reproof came from the leading men of Ipswich—Bradstreet, Saltonstall, and Ward—who wrote, "We have little hope to revoke resolutions so far transacted and ripened, but we presume it shall not be taken amiss if we labor to wash our hands wholly of this design and whatsoever ill consequences it may produce." In the ensuing criticism from all over Massachusetts, Winthrop was accused of inviting reprisals from D'Aulnay, of helping Papists, and of attempting to further Boston's commerce while endangering the lives and trade of fishermen, largely from Marblehead and Salem,

[24]Winthrop, *Journal,* II, 210.
[25]Mayo, pp. 162-70.

who plied the northern waters.[26] These criticisms were undoubtedly unfair, but they give a good indication of the suspicion of
Boston felt by both Essex towns and the inland settlements.

For Winthrop the consequences of this episode and other
factional pressures in 1644 was the loss of his and Dudley's places
in the United Colonies. The deputies replaced them with Hathorne
and Simon Bradstreet, now of Ipswich. Winthrop was incensed
because the other colonies "had chosen either their governors or
other chief magistrates" while Massachusetts picked two "younger
men." Plus, that, Hathorne was "the principal man in all these
agitations." Also Hathorne and Bradstreet were less aware of the
confederacy's problems and personalities, since they were "both
eastern men." By the 1645 election public reaction had cooled
enough to allow Winthrop back into the governorship and to
regain his place as a commissioner. Nevertheless, from then on
"eastern" or Essex men predominated on the commission from
Massachusetts.[27]

Matters of foreign policy and war and peace long remained
issues that deeply interested the Essex faction and their allies. As
early as July 1644, while the first argument over La Tour—
D'Aulnay raged in the General Court, the deputies sought
influence in foreign policy, especially in time of possible war, by
denying the magistrates the right to raise troops "without calling a
general court." That this requirement went against the written
articles of the confederation, "would put the country to great
charge," and "might occasion the loss of the opportunity" of
quick military action bothered the deputies not at all. In 1646, the
freemen, who gave the faction its most enduring support,
demanded and received a further curbing of the magistrates' power
in foreign policy by having the commissioners run in the annual
colonywide elections rather than be appointed by the General
Court.[28]

In these political struggles Hathorne, and through him the
community of Salem, was defining Salem's identity. The 1640s
were a time of great uncertainty for Massachusetts because the
Puritan successes in England were threatening its position as the
vanguard of the Puritan movement. Salem asserted its uniqueness
by deciding that if it could not be the leading community in
Christendom it would at least lead Massachusetts. As usual with
Salem's grander political and religious designs, this effort was

[26] Harry M. Ward, *The United Colonies of New England, 1643-1690* (New York,
1961), p. 92.

[27] Winthrop, *Journal,* II, 171-72; Mayo, p. 174.

[28] Winthrop, *Journal,* II, 173, 258-59; Ward, p. 64.

doomed to failure. Boston could not be permanently shunted aside. Yet the contest provided the community with another goal to help hold its disparate elements in relative harmony.

Because William Hathorne almost embodied the town's will to power, his ambitions and the town's view of itself were closely intertwined. The town's internal cohesion in the 1640s can be gauged by tracing the development of the delicate harmony of interests that allowed Hathorne to rise to a position of leadership. The changing selectmen and deputies are the most available evidences of power relationships.

In January 1637 the board of selectmen reflected the struggle between East Anglians and West Countrymen. The board had ten members, five from each of the two areas in England, if Endecott is considered a West Countryman. Four of the five East Anglians had difficulty adjusting to Hugh Peter's brand of non-Separatism, and two, Moulton and Scruggs, were soon excommunicated. By the end of 1637 the adjustment between the factions had been made and Hathorne was starting his career. Hathorne and the moderate East Anglian, John Holgrave, were added to the board. The astute Conant, who was inexplicably not a selectman in January, was also added, replacing Endecott. The board now had twelve members; five East Anglians, six West Countrymen, and Hathorne. It was a more temperate group of men. The composition of the board remained the same with only slight modification of one substitution for each side until December 1643, the year the Essex faction began its biggest effort.

The elections of deputies between 1637 and 1643 tell roughly the same story, except that Hathorne's influence was more pronounced and a new element was added, Downing, Winthrop's brother-in-law, who was deputy from 1639 to 1641. Besides Downing and Hathorne, eight men became deputies. Reflecting the East Anglians' weakening position, only two were born in that part of England, Moulton, who served in 1637, and Townshend Bishop, who was elected in 1637 and again in 1640. The West Countrymen showed more strength, electing three men, Jacob Barney and John Woodbury for a term each in 1638 and William Trask for 1637 and 1639. Hathorne and his allies did better than both groups. He was elected all seven years; his brother-in-law, Richard Davenport, was chosen once in 1637; and his friend Batter was chosen for four of the seven years, 1637, 1638, 1642, and 1643.

By December 1643 the East Anglians as an identifiable political interest disappeared, or rather were transformed into a mercantile interest. After 1636 the East Anglians tended to remain in and around the peninsula while the West Countrymen took up residence in more distant areas, most notably the Bass River region. By 1643 the peninsula was just beginning to become a significant port. Bartholomew, the young merchant who had been excommunicated under Hugh Peter, became a selectman that year after having rejoined the church. Another East Anglian merchant, William Lord, who began as a cutler with two acres in 1636 and had accumulated 120 acres by 1640, was also a selectman in 1643. Since the board was reduced to seven members in 1643, these two comprised a significant minority. In addition to Hathorne and Endecott, the board also contained three traditional West Country political leaders, Jeffrey Massey, Thomas Gardner, and Peter Palfrey. Until early in 1647 there were no further changes in the board.

Their large representation on the board indicated that the West Countrymen still were a force to be considered within the town. Hathorne's relations with them were cordial since he had played a significant role in the elimination of Separatism at Salem. On the other hand, the program of the Essex faction that he was pushing so strongly would have been of greatest economic benefit to the merchants, artisans, and innkeepers of the peninsula. In fact Bartholomew became one of Hathorne's close allies, joining him as deputy in 1645 and 1646 and fairly often thereafter until 1679. Although their interest in commerce was minimal by the 1640s, the West Countrymen showed little disposition to oppose a program which held such promise for the wealth and prestige of the town. The composition of the board shows that Hathorne enjoyed satisfactory if not passionate support. Endecott was a member, but he was often involved with his higher posts. Hathorne's fellow deputies, Batter in 1643 and Bartholomew in 1645 and 1646, were his dedicated allies. Downing, who served as the other Salem deputy in 1644, was the only sign of potential opposition within the community.

Such coalitions are often delicate, and Hathorne's was threatened in 1645 and 1646 by local militia politics. Since 1636 West Countryman Trask had been captain of the Salem trainband. Endecott exercised higher command and was only indirectly concerned with the local militia. Hathorne's brother-in-law Davenport was Trask's lieutenant until 1644 when he was promoted to captain and put in charge of Castle Island in Boston harbor. He moved to Boston to take up his new post during the winter. After his departure, the militia posts from sergeant up to captain, about

[29] Loggins, pp. 37-38.

five positions, became a West Country monopoly. With the removal of Davenport, whose military reputation was excellent, the Salem band became noticeably lax.[29] At this point both Endecott and the Essex faction were worried about possible attack from the sea because of the La Tour episode. So they decided on reform.

In the spring of 1645 Endecott, Hathorne, and some others from Salem and Lynn petitioned the General Court for permission to form another company "out of care for the safety of the public weal." The petition was granted. In the General Court's order only William Dixie and Endecott were former officers mentioned by name. William Clark, an East Anglian merchant, Hathorne, and Thomas Lathrop were new military names. It is not clear whether the petition or the General Court's order intended to abolish the old company, but in any case it survived.[30]

It soon became apparent that there were not enough arms to supply two companies, and the old company refused to surrender theirs. The local political situation became delicate. Endecott wrote to Winthrop in August that he was unwilling to push the clerk of the band on the problem but that the constables, both East Anglians, were willing "to press other men's arms to supply theirs, so that some will be disarmed amongst us." Endecott's suggestion was for the colony to send enough weapons for everyone.[31]

The General Court's solution, however, was that there should be but one company in Salem. Hathorne and Bartholomew, Salem's deputies, were faced with a nasty problem which they resolved by placing both Hathorne's and Trask's names in nomination for command. The court chose Hathorne and then, to make its reasoning as clear and as inoffensive as possible, declared that the leading officers should live near the harbor and, "considering that Captain Trask, who hath been many years their chief officer, dwell so remote from that part of the town as he cannot be helpful upon any such sudden occasion," proceeded to "discharge him of that office, with all due acknowledgment of his faithfulness and former good services to the country."[32]

Salem did not take the decision well. In April 1646 Downing wrote that "our town is much troubled by the putting out their old Captain." Hathorne wisely decided to hold an election, and Trask won "by almost twenty votes more." Both names were resubmitted to the General Court in May, and Hathorne was

[30] Sidney Perley, *History of Salem, Massachusetts,* 3 vols. (Salem, 1924-27), II, 169.
[31] *Winthrop Papers,* V, 41-42.
[32] *Mass. Recs.,* II, 133.

reappointed despite the sentiment in Salem.[33] Nothing further happened. The West Countrymen apparently gave up. But it was the sort of incident that may have rankled them, adding to the store of grievances that twenty years later led to the separation of the Bass River West Countrymen from Salem. Hathorne, however, had weathered the controversy fairly well, having picked up another office that would extend his political influence. He had not pushed, overtly anyway, his claim to command and had attempted to dampen local bad feeling. His position within the town, if anything, was strengthened.

As for the West Countrymen, it was their last impressive display of political strength until they began to move for independence. After 1640 none of the original Old Planters became deputies. Those positions were in the hands of Hathorne and his allies, with occasional forays by Downing. In 1647 the composition of the board of selectmen altered radically, reflecting the new political situation. For the first time in Salem's history not a single Old Planter leader nor any of their sons were on the board. Captain William Hathorne's name appeared at the head of the list, indicating that he had become its most prestigious member. His ally Batter was also a selectman, and Lord had been reelected.

There were four new selectmen, George Corwin, John Hardy, Sam Archer, and John Porter. Corwin, "a man of education and property," emigrated to Salem in 1638 from Workington, Cumberland. He arrived too late and came from too remote a section of England to be involved in the East Anglian–West Country struggle. Given twenty acres in 1638, he opened a store and quickly prospered. His interests were almost totally economic, and it was on that criterion that his fellow townsmen judged his usefulness. He did not join the church until 1650, three years after he became a selectman. Hardy, one of the few men who moved from the status of small landholder to large, was a mariner who owned his own craft and held 107 acres near Mackerel Cove in 1647. Although probably a West Countrymen, he did not settle in Salem until 1637 and did not join the church until a year after he became a selectman. Archer was a ship carpenter, a church member since 1636, who never prospered but who was apparently willing to speculate; he died in 1667 £119 in debt. These three men were more closely tied to the emerging mercantile interest of the community than the three landed merchants Hathorne, Batter, and Lord.

The agricultural side of Salem's changing economic structure

[33]*Winthrop Papers*, V, 47.

was represented by John Porter, who was well on his way to becoming the town's largest landholder. A West Countryman who had resided in Hingham since 1635, Porter purchased the 300-acre Skelton tract in 1643, moved to Salem in 1644, and began buying blocks of land from Downing and Sharp. His attitude toward the land was intensely commercial. He had a number of tenants, a large herd of cattle, and an estate of £2,570 when he died in 1676, a huge estate for a farmer. When Conant died three years later he left an estate of only £258. Porter, like Corwin, joined the church after becoming an economic and political power in the town. The Old Planters had lost influence and a new group of men more mercantile in their outlook had risen to power.

Hathorne and the other traditional leaders like Hugh Peter encouraged the development of commerce, seeing it as one more aspect of successful communal life. They did not foresee its disintegrative effects upon their hierarchical ideal, and indeed before 1647 there was little sign of the troubles to come. Hathorne and the other leaders simply took the new interests into account and conferred the other signs of status on the men who were accumulating wealth and prestige. During the 1640s Hathorne and a number of other landed leaders expressed politically the town's communal vision of itself, its pride, and its claim to be a leading orthodox community. Through their efforts Salem lived down its Separatist past and emerged as the second town in Massachusetts in economics, politics, and religion.

Chapter VII

The Transformation of Salem
1647-1668

During the period of 1647 to 1668 Salem underwent a profound economic and social transformation that doomed the fragile unity of purpose Hathorne had embodied in the 1640s. The commercial sector emerged as the dominant factor in the town's economic life. Before 1647 Salem's commerce was handmaiden to its agriculture. After that year the relationship gradually reversed itself as commerce and the attendant trades, like shipbuilding and coopering, expanded rapidly. This fast economic growth affected all aspects of the town's life, fundamentally altering and undermining the communal ideals envisioned in the 1636 covenant and the elaborations of that concept engendered by Hathorne and his allies.

The growth of commerce resulted in a more complex and pluralistic society. Under the impact of expanding trade, more distinctly mercantile behavioral patterns challenged and eventually subsumed the earlier ideals of unity and hierarchical order. Successful merchants, who accumulated great wealth and economic power, contributed significantly to the distortion and gradual collapse of the close correlation of the various signs of status so crucial to the Puritan experiment. The demands of commerce also transformed the patterns of land use in many parts of Salem, leading to further confusion, conflict, and disunity. The gaps between the various geographic sections of the town, between the rich and the rest of the population, and between occupational groups widened in the 1650s and 1660s. As Bernard Bailyn has succinctly remarked, "in many ways commercial success grew in inverse proportion to the social strength of Puritanism."[1]

Economic change, of course, was not the only factor that blighted the utopian hopes of Salem Puritans. Even in towns like Dedham, which did not undergo any fundamental economic transformation in the seventeenth century, there was a gradual dissipation of the utopian impulse under the normal pressures of human life.[2] Moreover, Salem had always been a divided com-

---

[1] Bailyn, *The New England Merchants in the Seventeenth Century* (paperback ed., New York, 1964), p. 105.

[2] Kenneth A. Lockridge, *A New England Town: The First Hundred Years, Dedham, 1636-1736* (New York, 1970), p. 79.

munity. The effect of economic and social change there was to
encourage divisions that could not be overcome within the
framework of the 1636 covenant and to accelerate the evaporation
of utopian concerns. Dedham's quest for perfection was thwarted
completely and irrevocably within fifty years of its founding. In
Salem the same process took only half as long.

During the seventeenth century commerce required surprisingly
small investments of capital and labor to start and maintain. Craft
of up to 100 tons, the staple of early New England shipbuilding,
could be built by any trained carpenter.[3] In early Salem such men
were plentiful. Among the eighty-seven small landholders of 1637
whose occupations are known, fifteen were carpenters or shipwrights. Another half dozen followed peripherally related trades
like smithing and joining. This work force, like the mariners
themselves, was largely casual and seasonal; carpenters, for
example, built other things besides ships. With this casual labor
and the abundance of timber, shipbuilding became increasingly
important. In 1641 Richard Hollingsworth completed a 300-ton
ship that sold, as did most craft made in New England, at about £4
a ton. When he died in the summer of 1654 he left "a great ketch
on the stocks" worth £130 and two smaller, less nearly completed,
craft together worth £25. At that date there were at least four
other yards, operated by equally skilled master shipwrights on a
similar scale. By the time of the Restoration, New England
shipbuilders were supplying all of North America's needs for small
vessels in the coastal and West Indies trades. In 1665 there were no
less than 300 New England vessels in those areas and 1,300 smaller
craft fishing off Cape Sable. New England yards were also turning
out many ships, both as carriers and products, for commerce to
Europe. It is estimated that by the 1660s one-third of New
England's shipbuilding was done in and near Salem.

Other physical signs of commercial expansion proliferated as
well. By the early 1660s warehouses, wharves, and "shops"
crowded the marshy banks of the South River near the center of
town. In conjunction with the warehouses a number of stores were
opened. Practically all the town's merchants kept such outlets for
the sale of imported goods and small quantities of local farm
produce, as well as odd lots left over from larger wholesale
exchanges. One of the most prosperous of Salem's early stores was
that of George Corwin. He owned a shop in this part of town as
early as 1651 and the warehouse on the site since before 1660.
Corwin sold a great variety of cloths, all manner of hardware, and

---

[3] Ralph Davis, *The Rise of the English Shipping Industry in the Seventeenth and
Eighteenth Centuries* (London, 1962), p. 45n.

household goods. Most of these stores were also allowed to retail and wholesale liquor.[4]

As the volume of trade increased and the settlement of inland Essex County expanded, the rivers and the small complement of roads no longer provided an adequate transportation system. In September 1657 the Salem selectmen authorized "settling of a highway" between Salem and the recently settled, landlocked town of Reading. Two years later the roads and bridges connecting Salem to Ipswich and Wenham were repaired and widened. During the early 1660s Topsfield, Andover, and Chelmsford grew into important agricultural areas and petitioned for better connections with Salem. So much traffic was passing between Marblehead and Salem by 1663 that the path through the South Field was made a common cartway which at its narrowest point was a full rod, or five and a half yards, wide.[5]

Samuel Maverick, a longtime resident of Massachusetts, crisply described Salem's economic position in 1660: "On the south side of Salem River stands on a peninsula the Town of Salem, settled some years by a few people before the Patent of Massachusetts was granted. It is very commodious for fishing, and many Vessels have been built there and (except Boston) it hath as much trade as any place in New England both inland and abroad."[6] He added that Marblehead, Salem's most important satellite town, was "the greatest Town for fishing in New England."

A computer study of the probate records, by William I. Davisson, has measured the extent and nature of economic growth in Essex County between 1640 and 1682. Despite the small sample of wills available for some years, this work is a valuable study of economic trends. It shows marked increases in the use of currency and credit while the prices of locally produced consumer needs, meat for example, remained stable. This pattern indicates real rather than inflationary expansion. In addition, the size of the average estate in the county rose from £85 for the period 1641-46 to £261 for the period 1677-82. By that gauge alone, Davisson said, "Essex County appeared to have grown by about 300 per cent between 1641 and 1682. I would regard this as a minimum growth figure for Essex County for the period." Combining all his indices reveals "at least 300%-500% increase in the size of the economy between 1640-1682." He posited a growth rate of 6

[4] George F. Dow, "Shipping and Trade in Early New England," *Proceedings of the Massachusetts Historical Society*, 3d ser., 64 (1932): 194-95; Bailyn, p. 100.

[5] *Town Recs.*, I, 204-5, 228; James Duncan Phillips, *Salem in the Seventeenth Century* (Boston, 1933), p. 214.

[6] Maverick, *A Brief Description of New England* (London, 1660), p. 12.

percent per year, using 1640 as a base, and concluded that "this rate of growth, itself, suggests a commercial or industrial rather than an agricultural economy."[7]

At the heart of the county's economic development was the shire town of Salem, and especially a relatively small band of merchants. These men who owned, either in whole or in parts, the stores, warehouses, and ships increasingly controlled the economy, not only of Salem but of the whole county. By 1650 good bills of exchange on English merchants could be found only in Charlestown, Boston, and Salem. The merchants were able to set prices and terms of credit to the farmers and fishermen, who had to supply constant mercantile needs by irregular, seasonal production. Thus the limited supply of money in New England tended to gravitate into the merchants' hands. By 1660 the basic ligaments of New England's permanent mercantile economy had been formed. From then to the American Revolution the main characteristics went unchanged, though their magnitude increased.[8]

Another statistical study of the probate records, by Donald Warner Koch, indicated not only that Salem was the chief beneficiary of the county's expansion but also that the absolute economic condition of all classes within the town improved markedly.[9] The increased prosperity was not, however, equally shared. Before the full impact of the transformation was reflected in the wills, around 1660, the wealthiest 10 percent of the town's residents left 21 percent of the inventoried wealth; after 1661 the same proportion of townsmen held 62 percent. Their share tripled.

This widening gap between the rich and the rest of the population occurred largely because the rich monopolized the basic tools of economic expansion, investment in shipping. In the century before the promulgation of laissez-faire, the organization of Salem's commerce encouraged cooperation rather than competition within the mercantile community. Hence the leading merchants were not only separated from their fellow townsmen by their enormous wealth but also bound closely together into a coherent economic interest that blossomed into a political and social interest as well.

The main device of economic cooperation was the ancient

---

[7]Davisson, "Essex County Wealth Trends: Wealth and Economic Growth in Seventeenth-Century Massachusetts," *Essex Institute Historical Collections* 103 (1967): 291-342; Davisson "Essex County Price Trends: Money and Markets in Seventeenth-Century Massachusetts," ibid., pp. 144-85.

[8]Bailyn, pp. 86, 96, 99.

[9]Koch, "Income Distribution and Political Structure in Seventeenth-Century Salem, Massachusetts," *Essex Institute Historical Collections* 105 (1969): 50-71.

maritime practice of owning shares in ships and cargoes in order to avoid overwhelming individual loss in the risky business of oceanic trade. Usually the title to a vessel, especially a larger one, was divided. The bulk of these shares were held by merchants, while smaller proportions might be owned by the master.[10] This is not to say that there was no sole ownership in ships. When William Jeggles, master mariner, died in 1659, his ketch *William*, worth £50, constituted over one-third of his estate. Even some of the town's leading merchants owned in whole some vessels, usually fishing craft. John Turner, for example, who owned his own wharf and two warehouses before 1670, also held four ketches ranging in value from £90 to £170. But in larger vessels he preferred shares. His third of the ship *William and John* was valued at £500, for instance. His investments in four other ships, ranging from one-eighth to one-half ownership, totaled £440.[11] The size of his investments shows that Turner could have afforded to own several large ships, but he chose the less dangerous practice of shares.

Investments in cargoes were similarly dispersed. Even in the unlikely event that a merchant had enough cargo bound along the same route to fill a ship, he was not apt to put it all in one bottom. He was much more likely to hire space in several vessels, all of which in their long rambles would reach the desired ports. Merchants rarely put cargo in ships in which they owned shares, since their interests as shipowners—highest possible freight charges—would conflict with their interests as merchants—highest possible profit on the cargo. Usually a group of merchants would band together to hire someone else's ships, splitting the costs and profits in proportion ot their investments.[12] The possibility of a rift within the mercantile community was eliminated, in Salem at least, by the fact that the same men tended to be both merchants and shipowners.

An ancient institution that had played a crucial role in the founding of New England, the shares system seems an ironic parody of the traditional covenant idea. Just as the covenants were designed to bind the community together and to reward individuals according to their value to the whole, the shares system tied together its participants and rewarded them according to their investments. Its goals were emphatically financial rather than spiritual or social. As the stakes and rewards within the commer-

[10]John W. McElroy, "Seafaring in Seventeenth-Century New England," *New England Quarterly* 8 (1935), 355.

[11]*Q.C.R.*, II, 164; Sidney Perley, *History of Salem, Massachusetts*, 3 vols. (Salem, 1924-27), II, 355-58.

[12]Davis, pp. 90-99.

cial system grew, it created a new communal interest with different ideals and values than those embodied in the covenants. A competing communal system grew up within the old, undermining the ideal of one communal order that embraced the whole town.

The Salem merchants of the 1650s and 1660s did not consciously seek the subversion of the covenant system. Commerce was considered an honorable and necessary calling. Many of Salem's religious and political leaders of the late 1630s and 1640s had not only encouraged trade, they had participated in it. Even Endecott tried his hand at copper mining, though with little success. Peter, Hathorne, Batter and Bartholomew all engaged in trade as an aspect of their obligations and perquisites within the communal system.

During the 1650s and 1660s the latter three of these busy political leaders owned warehouses and stores as well as farms. In the commercial sector they were soon supplanted as leaders by men of more dedication who by their diligence amassed greater wealth and economic influence. Endecott's inventoried wealth in 1665 totaled £815 and Hathorne's in 1681 was £754. Their estates are the largest known among the leaders of precommercial Salem. The merchants who became selectmen and deputies during and after the economic transformation of the town fared much better. Walter Price died in 1674 worth £2,058, and George Corwin left an estate of £5,965 in 1685.

With hindsight it is obvious that the phenomenal success of men like Corwin and Price distorted the status system. At the time, however, it was possible to ignore the problem because Salem's first generation of powerful merchants sought manfully to fulfill the expectations of Puritan society. Both Price and Corwin, for example, served the community in political offices that took time from their mercantile careers. They joined the church. Their effort to conform blurred the inherent conflict between the imperatives of the merchants' calling and the communal ideals of Puritanism. While their commercial activities were rapidly transforming the town and making it an impossible environment for the realization of Puritan social ideals, their own behavior and the respectability of their calling made it difficult to focus resentment against them or their economic function.

The attempt to reconcile Puritan ideals and commercial imperatives introduced some changes in the ideology and behavior of "the better sort." The merchants were unconsciously changing both the social environment and the intellectual content of the covenant. The difficulty was that large segments of the town and even some of "the better sort" dissented from all or part of the consequences of social change while accepting the necessity of commercial expansion.

The tacit mercantile covenant was simply an adaptation of the old to the new economic situation and its psychological results. One of its features was the hoary notion of stewardship, which justified the ever-increasing concentration of wealth while providing a means of avoiding the temptations inherent in it. The virtues that brought success in commerce—thrift, sobriety, frugality—were Christian to the Puritan mind. The first generation of wealthy merchants sought to use that wealth in ways they and most others thought would benefit the community as well as themselves. Part of the new wealth went into community services like loans to the town, welfare, and public works, but most of it was reinvested for continued economic development. Very little went into personal ostentation. One gathers from Corwin's will that his life style was not as grandiose as Downing's, for example.[13]

The merchants assumed that economic development was an end in itself, an attitude latent in the thought of, say, Hugh Peter. After the outbreak of the English Revolution and the consequent uncertainty over Massachusetts's purpose in history, this attitude was easier to accept. Some changes in the concept of calling were inevitable. The notion of general calling, which had meant an intense drive toward spiritual and social salvation for the community and the individual, lost must of its inspirational quality and hardened into a more mechanical conception of religious observance. A man's particular calling should be supplemented by acts of piety like church going, Bible reading, and daily praying. Religious life no longer organized and inspired daily life but became a separate set of values. Hence in this later period the particular rather than the general calling became paramount in defining a man and his value, and success in the particular calling became increasingly more significant.[14] With this shift away from a dynamic, integrated conception of religious life, wealth or the lack of it became the most important sign of status rather than just one among many. Of course piety, education, and family connections still counted, but not as much as commercial prowess. Wealth had always been seen as a gift of God, and poverty, a sign of His displeasure. The mercantile view gave the conception renewed emphasis, especially as commercial success began to show

---

[13] Bailyn, p. 120; Davisson, "Wealth Trends," p. 336.

[14] Robert S. Michaelson, "Changes in the Puritan Concept of Calling or Vocation," *New England Quarterly* 26 (1953): 326-27.

that individuals could control their own destiny to a greater extent than the notion of justification by faith had admitted. Good works had always been considered a sign of salvation, but gradually they came to be seen as a guarantee.[15]

The surface similarities between this view and that embodied in the 1636 covenant made acceptance easier and resistance more difficult. Both clusters of ideas were intensely moral or behavioral, stressing many of the same virtues. The notion of hierarchy was preserved and even simplified once wealth became the dominant sign of status. There was no overt rejection of any of the religious standards, and if anything, the new attitude was more relevant to the experience of men who were free of the social and religious tensions that racked early seventeenth-century England. The congregational churches had become established, an almost unquestioning acceptance of the values of the religious order was a more comfortable response than any sort of zeal.

As the composition of the 1647 board of selectmen showed, merchants came to exercise great political power within the town. The pattern of their growing influence is neither neat nor overwhelming, for the more traditional leaders were still influential and tensions aroused by the economic transformation blurred the political alignments. If a rigid distinction is drawn between the town's traditional leaders, those who first rose the political prominence in the 1630s and early 1640s, and the merchants, who came to political power in the late 1640s and the 1650s, the increasing power of the latter group during the years 1647-67 becomes evident (table 13). To further refine the comparison,

Table 13. Selectmen elections and mercantile representation, 1647-67

Years	Traditional leaders	Merchants	Special interests
1647-49	5	5	—
1650-51	4	4	1
1652-53	5	5	—
1654-55	6	5	—
1656-57	6	5	1
1658-59	3	3	1
1660-61	3	4	—
1662-63	3	5	—
1664-65	2	4	2
1666-67	2	3	2

Sources: *Town Recs.*, I, II; Sidney J. Perley, *The History of Salem, Massachusetts*, 3 vols. (Salem, 1924-27), I, II, biographical notes.

[15] Darrett B. Rutman, *Winthrop's Boston: Portrait of a Puritan Town, 1630-1649* (Chapel Hill, N.C., 1965), p. 244.

another category, "special interests," is used to include selectmen who represented the small farmers of the outlying areas and the Quaker sympathizers. The table is not intended to delineate strict faction lines since the two major groups agreed as much as they disagreed on policy. Throughout the period a rough parity in representation was maintained, with a slight shift to the merchants' favor after 1660. It should be noted that most of the men in these groups were of approximately the same age, and death did not begin to affect their ranks until the late 1670s and 1680s.

Another significant measure of power is the accumulation of political experience in office. Comparing tenure as selectmen among the three groups before and after 1647 provides a graphic picture of the growth of mercantile representation on the board of selectmen (table 14). Of the nine merchants who were elected

Table 14. Tenure of selectmen, 1636-67

Groups	No.	No. of years served (1636-46)		No. of years served (1647-67)	
		Range	Average	Range	Average
Traditional leaders	9	1-11	4.5	1-19	7.5
Merchants	9	0-4	0.9	1-17	8.8
Special interests	4	0	0	1-8	3.2

Source: *Town Recs.*, I, II.

selectmen between 1647 and 1667, only Bartholomew and Lord had previously served in that position, both for four years. Of these two, only Bartholomew continued to be an important political figure, serving as selectman for twelve years between 1647 and 1667. Lord, only a moderately successful merchant, held a selectman's post for just three years after 1647.

After 1647 the merchants quickly overcame their lack of political experience. Between 1647 and 1667 five of them—Corwin, Price, Porter, and William Browne Bartholomew—held office for more than ten years. Only two of the traditional leaders, Hathorne and Batter, had the same tenure, and they were the ones most likely to be sympathetic to the merchants' views. Men like Conant, who had more in common with the small farmers, held office much less regularly. Conant served seven years. Jeffrey Massey, Conant's neighbor and fellow West Countryman, was a selectman only five of the twenty years.

Salem's representation in the General Court from 1647 to 1667 followed a similar pattern of approximate parity between the two groups combined with accumulating political experience by the merchants (table 15). Bartholomew was the merchant who most often won election, eleven times in all. Browne was next with

Table 15. Deputy elections and mercantile representation, 1647-67

Years	Traditional leaders	Merchants	Special interests
1647-52	7	4	1
1653-57	4	2	1
1658-62	5	4	–
1663-67	3	6	1

Source: James Duncan Phillips, *Salem in the Seventeenth Century* (Boston, 1933), p. 358.

three. Corwin was chosen twice, in 1666 and 1667, and Price, once in 1665. Until his elevation to the upper house in 1662, Hathorne was the traditional leader most often chosen by the town meeting, also for eleven terms. Batter was next with six. The special interest deputy was Thomas Lathrop. He also was elected selectman eight times. A church member and a farmer on the Cape Ann Side since 1637, he accumulated land and political influence according to the expected pattern. In frequent alliance with the Old Planter leadership, he became one of the moving spirits in the separation of Beverly from Salem in the late 1660s.

The transformation of the town and the rise of full-time merchants to significant power caused tension and conflict. However, the tensions generally manifested themselves in religious and political, rather than economic terms. Those struggles and the resultant compromises and adjustments within the community are the subject of the next chapters. But before those tensions can be adequately understood, the impact of commercial expansion upon other groups besides the merchants must be examined.

The expansion of commerce improved the economic situation of all groups, in terms of absolute income. Judging from the town records there was little poverty in Salem. The town's poor were of the types to be expected in settled rather than frontier areas. All the town's relief that can be traced went to widows, orphans, and men aged or otherwise incapacitated. Only twelve separate cases occupied the selectmen or town meeting between 1650 and 1667. There were five widows, one orphaned family, one insane girl, and four aged men. The only "sturdy" man on relief was John Talby, the excommunicant whose insane wife had killed their daughter in 1638. In 1656 the selectmen determined that Talby "being commonly noted for a person spending his time Idle and Unprofitably, we think it meet that he should be sent to the next Magistrate to be employed accordingly." But when that expedient failed, the town continued to support him until his death.[16]

There may have been other men in Talby's economic plight, but not many. The people of Salem still had the ancient English fear of "sturdy beggars." Unlike Boston after 1640, Salem was a small enough community with a sufficiently intense Puritan ethos to keep enforcing the rules on inhabitantship and the "harboring of strangers."[17] Transient mariners and merchants were the only "strangers" tolerated by the town. Interestingly, a number of these people were French, another example of the pluralism engendered by commerce. At least one of these Frenchmen, perhaps a merchant, was in Salem often enough to rent quarters by the year. In June 1662 seven French seamen won a suit in Quarterly Court for wages against Thomas Wills, master of the Salem ship *Robert*. Five of these men lived or had relatives in Salem. Most of the town's mariners were, of course, Englishmen or New Englanders. Although often "strangers," they too were allowed to remain in town. But other persons who were not following the sea were "warned off."[18]

Supplying the needs of expanding commerce created much work for Salem's inhabitants. The chief beneficiaries, besides merchants, were artisans. As skilled labor became ever more vital to Salem's success, the town actively worked to procure and maintain coopers, joiners, tailors, glazers, and other workmen. In 1665 even a "translator" was settled in the town. The usual method of governmental encouragement was a grant or sale of land or even shop. A typical grant was made by the selectmen in August 1659: "Leave was given to Richard Harvey, Tailor, to mend up the little house Joining to the meetinghouse and make use of it for a shop at the Town's pleasure." On occasion lots were provided on a large scale. In 1661 the town meeting authorized the selectmen to dispose of a block of land "for shops." The next summer the selectmen divided the parcel into twelve lots which they sold for £5 each. On those lands houses and shops, largely for tailors, were built.[19]

Compared to most English artisans, Salem's workmen did well. In the Midlands, according to W. G. Hoskins, a "flourishing" artisan's estate amounted to about £20 sterling during the first decade of the seventeenth century. The income of artisans in Kent, historically one of the more affluent shires, was about £15 to £18

---

[16] *Town Recs.*, I, 193.

[17] Ibid., I, 209; Rutman, pp. 197-98.

[18] *Q.C.R.*, II, 385; *Town Recs.*, II, 11, 41, 50, 61.

[19] *Town Recs.*, I, 202, 231, II, 2, 19, 53; Perley, II, 308-11.

sterling a year. In Massachusetts the average Essex County artisan's estate was £152 over the period 1641-82 (£129 Massachusetts currency was valued at £100 sterling). In 1666 a Salem carpenter, Nathaniel Carrel, received £9 from the estate of a farmer for "repairing the house and some fence." The contrast is sharp, even taking into account the gradual inflation on both sides of the Atlantic.[20]

In the Midlands the general standard of living for artisans who owned small farms, like Salem's workmen, fell during the seventeenth century. Population increases, pressure on the available land, and heavy taxation created an increasingly large class of landless labor living on decreasing wages. In Salem, too, there was growing pressure on the town's available land, but a large landless class, other than mariners, did not develop until the 1680s and the wage levels remained high. Thomas Brackett, one of Salem's least successful artisans who owned only "a small parcel of land and timber," his carpentry tools, and his clothing, died in the summer of 1668. His tangible assets came to only £16. He owed £3, probably in house rent. But he was creditor for another £16 in wages. His total estate thus came to about £30.[21]

Farmers too profited from commerce since agricultural products were a staple of Salem's early trade. During the 1640s the average estate of small farmers, holding less than one hundred acres, was about £50. Land was plentiful, buildings were primitive, and money was scarce. Robert Pease's house, barn, and eleven acres were valued at £14 in 1645. The year before Richard Ingersoll's house and two-acre town lot were worth only £4. Ten acres of land he had cleared were worth £7, while his uncleared ten-acre lot was valued at £2 10s. Twelve years later in 1656 twenty acres on Ryal Side were valued at £1 an acre and a two-acre town lot with no buildings was worth £6. That same year a house and barn on a two-acre town lot belonging to a small farmer were inventoried at £35.[22]

As forests were cleared and new farm lands were opened, many townsmen moved off the peninsula to take advantage of the opportunities. By 1650 half the population was living on farms

[20]Hoskins, *The Midland Peasant: The Economic and Social History of a Leicestershire Village* (London, 1957), p. 173; C. W. Chalklin, *Seventeenth-Century Kent: A Social and Economic History* (London, 1965), p. 191; Manfred Jonas, "The Wills of the Early Settlers of Essex County, Massachusetts," *Essex Institute Historical Collections* 96 (1960): 229, 231; Curtis P. Nettels, *The Money Supply of the American Colonies before 1720* (rept. New York, 1964), p. 236.

[21]Hoskins, pp. 189, 213-15; *Pro. Recs.*, II, 132.

[22]*Q.C.R.*, I, 76, 77, 131, 241.

away from the peninsula.[23] During the 1630s the town had
granted much of the land in the area called the Farms in blocks
ranging from 30 to 300 acres. In order to satisfy the desire for
farms, the owners of these large grants sold or leased them in parts
or in whole. The Reverend Mr. Norris, for example, in 1654 sold
his 100-acre farm to Eleanor Truslar, whose son, Nicholas Phelps,
ran a portion of it and leased lots to Joseph Pope, Anthony
Needham, and the Southwick family. In so doing, Norris inadvert-
ently helped to create the geographic nucleus of the Quaker
movement in Salem. Another sale involved two blocks of land
totaling over 200 acres that had been granted to Elias Stileman and
Francis Weston in 1636. During the 1640s both blocks were sold
to three men who divided the land into smaller farms. By 1660
this acreage had ten families on it and formed the core of what
became Salem Village.

Often the large grants remained intact, but their ownership
passed to men interested in either leases or large-scale commercial
farming. There was even some concentration of ownership. In
1643 the ruling elder, Samuel Sharp, sold his 300-acre grant to
John Porter. The town gave Porter another 200 acres in 1647, and
he bought Townshend Bishop's 200-acre grant the next year. In
1649 Porter also acquired Samuel Skelton's 300-acre farm from
the General Court. He then bought over 500 acres from Emanuel
Downing in 1650. With well over 1,500 acres by 1650, "Farmer"
John Porter became the town's largest landholder. On those lands
he settled at least a dozen families. He also conveyed Skelton's
tract, still wilderness, to his son in 1660. Porter produced and
acquired, probably from his tenants, enough agricultural goods to
justify owning a warehouse on the peninsula. When he died in
1676 his estate was inventoried at over £2,570.[24]

Robert Goodale, who began with a 40-acre grant in the Farms,
followed a similar course of acquisition, but on a smaller scale.
While Porter was buying the large grants of the deceased or of men
who, like Sharp, desired to stay near the civic and religious center

---

[23]Phillips, pp. 171-72. Joseph B. Felt, *Annals of Salem*, 2 vols. (Salem, 1845), II,
410, contains these population estimates:

Year	Number	Year	Number
1626	30	1665	1,446
1629	336	1677	1,416
1639	950	1683	1,560
1644	1,200	1690	1,680
1654	1,068		

Note declines follow the creation of new towns out of Salem territory.

[24]Perley, II, 161-64, 333-35.

of the town, Goodale was purchasing smaller grants from artisans who needed lots nearer their trade. By 1652 he had acquired 480 acres from fourteen different families.

The farming lands of the interior were passing into the hands of both large and small farmers whose interests were primarily commercial. The situation subtly undermined the communal ideals behind the original land division. The leaders who designed the 1636-37 division attempted to combine commercial considerations with the more medieval concept of a stable status hierarchy reflected in the land. The emphasis, in their plans, was on the latter. As the economy expanded, the emphasis shifted and commercial considerations became paramount. The acquisition of land and the profits it brought became the prime sign of status in the countryside, just as mercantile wealth influenced the peninsula. Hence John Porter, the most successful commercial farmer, was almost invariably a selectman after 1647, even though he did not join the church until 1649.

As the farming areas expanded and the demand for more and larger farms grew, arguments between Salem and the bordering towns over boundaries increased. From 1653 to 1664 Salem found itself in various controversies with the recently formed and sparsely settled town of Topsfield. Topsfield complained of encroachment and even took its case to the General Court. The controversy was complicated by the Bellingham grant on the line between the towns, which was technically within the original bounds of Salem but never was under the town's jurisdiction. In 1659 Bellingham, then governor, complained that Salem farmers were appropriating his meadows. He confused the issue by selling the whole for £250 to two Lynn farmers, who then contested the jurisdiction of both towns. Minor disagreements also broke out with Lynn over other portions of the boundary.[25]

It is interesting that the West Countrymen of Bass River and the Cape Ann Side, being fewer in number and less speculative in temperament than the inhabitants of the Farms, had no disputes with the towns of Wenham and Manchester on their borders. Land transfers were also rare, and no evidence of tenantry can be found. During the 1650s and 1660s a village developed on the Cape Ann Side that formed the nucleus of Beverly later, but most of the owners were sons of the West Countrymen who owned the surrounding territory. In short, the settlers of the region across the harbor were little affected by the economic transformation taking place in the rest of Salem. The West Countrymen maintained a

[25]*Town Recs.*, I, 174, 205, 212, 213, 214, 223, II, 12, 24, 42, 46-47.

stable agricultural system by concerted and persistent political action, a subject of the next chapter. The contrast between the two farming regions intensified the sectionalism of Salem.

Another difference between the two agricultural sections related to the development of commercial agriculture in the Farms. Many of the traditional leaders who had lived in that region, at least during the farming season, began to abandon the countryside and move onto the peninsula permanently. Land sales by Norris, Sharp, and Downing have already been mentioned. Although Endecott did not sell his lands, he moved his household to Boston in 1655 in order to be near the center of colonial government. Hathorne lived on his extensive farm around what is now called Hathorne Hill in Danvers until the mid-1640s; there most of his children were born. Then, since he had nearly daily business on the peninsula, he moved to a smaller sixty-acre site with a sturdy two-story house on the border of the South Field, which he called the Mill Pond Farm.[26] In 1663 he sold all his lands in the Farms. By the mid-1650s all the traditional political and religious leaders who had lived in the Farms had moved to or near the peninsula, with the exception of Thomas Gardner, the only original Old Planter great landholder in the region.

As the problems of governing the burgeoning mercantile peninsula and maintaining Salem's power in the colony grew, the leadership lost touch with what happened in the countryside. Their removal created a social and political vacuum in the Farms that encouraged unrest and uncertainty in the section. The leadership vacuum was only partially filled by John Porter, who was more closely aligned to the merchants than to the small farmers. In this unstable situation where the hierarchy had broken down, a small farmer faction gradually coalesced around the numerous Putnam family.

The patriarch of the family, John Putnam, was granted 100 acres in 1641 but did not join the church until 1647. He participated little in the town's affairs. However, his three sons, Thomas, Nathaniel, and John, began to acquire land, prestige, and political power even before their father's death in 1662. They rose to power according to the accepted pattern, first becoming church members and then serving their political apprenticeships as jurymen and constables. All three eventually became selectmen. By the 1660s they were fulfilling the Purtian ideal of leadership, but their influence was restricted to the small landowners and

---

[26]Vernon Loggins, *The Hawthornes: The Story of Seven Generations of an American Family* (New York, 1951), p. 35.

tenants whose interests they defended. Their rise is strong evidence of the sectionalism that characterized Salem local politics during the period of transformation.

Salem's sectional problems were badly exacerbated by the failure of the agricultural sector's wealth to expand as rapidly as that of the town. Davisson's statistical series on the value of farm assets, the necessary implements of agriculture, gives some indication of the slowing growth rate. Between 1641 and 1655 farm assets comprised between 20 and 67 percent of estate values. Between 1655 and 1667 they varied between 17 and 48 percent. After 1667 the percentage fell drastically, never rising above 23 percent. The absolute value of the implements also declined. In a related phenomenon the prices of work animals, most notably oxen, declined after 1655.[27]

These indications of slowing agricultural development might seem to have been negated by the rising value of land. Measured on a 1652 base, land values began increasing steadily around 1658, and the trend continued through the century. Also, the percentage of the estates held as land increased from around 30 percent in 1640-50 to about 60 percent in 1660-70. But not all the land increased rapidly in value; the boom was largely restricted to the peninsula. As noted earlier, the two-acre house lots became more and more valuable. Salem merchants invested in peninsula lands not only for warehouses and other commercial necessities but also for speculative purposes. In 1672 a four-acre enclosed lot along the shore was inventoried at £90 and a house on five acres of peninsula land was worth £150.[28]

The value of agricultural land, even that in the North and South Fields, increased much more slowly than peninsula land, especially after 1658. During the 1640s ten acres of cleared arable land were worth about £7. From 1646 to 1656 the price per acre of arable land in the developed areas in the North and South Fields, the Farms, and the Bass River region rose to £1 and from 1656 to 1676 it remained at that value with little fluctuation. In the undeveloped portions of Cape Ann Side farthest from the peninsula the price was about three acres for £1 in the 1660s.[29]

This stability in land prices in the farming areas and the decline in the value of work animals and farm implements does not mean that there were fewer farmers after 1658 or that their absolute

[27]"Wealth Trends," pp. 325-26; "Price Trends," pp. 172-73.

[28]Davisson, "Wealth Trends," pp. 318-19, 324-25; *Pro Recs.*, I, 241, II, 275-78.

[29]*Q.C.R.*, I, 76, 77; *Pro. Recs.*, I, 185-86, 241, 256-57, 388-89, 420, 455-56, II, 48, 49-51, 90-91, 92.

income declined. Farms were still valuable property and there are indications that farm income rose during the transformation period. Henry Bullock, a North Field farmer who owned forty-six acres and leased eight more, died in July 1657 worth £121. His North Field neighbor, Thomas James, died almost ten years later possessing around thirty acres. His estate was nearly identical in value, £122, even with less acreage. Edward Randolph's observation on Massachusetts farmers in 1676 fits Salem as well: "The farmers are numerous and wealthy, live in good houses, are given to hospitality, and make good advantage by their corn, poultry, butter and cheese."[30]

Yet during the late 1650s and 1660s many of Salem's farmers, even some of the more substantial ones, were showing signs of unrest. Despite their material gains, the farmers were falling considerably behind the merchants. Before the transformation large farmers and merchants enjoyed similar incomes and roughly equal prestige, with a slight advantage to the landholders. After 1660 in Salem the most wealthy 5 percent of residents leaving wills accounted for 48 percent of the inventoried wealth, and this wealth was mercantile. More important, this relative loss of economic power meant an eventual decline in social and political influence as well, a development that many large landholders resisted in various ways.

Other groups besides the large landowners sustained relative losses of position despite the general prosperity. Opportunity for small farmers and artisans to obtain great wealth began to decline as mercantile families consolidated and perpetuated their power through expanded economic activity and intermarriage. Before 1660 the estates of artisans and small farmers valued between £25 and £149 comprised about 56 percent of the town's inventoried wills. After 1660 the figure fell to 32 percent, even though the number of individuals rose from thirty to thirty-four. The great increase in numbers of estates came at the upper end of the economic scale. Before 1660 only thirteen out of fifty-three wills were valued over £149, and none was over £400. After 1660 fifty-six Salem wills out of 108 were worth over £149, and sixteen of those exceeded £400.[31] As near as can be determined only six of the fifty-six men who died after 1660 worth more than £149 began their careers as artisans, and three of them were sons of

---

[30] *Q.C.R.*, II, 49; *Pro. Recs.*, II, 46; Robert N. Toppan and Thomas S. Goodrick, eds., *Edward Randolph, including His Letters and Official Papers . . .*, 7 vols. (Boston, 1898-1909), II, 235.

[31] Koch, pp. 56-57, 69.

large landowners. Only five others of the fifty-six started as small landholders. Peaking during the early years of Salem's transformation, around 1655, the possibility of rapid economic mobility for artisans and small landholders tapered off as Salem's merchants organized and fixed the pattern of the town's commerce.

From 1650 to 1667 the basis of Salem's economy shifted from agriculture to commerce. The expansion of commerce meant new wealth for most of the town's inhabitants, but it also brought with it important changes in the social, political, and religious life that were not so welcome to many townsmen. The rise of merchants, who acquired previously unimagined wealth, introduced new elements of complexity and conflict. Their activities sparked the transformation of the peninsula from a central farming village into a commercial town with all the attendant urban problems of crowding, rising land prices, and controlling fire, animals, and the water supply. Inded, from about 1655 on, the peninsula was generally referred to as the Town.

As the population spread over the township and as the various sections specialized their economic functions, farmers moved their homes out into the countryside while artisans and political and religious leaders, as well as merchants and mariners, concentrated on the peninsula. Increasingly the various sections of the town and portions of its population were separated in their daily lives. This physical separation of the farming population from their fellow townsmen exascerbated their sense of being left out as the town developed economically. It severely challenged their sense of unity and identity with the whole community. On the peninsula itself, merchants and traditional leaders found themselves in occasional conflict over policy questions. The greatly altered social and economic situation generated political and religious conflict and gradually forced a general adaptation of the covenant in both its tacit and explicit aspects to the new realities of Salem life.

Chapter VIII

The Collapse of Communal Unity
1650-1668

Salem was undergoing a profound economic alteration, encouraged and approved by the townsmen. They were seeking greater wealth for the community. This conscious effort was consistent with and an integral part of the more comprehensive attempt, so well embodied in William Hathorne's political career, to consolidate and extend Salem's influence through every sphere of the colony's life. While pursuing these ends, the town underwent social changes whose consequences went unforeseen. A good example was the abandonment of the countryside by almost all of the town's leadership except the West Countrymen. As a result, the people of the countryside felt an increasing sense of isolation and alienation which erupted into religious and political conflict when the agricultural sector of the economy failed to keep pace with the commercial.

Sectional conflicts were not unusual within New England towns as the population spread out. Even the successful Puritan utopia of Dedham faced this problem.[1] Also, it was difficult to maintain the necessary zeal when the conditions that gave rise to the utopian vision became far removed in time and space. As zeal ebbs and as societies develop, people naturally begin to lay more stress on the various social arrangements that bind them to some and separate them from others in their immediate surroundings. The New England churches periodically turned inward and ignored the problems and interests of the larger community. The Boston church went into a phase of this sort as early as 1635.[2] After the ideologically inspired inwardness of the Williams interlude, socially separating members from nonmembers, Salem underwent a similar episode during part of the pastorate of Edward Norris (1641-59), a situation that John Higginson sought to reverse after he became the minister in 1660. Conflicts arising out of these and other social distinctions such as occupation and family developed more rapidly

---

[1] Kenneth A. Lockridge, *A New England Town: The First Hundred Years, Dedham, 1636-1736* (New York, 1970), pp. 82, 100, 102, 131-32.

[2] Darrett B. Rutman, *Winthrop's Boston: Portrait of a Puritan Town, 1630-1649* (Chapel Hill, N.C., 1965), pp. 142-43.

in Salem than in some other towns largely because of the dislocations caused by economic changes.

The first signs of trouble after 1650 arose over the vestiges of communal agriculture: rights to the commons, general land use and distribution, and the town animal herders. In 1655 a group from the Farms won from the town meeting "liberty to herd their cattle themselves with a keep of their own hiring for this year"; the selectmen were to choose another herdsman for the peninsula.[3] This small incident is a paradigm of the problems caused by dispersion and the inevitable but subversive solution of subdivision. The town meeting, by allowing the farmers to choose their own keep, was undermining the selectmen's responsibility for, and interest in, a significant aspect of life in the Farms. The selectmen were surrendering one element of common experience and reinforcing the growing distinctiveness of the sections.

The problems of commons rights were much more complicated and controversial. Emotion often ran high since free use of the commons was important. During one of these discussions Francis Nurse was "fined twenty shillings for his abusive Carriage in the town meeting." On another occasion the town meeting was faced with a petition from a small farmer who wanted it to remit a fine assessed by the selectmen for cutting timber on a common. After deferring this controversial question "until there be a fuller Town meeting,"[4] the town meeting finally remitted the fine.

As the town developed, the boundaries between privately owned lots and farms and between them and the commons and highways became increasingly important. The townsmen, particularly during the frontier decades, had not clearly maintained the boundaries. The result was confusion, encroachments, and quarrels. By 1661 the problem was so severe that one town meeting dealt with seven different disputes. That same year the town meeting attempted to regain control by ordering "that all men that have any former Grants of land from the town are to come to the selectmen and make their claim within one year after the Day and Date hereof or else to lose it forever."[5]

The problems were compounded by the fact that so many selectmen were residents of the peninsula and often ignorant of exact conditions in the farm areas. They also occasionally made grants that cut into the common land beyond the intention of the town meeting. In February 1664 the town meeting authorized the selectmen to dispose of a section of land "for making good former

[3] *Town Recs.*, I, 182.
[4] Ibid., I, 204, 219.
[5] Ibid., II, 13, 18.

grants or to accommodate others as they shall see occasion." The selectmen "made good" four former grants totaling 160 acres and added eight more for another 210 acres. Because no one seemed sure of the bounds, even though the town meeting had assigned three men "to lay out the land," the grants caused a series of tangled disputes.[6] The confusion took several years to straighten out. This incident and the general pressure on land led the town meeting at the next election to put into the record the first explicit limit on the power of the selectmen. They were to have "full power to act in all the prudential Affairs that Concern the good of the town: only they are to dispose of no land."[7]

Resting the power to grant land exclusively in the hands of the town meeting did not guarantee protection of the interests of the people of the Farms. Even though their voice was more potent in that body than on the board of selectmen, it was not the only voice. They wanted to keep new people from sharing the lands and rights in their area, but the town meeting was not always sympathetic. It continued to grant land and rights in the Farms.[8]

The West Countrymen of the Cape Ann Side and the Bass River were more successful in gaining power over the land in their area, largely because of the greater prestige of their leadership. They carried out their intent by concerted political action. Early in 1650 only one of six selectmen was from the Cape Ann Side. After the election in July 1650 the board, reduced to five members, contained a West Country majority. Much of the selectmen's business over the next two years concerned fixing boundaries and adjusting private and common rights in that region. The decision reached in the new board's first meeting was probably its most important. It set aside as a common a vast tract stretching from the Bass River to Mackerel Cove and thence just inland down to "the head of the ten acre lots" located near the ferry landing. A year later upon petition the selectmen created another large common on the boundary between the Farms and the West Country farms. In this way the West Countrymen put aside practically all the available inland territory in their region and declared that it "shall be reserved for Common and none of it granted in propriety to any."[9] The West Countrymen had effectively restricted the Cape Ann Side to themselves and their

---

[6] Ibid., II, 42-44, 46.

[7] Ibid., II, 54.

[8] This finally led to an attempt by the Farms to circumvent the town meeting in 1678. The resulting case went all the way to the Court of Assistants. James Duncan Phillips, *Salem in the Seventeenth Century* (Boston, 1933), pp. 253-54.

[9] *Town Recs.*, I, 164, 167-68, 171-74.

children by defining with precision most of the virgin land as permanent commons.

In 1652, the size of the board of selectmen was once again increased to seven and, the West Countrymen were no longer the majority, holding only two of the seats until 1659 and dropping to one representative, Roger Conant, in 1659. This loss of representation was due partly to their minority status. Another reason was their growing lack of interest in the rest of the town. Recognizing that they could not control the board of selectmen and the town meeting, they sought autonomy by attempting to limit the authority those institutions exercised in their region.

Establishing control over the land on the Cape Ann Side and over disputes arising from its use and ownership was essential. The West Countrymen, a close-knit group, had already begun to keep their controversies over land to themselves. Quarrels among them rarely appear in the town records. The squabbles that did reach the selectmen after the West Countrymen lost control of the board occasionally led to imposed solutions. In 1654 Humphrey Woodbury, an Old Planter large landholder, found himself in a dispute with his neighbors over a swamp. Before the case came to the selectmen, Woodbury had consented to cede some of the land. The amount, however, was still in dispute. The selectmen chose "four indifferent men," only one of whom was a West Countrymen, to mediate. By 1657 the West Countrymen had somehow managed to gain jurisdiction over land disputes in their region. Thereafter when arguments reached the selectmen, they tended to refer them to West Country leaders.[10]

By 1661 the vastness of their commons gave the West Countrymen some influence even over the original granting of land. The selectmen determined that henceforth they would give a prospective settler only "so much land as the Inhabitants on Cape Ann Side shall be willing to give out of the Common on the East side of Bass River." By 1664 their local control over the land was complete, even to the laying out of roads. The few grants thereafter were made "by the inhabitants of Cape Ann Side."[11] The selectmen and town meeting were apparently willing merely to record West Country decisions. The people of the Farms were not able to attain this degree of autonomy until late in the century.

The West Countrymen's campaign for autonomy included other matters besides the land. In 1655 the town tax totaled £48 13s., an average assessment before 1660. But during the town meeting

[10] Ibid., I, 177-78, 196, 205.
[11] Ibid., II, 18, 44, 53.

at which the rate was determined, the West Countrymen objected and forced the meeting to call another session a week later "to confer with our brothers of Cape Ann Side about their rates." On their specific complaints the town records are silent.[12] But over the next four years a pattern of seeking control over their local taxes became clear.

To cope with the dispersion of population the town meeting in 1657 elected three constables, one from each section of town. Since each constable kept separate accounts, some comparison is possible. The Cape Ann proportion was always low but apparently fair. In 1658 the projected town budget was just over £80. Cape Ann's part was just under £12, which was about half the Farm's assessment and only a quarter of the peninsula's. Although the Cape Ann Side comprised over a third of the town's area, it contained only about one-seventh of the population (approximately 200 out of 1,300 people) and paid about one-eighth of the taxes.[13]

Yet their complaints were frequent, for little of the town rate was disbursed on Cape Ann. In 1657, for example, well over half the Cape Ann constable's disbursements was used for repair of the town meetinghouse. By this time the Cape Ann inhabitants had already built their own meetinghouse, although they did not have a minister. In December 1659, after calling a conference in August between Hathorne, Bartholomew, the selectmen, and the inhabitants of the Cape Ann Side, the town meeting exempted "our Brethren and Neighbors of Cape Ann Side" from all the town rate except that portion that went "to the maintenance of the Ministry." The town meeting, however, was unwilling to cede complete control over local taxes to the West Countrymen. That body still assessed the county and country rates for Cape Ann and declared that "all levies or Rates which concern them and all things about Ordering of fences shall be made by the Selectmen in being and if there be no Selectmen or man on their side than they have liberty to make choice of two or three of themselves to join with the selectmen in the premises abovesaid."[14]

This arrangement for setting local rates may have made the West Countrymen even more willing to do without significant representation on the board of selectmen. Having selectmen from other parts of Salem meeting with "two or three of themselves" in the

[12] Ibid., I, 186.

[13] Ibid., I, 225; Sidney Perley, *History of Salem, Massachusetts,* 3 vols. (Salem, 1924-27), II, 417-18.

[14] *Town Recs.,* I, 207, 222, 225-26, II, 2-3.

Cape Ann meetinghouse gave the West Countrymen more influence over their rates than sending even the prestigious Conant alone to the peninsula. It was also more convenient and more satisfying to their pride to have the mighty Hathorne come to them.

The West Countrymen's next step was to become a separate town. In 1664 they began sending Thomas Lathrop to the board of selectmen. They also mustered enough votes to elect him a deputy that year, and he carried to Boston a petition that Cape Ann become a town. The General Court, faced with the problems of the post-Restoration period, did not act on the petition until four years later. Meanwhile the West Countrymen formed their own church, the ultimate sign of their separate identity. In 1664 they settled a young minister, John Hale, giving him land and £70 per annum. Two years later they formally asked the Salem church "that they might have their consent to be a Church by themselves, and to have Mr. Hale for their Pastor." The petition "was left unto consideration" and the last day of February 1667 was declared "a day of solemn Fasting and prayer to seek unto God for his direction and presence in such a weighty matter." It was indeed a "weighty matter," for the West Countrymen were asking for a spiritual separation from the Salem community. The next summer, on July 4, their formal petition to the Salem church was made and accepted.[15]

All that remained was the formal, political separation. In March 1668 the town convened its most solemn secular meeting, a freemen's assembly, and declared, "In answer to a motion of our Brethren of Bass River presented to us from the General Court we think it the best expedient for them to be a Township of themselves; if they desire it, and there do Consent if Content with the present bounds already set them." In May the General Court laid out the terms of separation, granting the inhabitants of the Cape Ann region the right to choose their own officers. The petitioners, however, were not requesting total separation; "their desire is still to continue with that part of the town of Salem, *vizt*, in bearing with them, and they with us, common town and country charges in common interests and concernments, as choice of deputies for the General Court and such like, as hitherto they have proceeded together." On November 7, 1668, the General Court formally declared the Cape Ann area the town of Beverly.[16]

---

[15] Perley, II, 409-10; Daniel A. White, *New England Congregationalism in Its Origin and Purity, Illustrated by the Foundation and Early Records of the First Church of Salem* (Salem, 1861), pp. 71-74.

[16] *Town Recs.*, II, 87; Perley, II, 415.

Both the separation and the exceptions reveal just how self-interested the West Countrymen had become. They were seeking to avoid the expense of sending their own deputies and paying the colony rates as an independent town. Not until 1672 was this last tie severed. With the creation of Beverly, the West Countrymen completed their drive for autonomy. They were able to maintain a stable agricultural settlement made up almost entirely of themselves and their children.

The West Countrymen succeeded in establishing an arena in which they could pursue their vision according to their own lights. The people of the Farms, facing many of the same problems and pursuing many of the same ends, were nonetheless doomed to frustration. Their leadership was not as skillful nor as prestigious. Although they outnumbered the West Countrymen, they were dispersed over a wider area. There was no harbor neatly setting them apart from the peninsula, even though the distances between many of them and the meetinghouse were just as great.

The farmers also lacked a cultural unity to set them apart. Consequently they were often divided among themselves. For example, in 1666, a group of Farms residents, inspired by Cape Ann's successes, petitioned the church for permission to form a parish "by reason of their distance from the meetinghouse." The Salem church refused the petition partly on the grounds that the petition contained "the agitation of some things that did not concern it [,] more proper to a town meeting," meaning extraneous political and economic matters. But the main reason was the disagreement among the farmers themselves. "There was some consideration of the Farmers' motion for another minister, but another writing being at this time propounded by five of the near neighbors and brethren thereabouts desiring that they might not be engaged in that design, it did not appear they had a competent number." There was no minister for the Farms until 1672, and even then he served only the area that became Salem Village.[17]

In 1667 thirty-five "inhabitants of the farms belonging to Salem," led by two Farms selectmen, John and Nathaniel Putnam, petitioned the General Court to be exempted from "the Military watch at Salem Town, which considering how remote our Dwellings are from the Town, we did and do still conceive Law doth not require it of us." The issue was controversial; "the spirits of men seemed to be very high." Pressure from the peninsula to keep the farmers on the watch was intense. The Quarterly Court

[17]White, pp. 68-69; Phillips, pp. 222-24; *Mass. Recs.*, V, 247.

first declared for the farmers, but the leaders of the militia, who were Town residents, ignored the ruling. The next session of the court "was pleased not to determine the matter" and asked the farmers to petition the General Court. The incident itself and the tone of the petition reveal how badly the communal sense had deteriorated. The farmers complained that watching in Town often "cleared the strength of 2 or 3 miles about" in that rural area. They remarked, "It may also be Questioned, whether it be not, a profanation of the Lord's day, for persons to travel so far Armed, as before expressed, on the Sabbath, to watch a populous Town, in times of peace, consisting of near 300 able persons within the limits of the watch, and ourselves left out." Then they questioned bitterly "whether Salem Town hath not more cause to send us help . . . than we have to go to them . . . they a compact Town, we so scattered that 6 or 8 watches will not secure us, our dwellings are so scattered and remote one from another and so far from the Town, That Cambridge village, or Milton, may as easy go to Boston to watch as we may to Salem Town and leave their families in a great deal more safety, because they have Towns near to help them."[18]

It is within this context of growing alienation that the Quaker movement in Salem must be seen. Although Quakerism was an Anglo-American movement of great breadth, its appeal in Salem was largely restricted to a portion of Farm residents living in an area on the Lynn line often referred to as the Woods, located about seven miles from the peninsula. Only two of the more than forty Quakers whose place of residence at the time of their conversion is known came from other parts of Salem. There were thirteen husbandmen, twelve artisans, four mariners, and only one family of large landholders, the Gardners, among the early Quakers. Only later did a couple of these men become successful merchants and move to the Town.

Although its appeal in Salem was narrow in sectional and class terms, Quakerism gained enough converts to make Salem the core of Quaker agitation in the Bay Colony. Kai Erikson, using the Quarterly Court records, has identified fifty-one Quakers.[19] By supplementing those records, sixty-three Friends, thirty-seven men and twenty-six women, can be counted in the period 1657-67. In comparison to the individualistic heretical outbursts of the 1640s, The Quaker movement was most impressive. The size of the movement, its ideology, and the ferocity of the initial official

[18] *Essex Antiquarian* 2 (1898): 27-29.
[19] Erikson, *Wayward Puritans: A Study in the Sociology of Deviance* (New York, 1966), p. 176.

resistance indicate that something was seriously awry in Salem society.

Quaker ideology and practice embodied a reasonable, if highly emotional, form of religious and social criticism relevant to Salem society. However, this aspect was obscured, for both contemporaries and later observers, by the cycle of official repression and fanatical response. In essence the Quakers were demanding a frank recognition of the fact that the communal system had collapsed and that the Puritan experiment was a failure.[20]

The Quakers repudiated almost every aspect of the hierarchical ideal. The refusal to doff one's hat in the presence of magistrates may seem insignificant, but the Massachusetts leadership found it a convenient test for what they considered a deeper problem. According to Nathaniel Morton, "As to civil account, they allowed not nor practiced any civil respect to man, though superiors, either in magisterial consideration, or as masters or parents, or the ancient, neither by word or gesture."[21] The magistrates also used frequent absence from church, a punishable offense, and the tendency to hold private religious meetings as means of identifying Quakers. The Quarterly Court continued routinely to fine them for absence from church long after active persecution had ceased. This practice was maintained not only because it provided a means of circumventing the king's order of 1661 to cease the persecution but also because it punished a conspicuous facet of the Quakers' repudiation of the community's collective sense. The orthodox people of the Farms and Cape Ann Side asked for separate churches within the governing value system. The Quakers denied the validity of the whole system.

The Quakers felt that the Puritan system was a sham. It is hardly surprising, therefore, that Salem's earliest Quakers met in the home of Nicholas Phelps, son of the Gortonist dissenter Eleanor Truslar. The Quaker criticism of their fellow townspeople was bitter and sweeping. For example, in 1661 a tanner of the Farms interrupted a tense session of the Quarterly Court held in Gedney's tavern. "John Burton, coming into court in an uncivil manner, reproached the court by saying they were robbers and destroyers of the widows and fatherless, that their priests divined for money and their worship was not the worship of God, interrupting and affronting the court, and upon being commanded silence, he commanded them silence and continued speaking until the court was fain to commit him to the stocks."[22] The Quakers'

[20] Ibid., p. 130.
[21] Morton, *New Englands Memorial* (1669;facsimile ed., Boston, 1903), p.281.
[22] *Q.C.R.*, II, 337.

refusal to take an oath in court had great significance in Massachusetts. They denied any connection between God and the community's power structure. They repudiated the notion of a common and exalted destiny as a Chosen People which was the basic rationale for Massachusetts communalism.

As an effective counterpart to the movement's social and religious criticism, the Quakers offered in their institutions an alternative to the established order, something that the individual heretics of the 1640s could not do. The Society of Friends was one of many mystical sects that proliferated among the English lower classes during the Commonwealth period. Besides a deep dissatisfaction with the Presbyterian and Independent leaders and the programs of the English Revolution, these sectaries shared a common idea that God was in Man and that revelation was not yet complete. They constantly sought fresh light. The Quaker version of this idea was the "inner light," the belief that men could intuit the mind of God and need not submit their religious experience to the discipline of any church institution or official.

The Society of Friends was the most successful of the millenial sects because, paradoxically, they were able to create an institution that perpetuated their essentially anarchic conception of the spiritual life. This was the remarkable Quaker meeting. There was no "hireling ministry" to expound the complexities of Christianity, no formal disciplinary structure. There was only a gathering of the Society in which individuals, on an equal basis, spoke or prayed as the inner light directed. In the words of the noted Quaker historian Rufus Jones: "It gave those who formed the group an extraordinary sense of spiritual dignity and no less important consciousness of responsibility. A person was no longer an atom, a mere individual, to be 'lost' or 'saved' by a system."[23] The Quakers forged a new organicism related to but significantly different from that of their orthodox neighbors. As in orthodoxy, each person in the group was responsible for the others as a possible channel of enlightenment. The difference was the lack of an overt hierarchy, the absence of open judgment of the status and value of individuals within the Quaker system.

Being aware of the inner light and becoming members of a new society gave individual Quakers a new identity. They were freed of the burden of Original Sin and of concern over the opinions of neighbors and officers. Like the Puritans of the 1630s, the Quakers developed a sense of participating personally in a cosmic drama whose end was the Kingdom of God. The movement, tied

---

[23]Jones, *The Quakers in the American Colonies* (New York, 1966), p. xix; Erikson, p. 108.

together by "divinely sent messengers," provided a sense of belonging to a community that transcended the boundaries of the town and the individual Quaker meeting. The Quakers formed a spiritual community that was not only critical of the established order but also in competition with it.

Since Quakerism offered both a critique of and an alternative to orthodox society that contained strong millenial overtones, it is not surprising that orthodox spokesmen saw Quakerism as "that pernicious sect . . . whose opinions are a composition of many errors, and whose practices tend greatly to the disturbance both of church and state." The Salem leadership, especially the local Essex faction men, Hathorne and Batter, felt threatened. These men were the main architects and chief beneficiaries of the adjustments of the 1640s that preserved Salem's elan after the outbreak of the English Civil War. Unlike the merchants, whose status rested securely on economic power, their position depended on the traditional values that the Quakers sought to undermine. For their part Quaker missionaries as far away as Barbados pointed particularly to Salem and Plymouth as places where spiritual "seed" could be planted easily. Presumably they had in mind the early strength of Separatism there.[24] Consequently both to the Quakers, whether native or "visitor," and to the traditional leaders of Salem, the town was an ideological battleground.

In July 1656 the first two Quaker missionaries arrived in Boston. Over the next two years the General Court passed a series of laws designed to suppress the movement.[25] Meanwhile the Quaker cell, centered around Nicholas Phelps, made its presence felt in Salem. In June 1657 the selectmen reaffirmed the local law against harboring strangers without consent, affixing a stiff twenty-shilling-per-week penalty. The rule was impossible to enforce in the scattered Farms. On September 20 the Quakers, led by two "visitors," began their campaign by interrupting a church service. Incensed, Edmund Batter grabbed one of the missionaries by the hair and stuffed a glove and a handkerchief into his mouth as a gag. The missionaries were sent to Boston jail according to law. The cycle of provocation and repression had begun.[26]

The Quakers also attempted to use the town's civil institutions. In December 1657 they gathered enough votes to elect a small farmer and tanner from the Farms, Joseph Boyce, to the board of selectmen, the only member of his economic class to attain that position. Although a church member who avoided prosecution

[24] Jones, p. 64.
[25] *Mass. Recs.*, IV, pt. a, 277-78, 308-9, 345-46.
[26] Perley, II, 244-45.

until 1661, Boyce was strongly sympathetic to the Quakers at the time of his election. Two years later there was an election for which the town records give a tabulation.[27] Boyce was again a candidate but was not chosen, having 35 votes, eleven less than the lowest ranked winner, George Corwin. Young Thomas Gardner, whose wife was a Quaker, got 32 votes. Another candidate from the Farms, the merchant-farmer John Porter, was also unsuccessful, although he was not connected with the Quakers. While the mercantile representatives, Corwin, Price, and Browne, held a substantial margin over the Farm-Quaker candidates, the traditional leaders and chief opponents of the Quakers, Hathorne and Batter, enjoyed overwhelming support, 116 votes and 70 votes respectively. The balloting indicates that the political power of Quakers and their sympathizers was insufficient to threaten the influence of any of the town's leaders, with the possible exception of Porter. In fact, rough handling of the Quakers at first enhanced the popularity of Hathorne and Batter. From 1658 to 1660 Salem experienced what Erikson has called "a crime wave." "In the sense that the term is being used here, 'crime wave' refers to a rash of publicity, a moment of excitement and alarms, a feeling that something needs to be done."[28] Batter and Hathorne, the town's magistrates, could only benefit from this consolidation of orthodox opinion.

In turn, the vigorous raids on Quaker meetings and heavy fines strengthened the Quaker movement. The community became increasingly polarized. Having won in 1657, Boyce lost in 1659. Persons who were indifferent were forced to choose sides, and, of course, most chose orthodoxy. But a number of others took the opposite position. As George Bishop, a Quaker publicist, later wrote, "And indeed, these Cruel Proceedings so sunk down into the Hearts of many of Salem, that they withdrew more and more from your public Meetings, though they knew they should suffer; upon which the Court sentence them to pay Five shillings a Week, each that absented, by an Old Law made in 1646."[29] Bishop's account was correct. Thirty-one people were presented to the Quarterly Court during the initial period of prosecution in 1658 and 1659. From 1660 to 1667 thirty-two new persons were presented, usually for nonattendance at church services. Prosecution did not deter those arrested from further offenses. The initial group of offenders averaged 5.3 appearances in court between

[27]*Town Recs.*, I, 231.
[28]P. 69.
[29]Bishop, *New England Judged* . . .(London, 1703), p. 71.

1658 and 1667. The average would have been higher had not ten of the original thirty-one been imprisoned or banished. The second group of converts was almost as persistent, averaging 3.5 appearances. Also, judging from the court records, the movement grew steadily throughout the period. At each session involving Quakers, three to five new faces appeared.[30]

In the face of this persistence the Salem leadership had to choose between more severity or new leniency. An exasperated Hathorne even suggested that some younger Quakers be sold into slavery in the West Indies, but the other judges, including the venerable Endecott, were more temperate. The pressures for leniency were much stronger, especially after 1661 when a banished Salem Quaker, Samuel Shattuck, returned to Boston with a letter from the king demanding cessation of persecution. There were local pressures as well, even before Shattuck's arrival.[31]

As the crime wave psychology dissipated, there developed a sense that persecution was both a failure and a violation of other Puritan values. During 1660 the court began protecting Quaker rights against the orthodox leaders even while prosecuting the same Quakers. In June, it admonished Edmund Batter for calling a woman a "base quaking slut, with diverse other opprobrious and taunting speeches." The next year it returned a colt seized by John Porter to a Quaker farmer. Since attachment of property in order to meet fines was frequent, abuses were common, and these abuses were apparently unpopular.[32] The Quakers played on the accumulating sense that the magistrates were misusing their authority. One woman whose oxen had been seized asked the court why. Hathorne answered, "They will be sold, and the money will go to the poor." She observed that the money would most likely go to Mr. Gedney, in whose tavern the court met. Hathorne was reduced to replying, "Would you have us starve while we sit about your business?"[33]

The orthodox leadership found it difficult to justify persecution. When challenged, an Ipswich magistrate simply replied that since the Quakers could not be assimilated it was the right of the orthodox "to fend them off." George Bishop reproduced the Quaker assault on the Puritans' belief that they were a Chosen People. "But why not [allow Quakers] into your Jurisdiction? Are you entailed thereunto, you and your Heirs forever? How came ye

---

[30] Calculated from *Q.C.R.*, II, III.

[31] *Mass. Recs.*, IV, pt. b, 34; Vernon Loggins, *The Hawthornes: The Story of Seven Generations of an American Family* (New York, 1951), pp. 61-62.

[32] *Q.C.R.*, II, 219-20.

[33] Loggins; pp. 63-64.

so to be; and by what Right? Is it because ye came out of
Old-England? So did these. Is it because ye are English-Men? So
are they. Is it because ye Dissented from the Government
Established, and so fled from the Trial of your Principles? These
stand to their Principles, and through all Sufferings came to you to
Convert thereunto." After this aspersion on Puritan exclusiveness,
Bishop opened the ambiguous question of sovereignty, a painful
issue in the post-Restoration period. "If ye say, We are a People
Independent of ourselves, and so may make Laws within our own
Jurisdiction; then ye are not Dependent on England: If that from
Old England ye have such a Power, then show it." Then, in
reference to the king's letter, he quoted the requirement in the
charter that local law "be not Repugnant to the Laws, Statutes,
and Ordinances of this Realm."[34]

Because of these pressures the cycle of challenge and repression
began to level off during 1661. In February, for example, the
Quakers boldly held their meeting in a house next to the
meetinghouse during services. In August a Quaker challenged the
new minister, John Higginson, at his ordination and was promptly
arrested. But from then on the strategies on both sides became less
provocative. Ear-cropping and jailing became more selective while
fines for absence were continued. The new minister was one of the
architects of the new policy. In 1660, soon after his arrival,
Higginson and the ruling elder petitioned the court for a
suspension of prosecution against fourteen women. Under his
leadership the church began a persistent and patient campaign to
win back "in private discourse" members who had "withdrawn."[35]

It was not that Higginson felt any sympathy for Quakers. In
fact in 1663 he petitioned the General Court "to consider what
course may be taken for the dissolving of the Quaker meetings,
which we have frequent and constant." Characteristically,
Higginson, like the other traditional leaders, was deeply concerned
over the reputation of the town. He feared that "occasion may be
given for others abroad to look upon Salem as a nest of Quakers,
from hence to infect the rest of the country."[36] Yet, despite his
hostility to the sect, Higginson realistically pursued a policy more
likely to lead to reconciliation, albeit on orthodox terms. The
church, after a year of trial, found the strategy promising,
remarking of the withdrawn members "that they were some of
them in a more pliable way than formerly."

[34] Bishop, pp. 37-38.
[35] Perley, II, 262, White, pp. 50-53.
[36] Joseph B. Felt, *The Ecclesiastical History of New England*, 2 vols. (Boston,
1855), II, 306.

Even Hathorne acquiesced in the more lenient approach. He was deeply involved "in private discourse." In court the judges, including Hathorne, were sparing with fines and whippings, even in the face of such declarations as "Higginson is one of Baal's priests, and Major Hathorne was drunk, and I had to lead him home." Gradually the relative leniency calmed Quaker passion. The last spectacular outburst was Deborah Wilson's naked parade through the streets in 1661. Increasingly the Quakers refrained from blasphemy and evangelism and proved themselves economically valuable to the community. For example, Edward Wharton, a "native" Quaker who had "visited" all over coastal New England in the 1650s, used his contacts with spreading Quaker meetings to become a prominent merchant. Soon the growing Anglo-American Quaker trading pattern found one terminus in the port of Salem, increasing the respectability of the Society of Friends.[37]

Despite continued mutual hostility and recrimination, Quakers and the society at large slowly reached an accommodation. By 1667 Quakers were exempt from the church rate, although not from fines for nonattendance. There is evidence that by 1663 the Quarterly Court was occasionally accepting Quaker testimony by affirmation. More significantly there were marriages between prominent Quakers and respectable families of the orthodox society. Although pressure on the Quakers increased periodically after traumatic events like King Philip's War in the mid-1670s, a permanent detente clearly had been achieved by the mid-1660s.[38]

One outcome of the Quaker struggles, besides the permanent division of the town's spiritual life, was an uneasy tolerance of diversity of belief and behavior. With the removal of strict enforcement of Puritan standards, there developed "a new tendency on the part of the settlers to search inside themselves for the meaningful landmarks they needed to identify the boundaries of the New England Way." This new individualistic focus began to undermine another element in the community, the pattern of enforced emulation.[39] Although the mercantile community initially opposed the Quakers, the struggle and its outcome benefited them as much as the Quakers. Merchants, whose essential principles were mobility and economic growth rather than social stability and order, were able to act in ways more conducive to their ends.

After 1660 rising merchants from leading families began avoiding the onerous lower offices while usually accepting higher

[37] Loggins, pp. 64-66; Jones, pp. 103-4; *Q.C.R.*, II, 314.
[38] Perley, II, 289; *Q.C.R.*, II, 109; Erikson, p. 134.
[39] Erikson, p. 136.

posts. In 1665, soon after they became freemen, Eleazer Hathorne and William Browne, merchant sons of two prominent leaders, were elected constables and then "freed" from their posts by the town meeting. The town meeting did more than acquiesce in this rejection of tradition. Two years later young Browne was chosen selectman. Throughout the rest of the century merchant sons of important families became selectmen and deputies without serving on juries or as constables, while newcomers and sons of less prominent townsmen went through the expected apprenticeship. Of the thirty-seven men who became selectmen from 1668 to 1685, twenty-one were sons of former selectmen. Of these only five ever served in lower offices, and three of the five were not merchants. Only four of the sixteen sons who bypassed political apprenticeship were not merchants, and these four were from the Putnam and Porter families. The combination of wealth and a prominent surname had become a substitute for status gained by working through the lower offices.

Many of these people were less inclined toward the communal values of the older generation. Eleazer Hathorne, who married a daughter of George Corwin, studiously avoided all public service and was even fined for habitual absence from church. His younger brother John, also a merchant, aspired to the role played by his father and largely succeeded, becoming a leader of the orthodox, anticommercial party in colonial politics. His dedication to the old values was intense enough to make him one of the two merchant sons of leading families to serve in lesser posts. Hence he was an obvious exception. Yet, as the biographer of the Hathorne family noted, "to the spiritual forces mainly responsible for making the first Hathorne of Salem a man of distinction John Hathorne was wholly a stranger." The new form of leadership was provided by the two Corwin and three Browne brothers, all of whom were of the mercantile faction and lavish in their display of wealth and indifference to the church. Benjamin Browne left a fortune of over £30,000, while his brother William became an Anglican and a councillor under Sir Edmund Andros.[40] Many of the merchants of this generation were modeling their behavior after Restoration England rather than the New England Way.

A number of newcomers who rose to power in Salem after 1660 evinced a similar spirit. Philip English, for example, was an outspoken Anglican. Yet his economic prowess, excellent contacts in England, France, and the Caribbean, and marriage into the

---

[40]Loggins, pp. 84-85, 101-5; Bernard Bailyn, *The New England Merchants in the Seventeenth Century* (paperback ed., New York, 1964), pp. 138-39.

shipbuilding Hollingsworth family made him a power in Salem by the 1670s. The individualistic attitude toward public service even appeared among some of the older merchants. After the death of the ruling elder, the church chose John Browne to take the position, but he "was very loath to assume the responsibility as he was a merchant and mariner trading especially with Virginia."[41] Loosened standards were allowing townsmen, especially merchants, to put their particular calling over their general calling without losing status.

The earlier communal system had been shattered beyond repair; yet there were other men in the leadership of Salem who still treasured many of the traditional aspirations and sought to salvage as much of the badly fragmented system as possible. In this attempt they centered their efforts on the traditional institutions like the church and used the traditional tools like covenants. Necessarily the direction and the product of these efforts was a new order, a new adjustment whose main elements survived far into the next century.

[41] White, p. 58.

Chapter IX

Forging a New Order, 1650-1668

As the transformation of Salem continued, the leadership sought to preserve as much as possible of the covenant standards and institutions. Although remarkably successful in the end, throughout the 1650s they seemed to be fighting a futile rearguard action against the continuing disintegration of the order established in the late 1630s. On the economic front enforcement was sporadic and ineffective. In the Quarterly Court the notion of a just price was rarely enforced. The sumptuary laws were operative for only a couple of years after the General Court passed major legislation on the problem in 1651.

Judging from Erikson's statistics on presentments, the Essex grand jury was more interested in other challenges to Puritan ideals. Even before the Quaker outbreak "crimes against the church" and "Contempt of Authority" together generated more concern than offenses labeled "Persons, Property." Incidents like that involving the former town clerk, Ralph Fogg, in 1650 were either more frequent or more threatening than economic violations. Fogg was presented "for lying in face of open congregation on a Lord's day, slandering the church, and after the meeting was ended, complaining the honored Governor [Endecott] of wrong that he had done him both in church and court, saying that the Governor was the grand jury, and the grand jury, the Governor." From 1656 on, this type of offense contributed even more to the "crime rate," providing around half of the total presentments.[1] The leaders of Salem seem to have believed that the main threat was to their civil and ecclesiastical order.

The church, even after the Quakers split the spiritual unity of the town, remained the ideological citadel that provided the rationale and most of the energy for the formation of renewed religious and political order. Of all social arrangements, ideology is the most resistant to change. Men are reluctant to alter ideas central to their self-identity. Yet in any healthy society in which the dominant ideology is out of phase with the other elements of

---

[1] Kai T. Erikson, *Wayward Puritans: A Study in the Sociology of Deviance* (New York, 1966), p. 175; *Q.C.R.*, I, 185.

the community, ideology gradually adapts. However, as it adapts, spokesmen often use orthodox themes as social criticism and as a definition of and justification for institutional changes designed to meet the altered social situation.[2] Church leaders in Salem, especially after 1660, analyzed the threat and promoted changes in the institutions of church and state to meet the challenge.

The problems Salem faced were hardly unique. At one time or another almost every town in the colony encountered similar difficulties. In fact, after 1650, relating the old symbols and institutions to a new situation constituted a crisis in Massachusetts history. How successful church and political leaders were in adapting is a moot point among historians. Peter Carroll, for example, has said that "anachronistic patterns of thought" provided Puritans "with unsatisfactory answers to basic social questions," while Perry Miller held that the process of adaptation paved the way satisfactorily for acceptance of the eighteenth-century concepts of social compact and natural rights.[3]

For Salem both views have elements of truth. No real solution was found for the permanent collapse of religious unity. Neither the West Countrymen of the Bass River nor many of the people of the Farms were reconciled to the economic and social dominance of the peninsula. The imperatives of commerce continued to play havoc with the communal values of traditional Salem society. Yet the non-Separatist goal of an inclusive, peaceful, and pious community still animated many of the leaders. In pursuit of these goals the leadership undertook bold, innovative reforms within the church and the town's political life. Paradoxical as it may seem, these reforms were based on "anachronistic patterns of thought" that provided a basis for a viable compromise between the secular drives of a commercial and pluralistic society and the traditional non-Separatist ethos.

In this effort doctrine again was an important but secondary issue, subordinated to the goal of inclusiveness. The political and ecclesiastical problem, as always with non-Separatists, was to extend the signs and seals of communal unity without debasing the meaning of those signs. As time and events cooled the utopian zeal of many and as Salem developed into a more pluralistic society, the problem became more difficult. As early as 1652

---

[2] Richard T. LaPiere, *Social Change* (New York, 1965), pp. 293-94, 295-96.

[3] Carroll, *Puritanism and the Wilderness: The Intellectual Significance of the New England Frontier, 1629-1700* (New York, 1969), pp. 128-29; Miller, "Puritan State and Puritan Society," in *Errand into the Wilderness* (paperback ed., New York, 1964), p. 151.

Edward Norris was concerned about the fact that many young adults who were baptized children of original members were not presenting proof of their conversions and, consequently, could not gain admission to the Lord's Supper. Fearing for the continuity of the church, he proposed that their children also be baptized and taken under the discipline of the church. He was suggesting what became the Half-Way Covenant adopted by many New England churches between 1657 and 1662. The Salem church easily accepted the notion that the second-generation parents should retain the partial membership to which their baptism entitled them. They remained under the discipline of the church and, in the language of the times, "owned the covenant." But, despite several meetings, the full communicants could not agree on extending baptism to the third-generation children automatically. It was not until 1665, after a strenuous campaign by John Higginson, that the Salem church fully accepted the idea.[4]

In 1653 Norris and the ruling elder, expressing the old fears of Separatism, got the Salem church to petition the General Court that a "restraint" be put upon the choice of pastors "except upon certain approval." Norris, along with other Massachusetts pastors, believed that transient lay preachers who were beginning to serve frontier churches were a threat to both orthodox doctrine and the standards of an educated ministry. The danger seemed more acute since a number of Baptists, Quakers, and even English Puritans argued that a learned ministry was unnecessary. According to David D. Hall, lay preaching was "an expression of dissent from official practice and increasing formalism."[5] Norris seems to have feared both a diminution and an excess of zeal. But in both cases he was trying to prevent the development of religious bodies too restrictive or too unorthodox to communicate with the community at large. To gain that end he was willing to compromise other basic principles like visible sainthood and congregational autonomy. But in Salem he experienced little success. The full communicants resisted any program that seemed to lower the quality or meaning of membership. Lay preaching continued on the frontiers of the colony.

Although respected, Norris was not among the colony's most

[4] Robert G. Pope, *The Half-Way Covenant: Church Membership in Puritan New England* (Princeton, N.J., 1969), pp. 17-18, 23, 37, 166; Daniel A. White, *New Congregationalism in Its Origin and Purity, Illustrated by the Foundation and Early Records of the First Church of Salem* (Salem, 1861), pp. 49-50.

[5] Sidney Perley, *The History of Salem, Massachusetts*, 3 vols. (Salem, 1924-27), II, 216; Hall, *The Faithful Shepherd: A History of the New England Ministry in the Seventeenth Century* (Chapel Hill, N.C., 1972), pp. 183-84.

notable pastors. John Higginson was. Besides enjoying the prestige of being the son of one of the founding ministers of the Salem church, Higginson had the advantage of an education by Thomas Hooker and a reputation as one of Connecticut's leading divines before he came to Salem. Norris was also plagued by declining health, which became serious just as the Quaker crisis engulfed the town and led to his death in December 1659. Higginson in 1660 was at the height of his mental powers and new to, but not unfamiliar with, the nature and problems of the Salem community.[6] Also, the Quaker episode must have unnerved a number of laymen, removed their complacency, and perhaps encouraged some flexibility.

Almost immediately upon ordination Higginson too started the process of preservation by adaptation. Early in 1661 to mark the new year "the Church and people here assembled in a day of Fasting and prayer." Then Higginson preached "concerning the power of temptation." He discussed "the hour of temptation" of those "who kept the word." He also spoke on "our duty of covenant from Psalm 50:5": "Gather my saints together unto me; those that have made a covenant with me by sacrifice." He was trying to strengthen the sense of communal unity and purpose. Then at "the close of the day the Church covenant was renewed." When news of other disturbing events, such as the Restoration, reached the town, the pattern of covenant renewal was repeated.[7]

The renewing of the 1636 covenant was a reaffirmation of the traditional values. But a new clause was included in 1661: "By the help of Christ we would endeavor to take heed and beware of the leaven of the doctrine of the Quakers." This was Salem's first doctrinal statement, albeit a negative one. It was also an exclusionist and defensive remark, now embedded in the town's most important document, explicitly recognizing the split in the community. At the same time Higginson and the church were also declaring an evangelical crusade. They vowed in the church record "to seek the Lord for his presence with us in carrying on Church work, and for his mercy in reducing those that go astray." In general this policy was the traditional means of eliminating heresy, by isolating and branding the heretics and then working for their surrender.

The goal was still the extension of the community of belief. Reaffirming the covenant might encourage the orthodox, and the

---

[6] S. E. Baldwin, "Sketch of the Life of Rev. John Higginson," *Proceedings of the Massachusetts Historical Society,* 3d ser., 34 (1902): 505-7, 512.

[7] White, pp. 48, 57.

new clause on Quaker doctrine might warn the uncertain. But only evangelism could extend the membership and guarantee the church a continued role as Salem's ideological core. Higginson and most of the ministers of the Bay understood that the Half-Way Covenant and related steps would be necessary. It was more difficult for the laity to see the need. Higginson finally won the point in 1665, basically by threatening to resign. Even so, acceptance was not unanimous. Both Hathorne and ruling elder Henry Bartholomew attended the Half-Way Synod of 1662 and, in disagreement with their pastor, opposed "innovations." Hathorne remained dubious about the idea until his death.[8] Higginson, however, soon pushed through a more sweeping and controversial innovation.

An influential merchant and son of a full communicant, Batholomew Gedney, who had owned the covenant to get his children baptized, requested admission to the Lord's Supper. "This being considered of and spoken to by the Pastor and several of the brethren, it was in the issue consented unto with respect to himself, though with respect unto others it was left unto further consideration."[9] Gedney's admission, although judged an exception, prepared the way for less prestigious individuals. Gedney and subsequent new communicants who had been baptized in their youth met three requirements: a moral life, a confession of faith, and acceptance of the covenant. They no longer had to defend their conversion publicly. Acceptance of this process marked a return to the criteria of the implicit covenant of the early 1630s.

With this policy the Salem church was not adopting open communion, but it was moving in a definitely inclusive direction. Baptisms increased dramatically. In the decade preceding adoption of the Half-Way Covenant an average of fifteen children a year were baptized. After 1665 Higginson averaged more than thirty-six annually. Although membership increased after Gedney's entry, the trend was not impressive. From 1655 to 1660 only twelve new members were admitted; Higginson averaged seven new members annually before 1665. In the year after Gedney's admission there were twenty-four new communicants, but the average admission for the next five years fell to six. The laity was unwilling to go far beyond orthodoxy. Moreover, the number of children of original members who could be admitted was limited. Recognizing the problem in 1678, the church began extending baptism to children of families outside of the covenant.[10]

[8] Pope, pp. 52-53, 65-66; White, pp. 53-54.

[9] White, p. 67; Pope, pp. 143-47.

[10] Edmund S. Morgan, *Visible Saints: The History of a Puritan Idea* (New York, 1963), pp. 142-52; Pope, pp. 146-47, 247-48.

The need for conversions, the confusion over dogma brought on by Quakerism, and the evangelical tone of the church under Higginson led to a new emphasis on doctrine, but as an evangelical rather than an exclusionary device. In 1665, soon after Gedney's admission, Higginson wrote *A Direction for a Public Profession*, which was to serve as a confession of faith and a restatement of the covenant.[11] "In the Church Assembly, after private Examination by the Elders," persons owning the covenant were to repeat the relevant sections. In the introduction Higginson described the sections to be read aloud as "being the same for Substance which was propounded to, and agreed upon by the Church of Salem at their beginning," that is, the 1629 covenant. Higginson emphasized the continuity in the church's history because the *Direction* took the "substance" of the original covenant and elaborated it in an explicit, detailed confession of faith containing seven clauses giving the orthodox view on all the basic points of Christianity. Realizing how unusual a step this exposition was, Higginson explained: "The Genuine use of a Confession of Faith is, that under the same Form of Words they express the substance of the same common Salvation or unity of their Faith. Accordingly it is to be looked upon as a fit means, whereby to express that their Common Faith and Salvation, and not to be made use of as an imposition upon any."

The use of the confession was an adjustment to pluralism, a short, easily remembered statement that, like a catechism, had educational or evangelical uses. Such a device for adults had hardly been necessary during the 1630s and 1640s. Following the confession was a restatement of the covenant. The first part explicitly stressed the Covenant of Grace, another rarity for Salem. The second contained the member's covenant with the church "to continue steadfastly in fellowship with it." As might be expected after the Quaker episode, the statement emphasized the role of "Order Discipline" and the guidance and oversight of ministers and elders in the life of the individual.

In a remarkable election sermon, *The Cause of God and His People in New England*, printed in 1663, Higginson delivered a spirited rationale for the reforms he was implementing at Salem.[12] Like any good call to reform, the sermon contained a critique as well as an outline for action. The highly critical character of the sermon led Perry Miller to regard Higginson as one the first

---

[11] Williston Walker, *The Creeds and Platforms of Congregationalism* (1893; rept. Boston, 1960), pp. 119-20.

[12] Cambridge, Mass., 1663.

practitioners of the jeremiad.[13] The starting point for both criticism and reform was the covenant. As Higginson put it, "The Cause of God is the cause of his Covenant."

After stressing the necessity of covenant with God because of the weakness of men, Higginson began his social criticism by explaining what the "Cause" is not. "It is 1. Not the getting of the World's goods. 2. Not the Separation from other churches. 3. Not a toleration of all Religions." The values engendered by commercial expansion headed his list. He observed that "when the Lord stirred up the spirits of so many of his people to come over into this wilderness, it was not for worldly wealth, or a better livelihood for the outward man." Ironically, his father, Francis Higginson, had appealed for settlers on both spiritual and material grounds. But to carry his point the son had to help perpetuate a myth that exaggerated the religious motives of the first settlers. John Higginson was not questioning the desirability of economic development any more than his father had; he was objecting to its ethos. He was caught in the same intellectual dilemma that plagued other noncommercial leaders. To resolve it, he insisted on the priority of non-Separatist ideals, thereby offering an alternative and a challenge to the commercial ethos.

In the other two points on his list Higginson reiterated the customary warnings against toleration and Separatism. Then he went on to an affirmation of the non-Separatist emphasis on adaptability. He noted that the settlers had come "into this wilderness, with true desires and endeavors after a more full Reformation according to God's word." It was on this basis that he stated his definition of the imperatives within the covenant. This conception was the impulse behind reform efforts. He began the second half of his sermon with an outline of the "Cause." "It is 1. Reformation of Religion according to God's word. 2. A Progress in that Reformation. 3. The Union of Reformers." Under the second two headings Higginson stressed the importance of two reforms that he and other clerics had backed in the Half-Way Synod. "That Baptism be administered to the Children of Church Members who have right thereunto. And that the Communion of Churches be better improved amongst us. These are things we have been defective in, and therefore should be reformed in a practical way."

Higginson's suggestions on baptism were designed to strengthen the individual church's place within its town. His suggestions on

[13]Miller, *The New England Mind: From Colony to Province* (Cambridge, Mass., 1953), p. 36.

improving the "Communion of Churches" in turn would increase the influence of a unified church throughout the colony. To avoid "dividing names and parties amongst us," he advocated "that one Catechism, one confession of Faith, and one Covenant were agreed upon and used in the several churches as a means of consent." He saw this semipresbyterian method as a means to the higher end of an ideal community. More precise definition could combat the dangers of pluralism. His suggestion that "there should be a frequent use of councils amongst us, to inquire after the mind of God and his word" was a further move toward a unified, inclusive, evangelical church order. The doctrinal and ecclesiastical elements were a manifestation of the early explicit covenants, while, paradoxically, the individual admission requirements were drifting toward the implicit standards of the early 1630s.

Being a Puritan divine, Higginson knew that success rested with God. Thus the only way to "sanctify the Lord himself as the maintainer of this Cause" was to convince him of the sincerity of his people. Besides "Humble Prayer," "well-doing" was the most effective means. Under this rubric he justified the pragmatic temperament that had led him and other reformers to urge tampering with traditional beliefs in the interests of a higher good. "In the question of what is best, we are not only to consider what is best in itself, but what is best with reference to all the circumstances of a case."

Then he stated the non-Separatist standards, peace and good order, by which actions were to be judged. It was imperative to shun "whatever tends to faction, studying to be quiet, and every one to do their own work." Even though he was suggesting a greater emphasis on doctrinal unity, Higginson appended the traditional non-Separatist admonishment that among those "who profess the same cause, none should speak of themselves as if they were the Godly party and eminently Saints and faithful with despising others, nothing is more offensive amongst Christians, then to confine Religion to some singular Opinion, as if Religion did mainly Center there."

Besides being a mild rebuke to the opponents of the Half-Way Covenant, this statement reflected the inclusive temperament that helped preserve an effective church in Salem. Yet the danger was that "forbearance" might shade into "toleration," which to Higginson meant the subversion of the "Cause." In theory he applied the rule of forbearance only to those who shared the mission. "In one word; union is to be endeavored because the truth is but one, and forbearance is to be used because of the weakness of men, which yet is as far from a toleration of a false

Religion, as is the East is from the West." In practice the line was not so clear. Quakers were subjected to discrimination and sporadic persecution but, in effect, they were tolerated after 1663.

Higginson was bent upon reinvigorating the church and preserving the non-Separatist ethos. To be successful he was willing to compromise parts of the tradition. The general direction was toward a more inclusive church and a more defined system of belief. The effort he initiated continued throughout the rest of the century. The Salem church and its satellite churches of Beverly and Marblehead remained innovative in the attempt to preserve and adapt the New England Way.

The same drive toward a renewed inclusiveness and a more precise definition of the rules appeared in Salem's political life. The problem was participation, or at least communication, within the town over political matters. From 1647 to 1658, according to colonial law, freemen determined the degree of voting by inhabitants in town affairs. There is evidence of a gradually developing exclusiveness throughout most of the Bay, perhaps originating in the same lay conservatism that at first frustrated religious reformers.[14] In Salem in the early 1650s the distinction between freemen's meetings for colonial elections and the town meetings for local business was maintained, implying some difference in personnel. Yet in 1658 the deputies were chosen in town meeting. If Salem was complying with the law that restricted such voting to freemen, then it seems that the voters at that meeting were all freemen.[15]

There were also signs of trouble within the Salem town meeting. In 1654 it ordered fines reinstated for "all those persons that shall not seasonably attend town meetings either by their persons or proxies." In 1659 even the three constables were fined "for not appearing at meeting and not making return of their warrants."[16] By the late 1650s the town meeting was not as powerful as it had been. The problem seems to have been that the town's leadership, especially some of the selectmen, were overmanipulating the town meeting. In their sessions the selectmen were not only fixing the time of the town meeting but also the agenda. Scattered references in the town record indicate that some leaders, most obviously Edmund Batter, functioned as a caucus to present slates of officers and new statutes to be ratified by the town meeting.[17] As long as a

[14] Robert Emmet Wall, Jr., "The Decline of the Massachusetts Franchise, 1647-1666," *Journal of American History* 59 (1972): 303-10.

[15] *Town Recs.*, I, 183, 215.

[16] Ibid., I, 179, 223-24.

[17] Ibid., I, 216, 228, 231-32, II, 14, 22, 43.

consensus governed the town's politics, the arrangement did ¦ cause any serious difficulties. But after 1660 political as well as religious agreement became increasingly difficult to gain.

Issues arose that proved divisive. On occasion the town's leadership, as well as the populace, split passionately. An observer in Boston in 1668 described the people as "savagely factious," a situation that pertained in Salem too.[18] One result of the contentiousness in Salem was a resurgent town meeting that imposed a more defined and limited role on the selectmen. Another outcome was a pioneering suggestion that full rights be granted to some men outside of the church.

One sensitive barometer to these developments was the career of William Hathorne. A clever politician and a dedicated traditional leader, Hathorne found it almost impossible during much of the 1650s and 1660s to find a course that satisfied the ever more diverse desires of his constituency, and challenges to his leadership appeared. As a deputy in 1650-54 he temporarily undercut his strength in the General Court and within the Essex faction by advocating positions favored by the commercial sectors of the colony. The stands he took may explain why he was not chosen Speaker between 1651 and 1657.

The power of the Essex faction depended upon the countryside's suspicion of commercial Boston. As the Salem economy was transformed, giving local merchants more influence, Hathorne found it difficult to maintain his and Salem's power. In 1650 and 1651 he and Henry Bartholomew were two of only six deputies to oppose the burning of a book deemed heretical by many ministers and written by William Pynchon, a merchant and political leader of Springfield. By this time the merchants, in the minds of many freemen, were too closely identified with the principle of toleration. Hathorne also opposed the endorsement of a confession of faith and a book of discipline by the General Court. Hathorne and Bartholomew, along with thirteen other deputies, objected to any sanctions against the Malden church for calling a minister without the consent of the court.[19]

Although all three positions could be defended on orthodox grounds, Hathorne was flying in the face of those who were seeking more discipline and uniformity. His own pastor and church petitioned a couple of years later against allowing churches to choose ministers without consent. As a commissioner to the United Colonies, Hathorne again showed independence from his

---

[18] Erikson, p. 139.

[19] *Mass., Recs.*, II, 215, 240, 250; Bernard Bailyn, *The New England Merchants in the Seventeenth Century* (paperback ed., New York, 1964), pp. 108-9.

former allies. Indian discontent and the First Anglo-Dutch War precipitated a crisis within the confederation. He disregarded his instructions from the General Court and voted with the commissioners from the other colonies for war. The lone dissenter was another Essex man, Simon Bradstreet. Although supported this time by the Reverend Mr. Norris, Hathorne lost his seat to a new faction leader from Ipswich, Daniel Denison, and did not serve on the commission again until 1673. The New England merchants hoped to damage the massive Dutch commercial system, but the General Court was loath to war against fellow Calvinists. Massachusetts refused to be bound by Hathorne's vote, precipitating a constitutional crisis from which the confederation did not recover for many years.[20] Even his fellow townsmen were displeased by Hathorne's vote for between 1654 and 1656 he was neither a deputy nor selectman.

Hathorne had gone beyond the conservative wing of his constituency in his efforts to further the commercial interests. By his stance during the Quaker crisis, he rebuilt his political position, once again becoming Speaker in 1657. By 1662 he even augmented his colonywide influence when he was elected assistant, a position he held until 1679. Hathorne's troubles during the 1650s reveal a divided Salem, but one in which the greatest strength rested with the freemen antagonistic to the commercial ethos and to any sort of religious disunity. In the disputes of the 1660s Hathorne again played a major and controversial role, forced once again to choose between commercial and traditional interests. This time he was identified with the conservative church members.

Hathorne's troubles in the 1660s had their roots in the confusion over finding a proper response to Restoration policy. He belonged to that group least willing to compromise Massachusetts's independence. Although Salem had few royalists, many of its leaders, including John Higginson, favored a more moderate course than that advocated by Hathorne. The arrival of royal commissioners in 1664 to investigate the colonies made the issue inescapable. While the officials were still in the colony, Hathorne attacked them and their mission in a speech before the Salem militia, armed and assembled near the meetinghouse. Governor Endecott had to request that the General Court relieve Hathorne of his command and order him to

[20]Perley, II, 216; Harry M. Ward, *The United Colonies of New England, 1643-1690* (New York, 1961), pp. 172-73, 182.

compose a public apology.[21] Endecott died soon after the commissioners left in 1665, and Richard Bellingham became governor. Even though his opinions differed little from Hathorne's, Bellingham had the sense to quell much of the rebellious talk fostered by intransigents like Hathorne.

In 1666 a letter from the Crown arrived detailing the commissioners' charges against the colony and demanding that "four or five persons . . . attend upon His Majesty, whereof Mr. Richard Bellingham and Major William Hathorne are to be two, both of which His Majesty commands upon their allegiance to attend." Both men refused. The deputies, most of whom came from rural towns, strongly supported the decision. Yet many inhabitants of the seacoast towns, including Salem, urged compliance. The Salem petition was signed by thirty-three men, including Edmund Batter and most of the town's leading merchants. Instead the deputies implemented a policy of delay by sending masts for the Royal Navy and a flattering letter. When the petitions were debated and the signers were accused of maligning the General Court, both Salem deputies, George Corwin and William Browne, and some other former allies of Hathorne rose to their defense.[22]

Hathorne, now with a colonial rather than a merely local consituency, survived his alienation of both the merchants and the more compromise-minded traditional leaders of Salem and vicinity. He still commanded substantial support among the town's church members, evinced in his continual election as a selectman from 1661 to 1668 and his influence within the church. However, the consensus politics of the 1640s was no longer possible in the 1660s. The community was too pluralistic for any one political leader to represent it through any consistent program. The Essex faction in Salem broke into its constituent parts, Batter aligning with the merchants and Hathorne with the conservative laymen, who were becoming a minority in Salem but remained a majority in the colony at large.

A new pattern of consensus had to be found. Politics in the 1640s had been based upon a general agreement among the leaders to further the town's commerce and political power while preseving the religious settlement of the late 1630s. The mass of

---

[21] Vernon Loggins, *The Hawthornes: The Story of Seven Generations of an American Family* (New York, 1951), pp. 71-73; Paul R. Lucas, "Colony or Commonwealth: Massachusetts Bay, 1661-1666," *William and Mary Quarterly*, 3d ser., 24 (1967): 99-107.

[22] James Duncan Phillips, *Salem in the Seventeenth Century* (Boston, 1933), p. 208; Bailyn, pp. 123-25, 132.

people accepted the system. In the 1650s and 1660s the leadership could not agree on which part to emphasize, and significant blocks of the population, mainly West Countrymen and residents of the Farms, withdrew their consent.

Serious attempts to solve the political problem did not begin until 1664, after Higginson had started reform successfully within the church. Using the same rationale as Higginson in his election sermon, the freemen of Salem in their meeting of January 1664 chose Batter and Bartholomew as deputies and instructed them to suggest to the General Court a broadening of the colonywide political community by including "some that are not members of particular Churches."[23] On the surface the freemen were asking for a diminution of their own power, but actually they were advocating a strengthening of the consensual basis of colonial politics on the same pattern as had existed within the towns since 1647.

The problem of communication and participation in politics concerned them as much as it did in church affairs. A recent historian has calculated that the percentage of freemen in the adult male population of the colony dropped from 40 to 28 percent between 1647 and 1666. In Salem the decline was from 42 to 28 percent. [24] The Salem freemen hoped that broadening the prereguisites would align influential men, usually merchants who had not joined the church, with the colonial government and prevent them from appealing instead to English authority. It was no accident that the two men chosen to carry this suggestion were members of the church and leaders whose connections with both the mercantile and traditional freemen interests were good. The instruction was an attempt to bridge the gap before it widened even more.

In church reform the drive for inclusiveness was paralleled by a drive toward more explicit statements of belief. In Salem politics the movement took the form of limiting the power of the selectmen. Problems in land use and common rights precipitated the crisis. The selectmen had been granting a great deal of land for houses after 1660 even though, according to colonial law, no new "dwelling place shall be admitted to the privilege of common-age . . . but such as already are in being or hereafter shall be erected by the consent of the town." The selectmen gave that consent to pasturage since they had the power "to act in all prudential affairs." Also, in the interests of regulation the

---

[23] *Town Recs.,* II, 37.
[24] Wall, p. 304.

selectmen proposed and the town meeting accepted the practice of granting exclusive wharfage rights and providing particular places for the repair of vessels. Inevitably some townspeople resented these actions.[25] At last, after a bitter controversy over whether a privately owned mill could dam the South River and over land grants in the Farms, the town meeting in 1665 took away the selectmen's power to dispose of land. This stringent limitation was enforced for several decades.[26]

The town meeting had hit upon a solution to the problem of conflicting interests. The majority of the men who comprised the town meeting that curbed the board were farmers and artisans. Their interests were largely agricultural and their non-Separatist, communal spirit encouraged suspicion of the commercial ethos. By limiting the board's power in the areas that concerned them most deeply, they could safely continue to elect Salem's leading merchants as selectmen, for as the town developed it was clear to the townsmen the merchants could best cope with the commercial world they were creating. It behooved the town to give them political power commensurate with their social and economic influence, as long as that authority was carefully defined.

In 1668, the year of the separation of Beverly, their suspicions took the form of a set of instructions to the selectmen, voted in the election town meeting.[27] The order had five clauses. The first admonished the selectmen to "be careful to observe all those things that are enjoined by the Country Laws that so the Town may not suffer for your neglect therein." The town recently had been fined for not maintaining a proper watch. Then once again they were ordered to "neither give, sell or exchange any land belonging to the Town." The next two clauses concerned town rates and finances, matters close to the heart of the masses of townsmen. The town meeting proceeded to take away the selectmen's taxing power. "You shall raise no money nor town rate without the vote of the town." The second financial clause forbade the selectmen to "engage the Town so as to bring them into debt except in case of necessity of the poor etc. wherein we desire God to encourage you." The exception again revealed the communal ethos of the town meeting and the suspicion that some selectmen no longer shared it so deeply. The last section was a poignant commentary on the distance between the communal agricultural spirit and the commercial ethos of the selectmen:

---

[25] *Town Recs.*, I, 224; *Mass. Recs.*, IV, pt. b, 417.
[26] Phillips, pp. 210-12; *Town Recs.*, II, 47, 54-57, 68, 77.
[27] *Town Recs.*, II, 88-89.

lesire you to take care of the herd and Bulls." It was just the
f task that George Corwin, for example, probably neglected.
se instructions differed from those usually given by the
town meeting, such as those to deputies. The usual instructions
concerned specific matters, like the suggestion of extending the
suffrage. These instructions to the selectmen were meant to be
permanent. They were a form of covenant, indeed a written
constitution, that carefully delimited the exercise of power by an
institution that increasingly represented only one interest. All the
efforts to resolve the political problem did not succeed; the
General Court did not pass the extension of the colonial ballot to
selected nonfreemen. But the limitations on the selectmen were a
successful adjustment to local diversity.

More importantly, this reform, like Higginson's efforts, was an
explicit recognition of conflicting interests. In Salem's religious
life, standing outside the dominant order was still not fully
respectable, even though tolerable. Reforms in the church were
designed to include outsiders within the system with minimal
sacrifice of its values. Unity was still the ideal; adaptation is for
sacred institutions a slow process. The changes in the political
order were much more sweeping. The political reforms involved
the acceptance of equally respectable but nonetheless varying
interests, and the political institutions were adapted to give
legitimate expression to those interests within their own realms. In
Salem politics, unlike the town's religious life, the ideal of
unanimity was abandoned in favor of a rudimentary federalism, a
frank acceptance of the consequences of pluralism. With this
decision Salem surrendered the hope of being a Puritan utopia in
which all aspects of life were coordinated toward spiritual ends.
Salem was passing from a Puritan community to a Yankee town, a
transition every New England town made. It was Salem's fate to
cross that line earlier than most.

Chapter X

Commercial Salem, 1668-1685

Although the tensions within Salem were not resolved, a new economic and social structure, based more fully on commerce, had emerged by 1668. The townsmen had begun to adapt their religious and civil institutions to the new realities. In 1683 the General Court, reacting to pressure to conform to the Navigation Acts, officially confirmed the town's important role in the Massachusetts's economy by declaring Boston and Salem the only legal ports of entry for foreign goods.[1] It was in this approximate period, 1668 to 1685, that Salem exercised its greatest independent commercial power. After 1685 the town fell increasingly under the economic sway of its powerful rival, Boston. In 1683 the town's assessors compiled the only extant country tax rate list for Salem before the Glorious Revolution of 1689.[2] Since the country rate was a roughly graduated property tax, use of the list, together with other records, makes possible an economic and social portrait of Salem on the eve of the loss of Massachusetts's charter in 1684.

The list is not a reliable measure of absolute wealth nor of population since certain classes of people and property were exempt. The basic assessment paid by 43 percent of Salem's taxpayers on this list was two shillings. The estate of a recently deceased carpenter probated at just over £160 paid that amount, so that a tax of two shillings seems to indicate a reasonably comfortable living. Further up the scale, a mariner died in 1683 and left an estate of about £1,100 to his only surviving son, who was taxed at eight shillings. The higher rates, above five shillings, signified relative affluence.

This list cannot indicate the degree of poverty since a tax list is not a census of the poor. In 1682 the town raised £65 "for the relief of the poor." At the town's general level of support, £5 per year a head, this sum would have aided some thirteen people, a

---

[1] James Duncan Phillips, *Salem in the Seventeenth Century* (Boston, 1933), pp. 282-83.

[2] Sidney Perley, *The History of Salem, Massachusetts*, 3 vols (Salem, 1924-27), III, 419-21. The list gives only name, tax, and ward.

figure which accords with the twelve names of those listed as receiving relief in the town record. Yet thirteen added to the thirty-one families (see table 16) for whatever total of persons who were on relief or whose taxes were completely abated would not be an adequate measure of all the poor since the town probably helped only acknowledged residents, "the poor amongst us." However, there probably was not much poverty among "strangers" because Salem was still stringently enforcing the law against "entertaining" transients who might become public charges.[3]

The list does provide a useful index of relative economic position among the taxpayers of Salem. There were 541 men rated in 1683 who were taxed from zero to sixty-six shillings. Table 16 gives the distribution of the rate. Nearly three-quarters paid from two to four shillings. Just as in the period before the economic transformation of the town, Salem was essentially a society of "the middling sort."

Table 16. 1683 Assessment

Rate	Taxpayers		
(Shillings)	No.		%
0	31		6
1 - 1/8	39		7
2	238		44
2/6 - 4	159		30
5+	74		13

Source: "Appendix: Tax Lists" in Sidney J. Perley, *The History of Salem, Massachusetts*, 3 vols. (Salem, 1924-27), III, 419-21.

Dividing the ratepayers by occupation and comparing the total in each category with the number who paid five shillings or more, those of the economic elite, reveals much about Salem's commercial economy (table 17). The merchants were by far the wealthiest class. Their average tax was better than triple the community average. Although only 6 percent of the taxpayers, they comprised nearly a third of the elite. Even this measure probably understates their economic position, for mercantile property was more difficult to assess and easier to conceal than other property. The clustering of the average taxes of the other more numerous classes at two to three shillings is another graphic indication of the merchants' relative wealth.

Even though many townsmen were still part-time farmers, the fact that both the known mariners and artisans outnumbered the

[3] *Town Recs.*, III, 68, 88, 100-101.

Table 17. Occupations and relative economic standing of taxpayers, 1683

| Occupation | No. | % | Average tax | Elite paying 5s.+ | |
				No.	%
Merchant	32	6	9.1	23	72
Mariner	122	23	2.7	12	10
Artisan	150	28	2.6	15	10
Farmer	114	20	3.2	24	21
Unknown	123	23	1.9	0	0
Total	541		2.8	74	13

Source: Sidney J. Perley, *The History of Salem, Massachusetts*, 3 vols. (Salem, 1924-27), "Appendix: Tax Lists," III, 419-22, and biographical notes throughout the three volumes.

full-time farmers is indicative of Salem's commercial identity. Yet equally obvious is the continued strength of the agricultural sector of the economy. One farmer out of five was among the elite taxpayers, compared to only one of ten among the artisans and mariners. The wealthiest farmers were from the long-established families of the Farms, the most prominent being the Porters and Putnams, whose holdings dated from the 1640s.

Table 18. Occupations of taxpayers by ward, 1683

Ward	Merchant	Mariner	Artisan	Farmer	Unknown	Total
Pope	—	2	13	59	9	83
Howard	—	4	14	38	11	67
Lambert	9	12	33	6	13	73
Herst	12	19	31	6	16	84
Phelps	5	38	38	2	16	99
English	6	57	21	3	58	145

Source: Sidney J. Perley, *The History of Salem, Massachusetts*, 3 vols. (Salem, 1924-27), "Appendix: Tax Lists," III, 419-22, and biographical notes in all vols.

Table 18, showing the taxpayers' occupations by ward, provides eloquent testimony about the geographic as well as economic divisions of Salem in 1683. In 1683 the town was divided into six wards. There were two predominantly agricultural wards, Salem Village, located in the northerly portion of the township, whose constable was Joseph Pope, and the rest of the Farms and the Ryal Side under Nathaniel Howard. There were four wards covering the residents of the peninsula and the uninhabited lots in the North and South Fields. John Lambert was constable for the north-westerly base of the peninsula and the North Field while William Herst covered the southwest portion and the South Field. Christopher Phelp's ward was on the lower peninsula, and Philip English's ward, also on the lower peninsula, covered the banks of the South River from the Point of Rocks out to the Neck. In table 18 the wards are ranked from the Village down through the Farms and onto the peninsula. The degree of economic specialization by regions is striking.

In 1650 only about half the population on the peninsula. That was no longer the case in 1683. As commerce expanded, so did the population of the peninsula. The taxpayers of English's ward alone nearly equaled the combined total from the two agriculatural wards. Another sign of the relative decline of agriculture is that there were only twelve full-time farmers in the wards covering the old open fields. English's portion of the bustling waterfront contained not only about half the town's known mariners but also nearly half of the men of unknown occupation. The is group of unknown occupation must have supplied much of the unskilled labor—carpenters' assistants, dockworkers, occasional mariners—necessary to maintain extensive commerce. These men were predictably more transient. While almost half the taxpayers on English's list reappeared in the same ward in the 1689 rate (table 19), only a third of the taxpayers of uncertain occupation showed up again. Another sign of instability unique to this portion of the

Table 19. Ward growth and stability, 1683-89

Ward	No. of taxpayers		No. of taxpayers on	% of taxpayers
	1683	1689	both 1683 & 1689 lists	on both lists
Pope	83	109	65	78
Howard	67	88	50	75
Lambert	73	76	47	64
Herst	84	94	54	64
Phelps	99	86	73	74
English	145	124	70	48

Sources: for 1683 list, Sidney J. Perley, *The History of Salem, Massachusetts*, 3 vols. (Salem, 1924-27), "Appendix: Tax Lists," III, 419-22, and biographical notes in all vols.; for 1689, Salem Book of Taxes from 1689 to 1724, pp. 2-7, Essex Institute, Salem, Mass.

peninsula was its relatively few resident artisans. Besides being the site of wharves and warehouses, this populous section of the water-front served another highly specialized function, providing housing for many of the transient unskilled workers and mariners. Most of the artisans and merchants who built and directed the town's commerce lived elsewhere on the peninsula. The ward contained the lowest percentage of men paying five or more shillings and the highest percentage of those paying zero, and consequently it paid the lowest average rate in Salem (table 20). The waterfront

Table 20. Ward taxpayers, 1683

Ward	No.	Average tax (in s.)	Elite paying 5s.		Church members		Average births*
			No.	%	No.	%	
Pope	83	3.1	15	18	23	28	5.0
Howard	67	2.8	5	7	13	18	5.0
Lambert	73	3.6	11	15	14	19	3.7
Herst	84	3.5	22	26	15	18	4.2
Phelps	99	2.8	13	13	13	13	3.7
English	145	2.5	8	6	16	11	3.5

Sources: Genealogical data from Sidney J. Perley, *The History of Salem, Massachusetts*, 3 vols. (Salem, 1924-27), I-III; church membership calculated from James Duncan Phillips, *Salem in the Seventeenth Century* (Boston, 1933), for the period through 1650 and from the Records of the First Church, Essex Institute, Salem, Mass. for the later years.
*Births in 366 taxpayer families were known.

seems to have played a crucial economic role in the town without being an integral part of its political or religious life. English's ward, despite its large population, supplied only two of the twenty-eight selectmen who served from 1668 to 1683 and who were alive in 1683 (table 21). Only 11 percent of the taxpayers

Table 21. Selectmen by ward and occupation, 1668-83

Ward	Merchant	Mariner	Artisan	Farmer	Total
Pope	—	—	—	4	4
Howard	—	—	1	2	3
Lambert	5	1	1	—	7
Herst	4	—	2	1	7
Phelps	3	1	1	—	5
English	2	—	—	—	2

Sources: Sidney J. Perley, *The History of Salem, Massachusetts*, 3 vols. (Salem, 1924-27), II, 401, III, 419-22, and biographical notes throughout; James Duncan Phillips, *Salem in the Seventeenth Century* (Boston, 1933), 361-62.

joined the church. The other waterfront ward, Phelp's, had the next fewest church members, 13 percent. The other two peninsula wards had nearly 20 percent.

Herst's and Lambert's wards, paying the highest average assessment in the town and containing most of the merchants, were the heart of commercial Salem. Here lived the bulk of the political and mercantile elite. A full quarter of the taxpayers on Herst's list, for example, paid five shillings or more (see table 20). In these wards George Corwin and his two sons, both merchants and political powers in their own rights, were taxed. The merchant John Hathorne, who inherited his father's political role as well as much of his property, lived in Herst's section. Phelps's ward had a substantial share in this power, although the area was transitional in both geography and social structure. Like English's ward, about a third of its taxpayers were mariners, but like the other two peninsula wards, another third were artisans. Over seventy percent of Phelps's 1683 taxpayers appeared again in the same ward in 1689 (see table 19). The merchants of the ward were longtime residents of Salem, as established as their peers on Lambert's and Herst's lists. Political and economic power appeared among Phelps's people, therefore, but not to the same degree (see table 21). In politics, experience usually enhances power. By 1683 the selectmen of the merchant-artisan wards had averaged eight years in the office. Among the selectmen in Phelps's artisan-mariner ward the average was four years. In the agricultural section and in English's ward the average was just over two years.

Political and economic power in Salem was now centered socially in the merchant class and geographically on the peninsula. Nearly half the town's merchants had served as selectmen by 1683. But that power was hardly absolute. As shown in the previous chapter, the selectmen were empowered to handle the financial business of the town but not to grant land or to determine policy "for the relief of the poor" without specific authorization from the town meeting.[4] The farmers, despite their relative decline in numbers and influence, still maintained a strong representation on the board.

Salem was, as it had been for decades, a complex and divided community. In the 1683 voting for selectmen, the townsmen once again showed that gaining and maintaining political power in Salem was not automatic.[5] With about seventy men casting ballots, eighteen names were placed in nomination for the seven posts. No candidate got less than ten votes except one man whose name was withdrawn before it could be completely written in the record. Although nearly all were of the elite, the names ran the gamut of occupations and wards. They ranged in age from thrity-five to seventy-five. They must have all been well known to the voters, for they had all been in the town at least twenty years. Yet the decision was not easy. Only two votes separated the lowest ranked winner from the highest ranked loser. That loser with thirty-three votes was Edmund Batter. Other losers were

----

[4] Ibid., III, 87-88.
[5] Ibid., III, 83.

John Putnam, the political chieftain of Pope's ward, Salem Village, who had been a frequent selectman and an occasional deputy, and John Higginson, merchant son of the minister, who had served as selectman three times in the previous five years and who regained his post in 1684. Unlike most politically stable Massachusetts towns, Salem experienced frequent turnovers on its board of selectmen during the late seventeenth century.

Leading the winners of the 1683 vote with fifty-four ballots was John Hathorne, who had inherited not only his father's particularist political views but also his constituency. Young Hathorne was the only Salem politician of his generation whose career was both meteoric and consistent. He never lost an election. His success was due partly to his father's fame, of course. But it was also supported by many townsmen's continuing commitment to William Hathorne's attempt to reconcile Puritan values with the commercial system. Although more of a merchant than his father, young Hathorne built his career on at least outward piety and the traditional pattern of public service. He also aimed at maintaining Massachusetts's independence from England and Salem's independence from Boston.[6] Hathorne's position was supported by a dependable majority. Merchants who shared his views, young John Higginson for instance, were elected almost as dependably through the late 1670s and 1680s. Other mercantile leaders of equally prominent name who favored conciliation, like Jonathan Corwin and William Browne, Jr., were nominated regularly for selectman but won more occasionally.

Local issues, personalities, and divisions, however, were probably more significant in determining the membership of the board of selectmen. The electorate consistently maintained some Farm and agricultural representation while allowing merchants a majority of seats. On the 1683 board there two farmers, a mariner, and four merchants. Representation by geography was also roughly equal. With the exception of English's ward, no part of town was excluded. Consistent with the rather federalist approach to local politics that emerged in Salem in the 1660s, the membership of the board faithfully reflected the relative economic power of the various segments of the town's elite.

Salem's leadership, while divided by issues, interests, and geography, were still an identifiable group. They had more in common than the experience of officeholding and relative affluence. More so than their fathers, the generation of political leaders that came to maturity after 1660 were born and bred to

---

[6] Phillips, pp. 269-71.

exercise power. Although a few newcomers won places among the Salem elite, most prominent local politicians of the 1670s and 1680s were sons who inherited positions attained by their fathers. It was not unusual for a father and son or two brothers to serve simultaneously as selectmen.[7] Twenty-one of the thirty-seven men who were elected to the board between 1668 and 1685 were sons of former selectmen.[8] Another nine were surviving members of the first generation, having arrived in Salem before 1645. Only three were immigrants of the 1660s, and they each served only one term. A mere four selectmen, all farmers, were sons of townsmen who had never served on the board. Through deference politics the board was practically the preserve of powerful fathers and sons of prominent families. Two of the rising sons, John Putnam and John Pickering, were frequent selectmen of considerable influence. More common were men like John and Jonathan Corwin, merchant sons of George Corwin, and John Price, whose father Walter had been a prominent merchant and selectman of the 1650s. Twelve of the twenty-one sons of former selectmen were merchants. Five were farmers, two were artisans, and the remaining two were mariners. This second generation of political leaders, while representing all the town's economic interests, constituted a definite social class in which inheritance played a large role.

As in the town's politics, the men at the pinnacle of the economic structure, those twenty-nine assessed at eight or more shillings in 1683, had either settled in Salem before 1645 or had inherited significant wealth. Only four were more recent immigrants, three of them merchants. Three others were Salem-born sons of "middling" farmers or artisans, eight had inherited portions of large agricultural estates, and five more were sons of wealthy merchants. Nine were members of the first generation. Since the men at the top of both the economic and political structures were of roughly similar background, it is hardly surprising that seventeen of the twenty-eight selectmen or former selectmen were among the twenty-nine wealthiest townsmen in 1683 and that another three, although assessed at less than eight shillings, were sons or brothers of men who occupied this exalted economic position. The correlation between economic and political power was as close as it ever had been in Salem, despite the wide disagreements over issues and the divisions of interest among the farm and mercantile elites.

[7] *Town Recs.*, III, 34, 83, 104, for examples.

[8] Phillips, pp. 361-62, provides a convenient but incomplete list of selectmen. See also Perley, II, 401, and *Town Recs.*, II, III.

Even the third of the traditional criteria for high status, church membership, was still in evidence in 1683 (table 22). Those men

Table 22. Occupation and church membership of taxpayers in 1680s

Occupation	No.	No. in church	% in church	No. in church paying 5s.	% in church paying 5s.
Merchant	32	15	47	15	65
Farmer	114	32	28	13	54
Artisan	150	31	21	6	40
Mariner	122	11	9	2	17
Unknown	123	5	4	—	—
Total	541	94	17	36	49

Sources: Sidney J. Perley, *The History of Salem, Massachusetts*, 3 vols. (Salem, 1924-27); James Duncan Phillips, *Salem in the Seventeenth Century* (Boston, 1933); and the Records of the First Church, Essex Institute, Salem, Mass.

following occupations likely to exert political and economic power were proportionately apt to be church members. In contrast to the traditional order of the 1640s, church membership in the later period was often a seal of status already gained rather than a prior qualification for recognition. Twenty-two of the thirty-seven selectmen were church members, so that membership may have been desirable for election, but it was not essential. More pointedly, nine of the twenty-two joined the church after their first election to the board. Of the seventy-four men who paid a tax of five shillings or more, thirty-six were church members, comprising more than a third of the communicants.

Although church membership had become an optional step in accumulating status, rather than a mandatory one, the Salem church remained influential. Having recognized during the 1660s that the doctrinal consensus had dissipated, the church leaders in the 1680s still sought to retain the church's role as the ideological core of the community. The Reverend Mr. Higginson tried to preserve as much as possible of the traditional values by exhortations to evangelism and brotherly discipline. "Also the Pastor did speak to the Church, about their duty of observing and encouraging such as they knew to be godly to join to the Church. And that they should watch over such as were reported to be given to drinking and company keeping to deal with them in a regular way."[9] More than in the early years the church depended upon the individual influence of members to maintain and extend the effectiveness of Puritan values in the society. Also the church

[9] Records of the First Church, p. 269 (June 5, 1682), Essex Institute.

remained institutionally innovative. For example, baptism was
extended in 1678 to inhabitants born outside the covenant.[10]

The effect of these efforts on the behavior and values of the
townsmen at large is moot. There can be little doubt, however,
that church membership conveyed status and that many members
had influence that they were willing to use to maintain traditional
attitudes and mores. Membership rolls provide somewhat
equivocal measure of the impact of the church. That only 17
percent of the 1683 taxpayers were listed as members is certainly
an indication that the church as an institution had weakened
considerably since the 1640s. On the other hand, the fact that
almost half of the men of power and wealth were members seems
testimony to the continuing influence of the church, at least
among the elite (see table 22). Neither statistic says much about
the degree and character of individual piety of either the elect or
nonmembers. Yet fluctuations in church admissions from the
period just before the adoption of the Half-Way Covenant in 1665
to 1685 indicate, as Robert G. Pope has suggested, that "reli-
giosity" at least was strengthened by the crises of the post-1675
era (table 23).[11]

Table 23. Church admissions, 1661-85

Years	Men	Women
1661-65	17	24
1666-70	8	17
1671-75	2	10
1676-80	26	30
1681-85	29	46

Source: Records of the First Church of Salem, Essex Institute, Salem, Mass.

As had long been the case in Salem, women were more likely to
join the church than men. That male admission nearly equaled the
female in the years during and just after King Philip's War is
further evidence of the importance of insecurity and societal
confusion in provoking respect for the traditional communal
values. Judging from Higginson's remarks on the "godly" who
were not members, individual piety was still potent in this growing
commercial society where the communal sense was gradually
eroding. Church membership was valued, and the older pattern of

---

[10] Robert G. Pope, *The Half-Way Covenant: Church Membership in Puritan New
England* (Princeton, N.J., 1969), pp. 247-48.
[11] Ibid., p. 236.

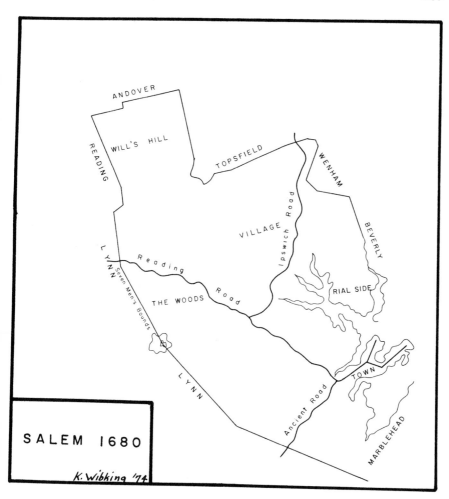

ANDOVER

WILL'S HILL

READING

TOPSFIELD

WENHAM

VILLAGE

BEVERLY

Ipswich Road

LYNN

Reading   Road

Seven Men's Bounds

RIAL SIDE

THE WOODS

LYNN

TOWN

Ancient Road

MARBLEHEAD

SALEM 1680

K. Wibking '74

correlation of the signs of status remained, despite the challenges. Thomas Maule, an outspoken Quaker immigrant of 1668, won financial success as a tailor turned merchant and was assessed twelve shillings in 1683; but it was not until 1688 that he gained the minor post of constable. Philip English, the Anglican merchant, was kept off the board of selectmen until the 1690s. Salem sons of respectable behavior and prestigious families could acquire political power without strictly following the traditional patterns of piety and political apprenticeship, but it was extremely difficult for outsiders or dissenters to take that route. Competition for place, as indicated by the turnovers on the board of selectmen, was intense, but it was competition among an elite formed basically by wealth and family and divided by interest, issues, and ambition.

In the 1680s this divided elite presided over three fairly distinct communities rather than the unified society sought by William Hathorne. First there were English's and Phelp's wards, a waterfront populated by laborers, mariners, and artisans (see tables 17 and 20). There was social mobility; ropewalkers became affluent sea captains and tailors, wealthy merchants. But generally the people of the waterfront were not an integral part of the social and political life of Salem. They were somewhat poorer, more transient, less apt to be church members or political participants.

Beyond the peninsula were the two agricultural wards, Pope's and Howard's, whose population was more affluent than the waterfront's and more stable. They participated fully in local politics. But at least Pope's ward, the farmers of Salem Village, felt deeply estranged from the commercial peninsula. Since 1672 their sense of separate identity had been embodied in their own church, which helps explain why their rate of church membership was higher than that of the other Farms ward (see table 20). Involved in frequent clashes with the people of the peninsula, they had never stopped agitating for independence as a separate town. The town meeting refused just as regularly. Even answers to their petitions of grievances were politely delayed.[12] An agricultural elite, dominated by the Putnam family, led these futile attacks on the power structure of the town center. Although the merchant-artisan core attempted to placate the farmers by granting offices to the Putnams, they were unwilling to lose the taxpayers of the Village and kept that section part of Salem until 1754. Despite their formal unity the peninsula and the Village had ceased to constitute a community of interest and sentiment in the 1650s.

[12] *Town Recs.*, III, 64-65, 67-68, for examples.

Another possible source of discontent in the Village was its rapidly growing number of taxpayers (see table 19). In 1683 it had 83 taxpayers; in 1689 there were 109, an increase of twenty-six. In Lambert's ward the increase was only three, in Herst's ten. In English's ware there was a loss of twenty-one. The fiscal value of the Village to Salem was increasing markedly, making separation in the peninsula's view more undesirable as time passed. Twenty-two of the newly assessed were sons or brothers reaching maturity; families were finding opportunity to settle children in the Village. But to do so, lands had to be divided, or at least empty tracts owned by these families had to be brought under cultivation. Families in the Village were larger also, averaging 5 births per family compared to the 3.7 births in Lambert's ward, for instance (see table 20).

With their agricultural economy and the highest rate of church membership in Salem, the people of the Village may have preserved more of the traditional values than their fellow townsmen. This is an imponderable question. The leadership of the merchant-artisan wards too showed signs of continuing piety, although church membership among the artisan population was 7 percent lower than that of the farming taxpayers (see table 22). The Village's conflict with the peninsula centered around use of the remaining common land, taxation, and distance from the town center, not religious or behavioral issues. The Village simply felt separate interests. The merchant-artisan wards did not have to pay much attention to these complaints; they merely outvoted the farmers and ran the town on the federalistic pattern established in the 1660s. Typical of the town center's exasperated attitude toward the Village was the advice sent to the Village parish from the officers of the Salem church in 1687 during one of the perennial Village squabbles over support of their parish ministry. After setting forth a long list of proposals to gain peace, the church officers noted, "But if our advice be rejected we wish you better and hearts to follow it, and only add if you will unreasonably trouble yourselves we pray you not any further to trouble us."[13]

Both the Village and Bishop's waterfront ward were, in a sense, excluded from the community. The heart of Salem was located in the three merchant-artisan wards of the peninsula. There the mercantile influence, led by established commercial families, was strongest. From this region came the bulk of Salem's economic,

[13]"Letter of Advice to Salem Villagers, February 1686/87," in *Salem-Village Witchcraft: A Documentary Record of Local Conflict in Colonial New England*, eds. Paul Boyer and Stephen Nissenbaum (Belmont, Cal., 1972), pp. 344-45.

political and religious leadership. Yet despite the preeminence of inherited wealth and status, the social system of these wards was hardly static. Twenty-five of the fifty-three men who were assessed at three to four shillings in these wards had immigrated to Salem during the 1660s and 1670s. Sixteen of the forty paying five or more shillings were also immigrants of the same period. However, only three of these immigrants, Thomas Maule, Timothy Lindall, and William Herst, paying twelve, twelve, and ten shillings respectively, rivaled the affluence of the longer established merchant families. Some of the newcomers, like Herst, must have brought capital with them. Yet others, like Maule, the Quaker tailor turned merchant, began humbly. As table 24 shows, the route to success was through occupations related to commerce. Twenty-one of the forty successful immigrants were merchants or mariners. Of the seventeen successful immigrant artisans, twelve practiced trades like shipbuilding, coopering or blockmaking, that

Table 24. Occupations of successful recent immigrants in the three
merchant-artisan wards, 1683

Occupation	Taxed 3-4s.	Taxed 5s.+	Total
Merchant	3	5	8
Mariner	7	6	13
Artisan	13	4	17
Farmer	1	–	1
Unknown	1	–	1
Total	25	15	40

Source: Sidney J. Perley, *The History of Salem, Massachusetts*, 3 vols. (Salem, 1924-27), "Appendix: Tax Lists," III, 419-22, and biographical notes in all vols.

directly supported commerce. Of course immigration to Salem was not a guarantee of financial success. About a third, at least 85 of the 256 taxpayers of this area, were recent immigrants and less than half of them, forty, paid three shillings or more. The median tax for this group of immigrants living in the merchant-artisan wards was between two shillings and two shillings, sixpence, about the same as that of the native sons. The immigrant population of English's waterfront ward may not have fared as well. But, since so many taxpayers in that ward left so few traces, it is impossible even to separate the immigrants from the natives with certainty. Yet that fact, along with the comparative transience and relative poverty of the waterfront during the 1680s indicates that there were a large number of immigrants in the ward in 1683 and that they were not as prosperous as the immigrants in the other peninsula wards. Nonetheless, the general impression remains that the peninsula wards offered the newcomers a reasonable chance to better themselves.

Compared to the merchant-artisan wards, there was less economic opportunity for recent immigrants in the farming sections. Only five of the eighteen men rated at five or more shillings and six of the forty-four assessed at three to four shillings were known newcomers. The agricultural sector of the economy was not as expansive, and the lands of the region were controlled by the families who settled the Farms in the 1640s and 1650s. At least two of the successful immigrants were leasing land.

Economic mobility in the commercial wards did not threaten the political or social dominance of the older families. Only four of the forty successful immigrants of the peninsula and only one from the Village ever became selectmen. Twelve of the forty became constables, a position not generally sought by the sons of prominent families. Only seven ever became members of the church, well below the average of native sons of their economic status. Indeed, a number of these immigrants were Quaker and Anglican dissenters from the standing order. It appears that by the 1680s being a native or longtime resident of Salem had become another criteria for status that tended to balance off financial success. Most of these productive and successful immigrants seemed willing to follow their callings, serve the community in minor offices, and accept the leadership of the Corwins, Brownes, and Hathornes who ran Salem. Salem was no longer a Puritan utopia, if it ever had been, nor was it even a unified community. But it was a successful commercial town with a skilled and relatively stable leadership. The reforms of the 1660s had been partially successful. There may have been little unity, but at least there was relative peace.

Chapter XI

The Salem Symbols

"The Salem Symbols," as Williston Walker fittingly entitled the town's church covenants,[1] were more than creeds. They defined mutual obligations not only among church members but also within the whole community, thereby embodying the town's sense of identity. Since the contents of the covenants changed as conditions changed, they were more than statements of ideals. Through them the church members attempted to interpret shifting reality and to cope with new conditions. These agreements linked aspirations and reality, perceptions of problems with methods for resolving them. They were social contracts.

Each covenant, after the first, also revealed a strong sense of continuity. The signers of each new agreement saw the document as an elaboration on, rather than a rejection of, the earlier covenants. elaboration on, rather than a rejection of, the earlier covenants. The signers were reinterpreting their past, retaining elements that remained useful and revising others in the light of experience. The process of reinterpretation reflected in the covenants provides valuable clues to intellectual and social life of the town. The changes in the covenants during the century revolved around a number of conflicting tendencies and ideas whose basic elements were rearranged to fit new conditions. Should the agreements reached be tacit to allow flexibility "over things indifferent" or explicit to encourage clarity? Would the ideal of "peace and unity" be better served by an inclusive civil and religious policy or by an exclusive one?

Salem's first covenant, Francis Higginson's simple one-sentence statement of 1629, was both implicit and inclusive. "We covenant with the Lord and one with an other; and do bind ourselves in the presence of God, to walk together in all his ways, according as he is pleased to reveal himself unto us in his Blessed word of truth." With this statement the Salem church and the town's sense of community was born. The people who signed it knew each other well and, with the assurance of mutual "good intentions," were

[1] Walker, *The Creeds and Platforms of Congregationalism* (1893; rept., Boston, 1960), pp. 116-22.

certain that as the Lord revealed his will they could interpret it in "peace and unity." Their covenant, therefore, expressed the signers' faith in their mission and confidence in their capacity to maintain a consensus. This optimism was not restricted to Salem. The initial covenants of both Boston and Charlestown were similar.

The consensus soon collapsed. The great migration beginning in 1630 made easy agreement increasingly difficult. The arrival of John Winthrop and the founding of Boston and nearby towns took away the preeminence that Salem and its leadership had expected. Salem's jealousy and suspicion of Boston helped fuel Separatism in the town, especially during the pastorate of Roger Williams. Salem experienced internal tensions as well. After 1633 large numbers of immigrants settled in the community. The older settlers had to grant them land, church membership, and political power quickly without intimate knowledge of their personalities. The problem was aggravated by the differing agricultural and religious backgrounds of the largely East Anglian immigrants and the predominantly West Country residents.

The early implicit covenant provided little guidance in the confusion. Not only in Salem but throughout the colony the influx of people opened a number of issues. What was the proper relationship of the Elect to the unregenerate, of the churches and towns to central authority? More prosaic questions of land use and mercantile ethics also complicated the colony's life. The lack of consensus and the belief in the need for some uniformity resulted in a number of disturbances, of which the Williams episode and the Antinomian Crisis were the most spectacular.

In 1636 the Massachusetts leadership began forging the necessary consensus and creating institutions designed to maintain and enforce it. The General Court formed the Quarterly Court system and encouraged the towns to make the town meetings and the boards of selectmen more formal institutions. Hugh Peter in December wrote for Salem the capstone of their effort toward consensus, a new church covenant. This document, with its lengthy preamble and nine articles, marked the lessons learned "by sad experience." After renewing the old covenant, the new one determined "more explicitly" what it meant "to walk together." The Elect were responsible for each other and the unregenerate. The "sister Churches" were to be respected "using their Council as need shall be." Those in authority "in Church or Commonwealth" were due all "lawful obedience." Communal ethics of civility, deference, and diligence "in our particular callings" were all explicitly reaffirmed.

The 1636 covenant, combined with adjustments in political institutions and land distribution, set the tone of Salem's life and provided a tolerable "peace and unity" for about twenty years. During this period the townsmen of Salem got their only taste of Puritan success. Ironically their commitment to non-Separatist orthodoxy allowed a number of Salem leaders, especially William Hathorne, to renew the town's challenge to Boston's leadership. Allied with the agricultural townships of Essex County, Salem sought to supplant a Boston grown "corrupt" by commerce.

But during the 1650s Salem too grew into a mercantile center. Commercial development drastically affected almost every aspect of the town's life. The peninsula was transformed from a central farming and fishing village into a trading town of wharves, warehouses, shipyards, and shops. Commercial farming became increasingly important in the agricultural area called the Farms. Only the West Country residents in the Cape Ann region remained relatively untouched. This transformation aggravated the sectionalism of the town, undermining the unity of the community. Sectional suspicion caused movements toward independence in the Farms and on the Cape Ann Side and contributed the development of Quakerism. The survival of the Society of Friends permanently shattered the religious unity of the town.

Economic development also undermined the status system envisioned in the 1630s. Commercial opportunity complicated the relationship between wealth, land, church membership, and political influence. Although not consciously opposed to the traditional order, the town's merchants gradually imposed new values, a stress on the particular over the general calling, for example. Their tendency to form a separate, identifiable group within the town subverted both communal unity and the social mobility assumed by the founders. By 1668 there was no longer any possibility that Salem could retain much of the communal system.

The people of Salem had to adapt their political institutions to the new realities. The town meeting, still concerned with agricultural interests and problems, placed explicit restrictions on the increasingly mercantile-minded selectmen. It instructed the deputies to move for an extension of the privileges of freemanship to selected men outside of the church. The town meeting was reinterpreting the covenant, making it more secular and even more explicit. It was operating under more modern federal assumptions that there were separate interests in the community and that the function of politics was to balance these interests against one another rather than absorb them into a communal unity.

"To walk together" had taken on a new meaning combining elements from both the earlier implicit and explicit covenants. Clarification and definition of political power were used as means to an inclusivist end. Allowing interests to clash while expecting the community to survive was a return to the flexibility and tolerance over "things indifferent" that had characterized the implicit covenant of the early 1630s. It was an intelligent, even if somewhat anachronistic, adaptation to a more secular and pluralistic society.

While recognizing the lack of unity, the church was unwilling to surrender the communal ideal, but it too followed the same pattern of adapting elements of the earlier covenants to include more people. Under the able leadership of John Higginson, Francis's son, the church members embarked on a campaign to renew the church as the vital center of town life. They started in 1660 by reaffirming the 1636 covenant and adding an article "to take heed and beware of the leaven of the docrine of the Quakers." But simple affirmation and warning were not enough to meet the situation. The Salem church helped pioneer the Half-Way Covenant as an effort to be more inclusive. In 1665 the members authorized *A Direction for a Public Profession*, which contained the town's first confession of faith, explicitly discussing the essential doctrines of Calvinism and a new church covenant. The *Direction* was an educational and evangelical device that made it easier for people to own the covenant. The new covenant did not replace the 1636 document any more than the 1636 covenant replaced the earlier one. It was an elaboration of only one point, the individual member's responsibility to God under the Covenant of Grace and to "this particular church." It was an accommodation to the more individualistic and secular pattern of the town's life.

By the 1680s, as a new generation replaced the last of the founders, the order forged in the 1660s had become accepted and relatively stable. Clashes of diverse interests and opinions were taken for granted, at least in the civil realm. The church strived to retain and adapt a core of orthodoxy relevant to the community's life. In April 1680 the church, still under the direction of John Higginson, affirmed a new covenant "as being more accommodate to the present times, and state of things amongst us."[2] As befitted their sense of continuity, the church members began by renewing the former covenant and restating their confession of incapacity to conform fully to the role of "the Lord's Covenant People." There

---

[2] *Salem Church Covenant* (Boston, 1680), Evans Microcard no. 295.

followed an explicit, if short, statement on the doctrine of the Trinity, a reaffirmation of the spiritual importance of child baptism, and a restatement of the importance of church discipline.

Then in the last operative section of the new covenant came the church's official response to the developing individualism and secularism of Salem. This last part contained three pledges. The first concerned reform of the self, promising to "worship" in the broad Puritan sense "without formality and hypocrisy, and more fully and faithfully than heretofore, to discharge all Covenant duties one toward another in a way of Church Communion." If the society was no longer a communal order, then the church had to be, and the reform of individual behavior was the means. The second pledge was to reform behavior within families. Children and servants were to be catechized, taught the rudiments of the faith. Finally, the drive to reform was passed from self to family to society. The church members realistically asserted that the means to wider reform was no longer the church as an institution but reformed individuals. We do further engage (the Lord helping of us) to endeavor to keep ourselves pure from the sins of the Times, and what lies in us to help forward the Reformation of the same in places where we live, denying all ungodly and worldly lusts, living soberly, righteously, and godly in this present world, making Conscience to walk so as to give no offense nor to give occasion to others to sin or to speak evil of our holy Profession." This was not a call to Separatism in any form; it was rather an appeal to individual effort to reform within a secular society.

Dedication to tradition and the prestige of being the official ideological core of the community allowed the church leadership to become social critics who harkened back to the supposedly pristine virtues of earlier years. Higginson in particular was critical of the spiritual impact of commerce on New England. The standard by which he judged his times was his interpretation of the covenant God made with the Chosen People and more specifically his understanding of the "Salem Symbols." He assumed that each covenant was an elaboration on, not a departure from, the original church covenant. In the words of the *Direction*, each statement was "the same for substance which was propounded to, and agreed upon by the Church of Salem at their beginning."

The orthodox people of Salem viewed each new document as a clarification rather than a repudiation of its predecessor because the covenants were social contracts, rudimentary constitutions. Despite significant social changes, the residents of Salem were no more willing to abandon their covenants than later generations of

Americans wished to replace their Constitution. The covenants, elaborated, extended, and reinterpreted, took on new meanings in new contexts. They and related documents of Salem reveal as much about Salem's early history as the Constitution and its amendments tell of the life of the Republic.

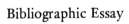

Bibliographic Essay

Bibliographic Essay

This essay discusses only those works and sources most essential to the central arguments of this volume. A more general and quite useful bibliographic essay can be found in Darrett B. Rutman, *American Puritanism: Faith and Practice* (New York, 1970). Michael McGiffert has surveyed scholarly opinion on significant issues and problems in "American Puritan Studies in the 1960's," *William and Mary Quarterly*, 3d ser., 28 (1970): 36-67.

Contrary to the legend of the "scientific method," most research begins with concepts rather than raw material. Darrett Rutman in the book mentioned above stresses the "exaggerated traditionalism" of Massachusetts Puritanism, that is, the attempt to form a new society based on an ideal "organicism" that was disappearing in England. The key to forging this organicism for Puritans was covenant theology. A most lucid description of the origins and implications of the covenant idea is David Little's *Religion, Order and Law: A Study in Pre-Revolutionary England* (New York, 1969). Difficult to read but rich in passion and insights, Perry Miller's works, especially *The New England Mind: The Seventeenth Century* (New York, 1939) and *The New England Mind: From Colony to Province* (Cambridge, Mass., 1953), are basic to an understanding of the "official mind" of the leadership and its permutations. Other significant works on the covenants and related issues are Edmund S. Morgan's *Visible Saints: The History of a Puritan Idea* (New York, 1963); Norman Pettit's *The Heart Prepared: Grace and Conversion in Puritan Spiritual Life* (New Haven, 1966); Robert G. Pope's *The Half-Way Covenant: Church Membership in Puritan New England* (Princeton, N.J., 1969); and Larzer Ziff's "The Social Bond of the Church Covenant," *American Quarterly* 10 (1958): 454-62. A convenient collection of covenants and other church documents is Williston Walker's *Creeds and Platforms of Congregationalism* (1893; rept. Boston, 1960).

The communal society that the settlers envisioned was congregational and town-centered. The histories of other Massachusetts towns provide comparisons that illuminate Salem experience. Kenneth A. Lockridge in *A New England Town: The First Hundred Years, Dedham, Massachusetts, 1636-1736* (New York, 1970) describes a successful "Puritan utopia," an organic and stable agricultural commune for its first fifty years. Another successful Puritan community is pictured demographically by Philip J. Greven, Jr., in *Four Generations: Population, Land, and Family in Colonial Andover, Massachusetts* (Ithaca, N.Y., 1970). On the other hand Darrett B. Rutman's *Winthrop's Boston: Portrait of a Puritan Town, 1630-1649* (Chapel Hill, N.C., 1965) is a tale of rapid economic growth and instability that doomed communalism. Even in farming towns organicism could be compromised or destroyed by arguments among settlers from differing parts of England with differing agricultural traditions. This possibility is illustrated by Sumner Chilton Powell's *Puritan Village: The Formation of a New England Town* (Middleton, Conn., 1963) on Sudbury and by John J. Waters's "Hingham, Massachusetts, 1631-1661: An East Anglian Oligarchy in the New World," *Journal of Social History* 1 (1968): 351-70.

Salem shared in varying degrees these characteristics. James Duncan Phillips, *Salem in the Seventeenth Century* (Boston, 1933) is the standard narrative history. Its appendixes, listing immigrants and church members to 1650 and officials through the century, are valuable. Sidney Perley's *The History of Salem Massachusetts*, 3 vols. (Salem, 1924-27) proved essential. Although poorly organized and therefore exasperating, these three volumes are a monument to careful genealogical research; they also contain a wealth of social and economic detail not easily available elsewhere. Unfortunately, Paul Boyer and Stephen Nissenbaum's *Salem Possessed: The Social Origins of Witchcraft* (Cambridge, Mass., 1974) came to hand too late to be consulted for this work.

The town records of Salem in the seventeenth century are published. The first volume (1634-59) is in the *Essex Institute Historical Collections* 9 (1868). Volumes 2 (1660-80) and 3 (1681-91) were published by the Essex Institute under separate cover in 1913 and 1934 respectively.

The Salem church records in their entirety are available in typescript at the Essex Institute. Significant excerpts can be found in Daniel A. White, *New England Congregationalism in Its Origin and Purity, Illustrated by the Foundation and Early Records of the First Church of Salem* (Salem, 1861). Robert G. Pope in his book provides important commentary on the changing character of the Salem church and its neighboring congregations in Marblehead, Beverly, and Salem Village.

The problem of economic and social development and its relationship to politics is central to this study. Two articles by William I. Davisson, "Essex County Price Trends: Money and Markets in Seventeenth-Century Massachusetts," *Essex Institute Historical Collections* 103 (1967): 144-85, and "Essex County Wealth Trends: Wealth and Economic Growth in Seventeenth-Century Massachusetts;" ibid., pp. 291-342, are computer analyses of surviving wills extracted in *Probate Records of Essex County, Massachusetts*, ed. George F. Dow, 3 vols. (Salem, 1916-20). These wills, along with masses of other important information, can also be found in *Records and Files of the Quarterly Courts of Essex County, Massachusetts, 1636-1692*, ed. George F. Dow, 8 vols. (Salem, 1911-21). As Davisson carefully states, analysis of wills, due to limited samples and the bias inherent in class origins and survival, can only reveal "trends," not a clear picture of an economy at any one time. However, since other forms of economic data for the period are scarce, no one interested in these topics can afford to ignore these wills.

Although some of his conclusions differ markedly from my own, Donald Warner Koch in "Income Distribution and Political Structure in Seventeenth-Century Salem, Massachusetts," *Essex Institute Historical Collections* 105

(1969): 50-71, has made effective use of the wills to describe the growing power of Salem mercantile wealth not only in the town but throughout the county. One problem in both Koch's work and Bernard Bailyn's brilliant and seminal *The New England Merchants in the Seventeenth Century* (paperbacks ed., New York, 1964) is clear identification of merchants. In that age in which vocations were not as elaborately differentiated as in our own, some men, most significantly the Puritan leadership of the early years, indulged in trade as only one aspect of their larger role in the community and consequently were not really "mercantile" in their attitudes. The distinction is not always clear but is important in understanding the tensions and politics of the era. There are similar difficulties in distinguishing mariners, farmers, and artisans. Fashioning useful models from often vague materials requires critical judgment and the realization that statistical paradigms, despite their seeming numerical exactness, are not precise reproductions of reality, only honest approximations.

A number of the models I have used are quantitative, inspired partly by the more recently published town histories and articles on economic development. These works illustrate how much can be shown through use of wills and tax and land grant lists. Peter Laslett's *The World We Have Lost: England before the Industrial Age* (London, 1965) is a good example of statistical method and a fine introduction to Tudor-Stuart society. Another excellent analysis of English society that is basically traditional social history incorporating some of the newer demographic techniques is Carl Bridenbaugh's *Vexed and Troubled Englishmen, 1590-1642* (New York, 1968). The descriptions of social structure and tension, particularly in differing social regions of England, were important to this study. Other works on English society that proved especially useful are C. W. Chalklin, *Seventeenth-Century Kent: A Social and Economic History* (London, 1965) and W. G. Hoskins, *The Midland Peasant: The Economic and Social History of a Leicestershire Village* (London, 1957).

Because of the dearth of other sorts of economic data, demography is proving to be an indispensible device for describing both social and economic conditions. Several of the works mentioned above make extensive use of demographic techniques. A good survey of the literature and the possibilities is Philip Greven, Jr.'s "Historical Demography and Colonial America," *William and Mary Quarterly*, 3d ser., 23 (1966): 234-56.

Index

Index